KARL FRIEDRI

JOURNAL

OF

THREE VOYAGES

ALONG THE

COAST OF CHINA,

IN

1831, 1832 & 1833

WITH NOTICES OF

SIAM, COREA, AND THE LOO-CHOO ISLANDS

Elibron Classics
www.elibron.com

Elibron Classics series.

© 2005 Adamant Media Corporation.

ISBN 1-4021-8767-X (paperback)
ISBN 1-4021-4686-8 (hardcover)

This Elibron Classics Replica Edition is an unabridged facsimile
of the edition published in 1834 by Frederick Westley and A. H. Davis,
London.

Drawn & Engraved by R. Sears, 65, Paternoster Row.

RESIDENCE OF THE REV.ᴰ M.ᴿ GUTZLAFF AT BANKOK.

London, Published by Westley & Davis, 1831.

JOURNAL

OF

THREE VOYAGES

ALONG THE

COAST OF CHINA,

IN

1831, 1832, & 1833,

WITH NOTICES OF

SIAM, COREA, AND THE LOO-CHOO ISLANDS.

BY

CHARLES GUTZLAFF.

TO WHICH IS PREFIXED,

AN INTRODUCTORY ESSAY ON THE POLICY, RELIGION, ETC.

OF CHINA,

BY THE REV. W. ELLIS,

AUTHOR OF "POLYNESIAN RESEARCHES, ETC."

LONDON:

FREDERICK WESTLEY AND A. H. DAVIS,

STATIONERS' HALL COURT.

1834.

LONDON :

R. CLAY, PRINTER, BREAD-STREET-HILL.

CONTENTS.

INTRODUCTION.

JOURNAL OF THE FIRST VOYAGE.

JOURNAL OF THE SECOND VOYAGE.

RELIGIONS OF CHINA.

CHRISTIANITY IN CHINA.

JOURNAL OF THE THIRD VOYAGE.

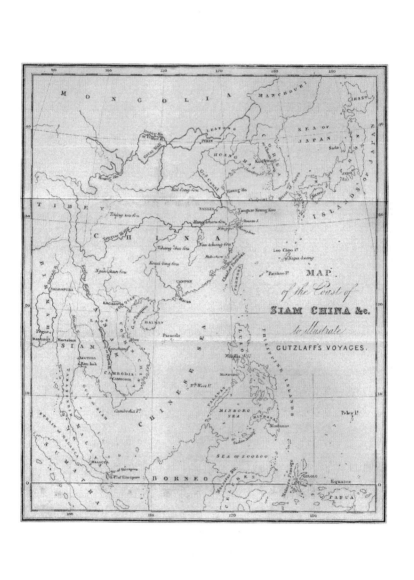

MAP.

of the Coast of

SIAM CHINA &c.

to illustrate

GUTZLAFF'S VOYAGES.

BRIEF NOTICE OF

CHINA AND SIAM,

AND THE LABOURS OF PROTESTANT MISSIONARIES IN
THESE AND THE ADJACENT COUNTRIES.

BETWEEN five and six hundred years have
elapsed since the publication of the travels of
Marco Polo made the nations of Europe acquainted with the northern portion of the empire
of China. Two hundred years afterwards, the
Portuguese, impelled by the spirit of maritime
enterprise, for which they were then so distinguished, pushing their adventurous way along
the African shore, passed the Cape of Good
Hope, and discovered the highway by sea to
the East Indies. Under the direction of the
celebrated Albuquerque, they visited Malacca,
Siam, Pegu, and Canton, and made the countries

b

of south-eastern Asia known to the inhabitants
of the western world.

In 1516, the Portuguese commenced their
traffic at Canton; but it was not until 1614,[*]
that the servants of the English East India
Company sought the trade of China. In 1637,
the Company's ships anchored off Macao, and
afterwards proceeded up the river towards Canton, to open a direct trade with the Chinese; but
they were obliged to abandon the project, and
were treated as enemies. Their commercial intercourse with this singular nation commenced
in 1683;—this intercourse, though attended with
many difficulties at first, was afterwards firmly
established, and has been maintained with few
interruptions ever since. " The English," as
Mr. Auber observes, " when they first adventured
in the China trade, presented themselves to the
notice of the Chinese necessarily under the
double disadvantage of being foreigners and
merchants: nevertheless, since they have been
invested with the character of representatives
and servants of a great Company, enjoying the
declared and immediate protection of the sovereign of their nation, they have succeeded, by

* Auber's Analysis of the Constitution of the East India
Company, p. 148.

sure though gradual advances, in raising the British trade to a pitch of prosperity, and themselves personally to a degree of respectability in the estimation of the Chinese, which the most sanguine expectations, under a due knowledge of the circumstances of the case, would hardly have anticipated; securing at the same time to the revenues of Great Britain an annual sum, exceeding 3,500,000*l.* without any charge of collection."* The justness of the above remark will further appear, when we consider that, according to the statement of Dr. Morrison, the Chinese rank in the scale by which they estimate the several classes of society,—the cultivators of the mind in the first class; the cultivators of the land next; in the third place are ranked the operators on the earth's produce, or the artizans and mechanics; and finally, the trader or merchant. †

During the greater part of the period since 1683, our commerce with China has been progressively increasing and prosperous. The finest ships which British industry and skill have constructed, and which British wealth and enterprise have employed in varied and extending commerce, have traversed half the circuit of the

† Analysis, p. 151.　　† Chinese Miscellany, p. 43.

b 2

globe to the market of China, and have returned
freighted with its merchandize. Of this merchandize, the only port which the unparalleled
jealousy of the Chinese government allows
foreigners to visit, has for some time past exported to England one single commodity, —
namely, tea, to such an extent, that the annual
sale in England, including what is exported
to the continent of Europe, amounts nearly to
30,000,000 pounds weight. The annual sale
of this article, in 1825, produced a gross return
of upwards of 7,000,000l. sterling, with a net
revenue to the government of three millions and
a half; besides a stock kept on hand, in the
warehouses, equal in value to the above.

Two hundred years ago, its use was unknown in England; but since that period it
has been imported to an extent that has entirely changed the domestic habits, not only of
our own country, but of many parts of Europe.
The gratification of the taste thus acquired, has
made us dependent on our traffic with China for
much of the comfort of a large portion of every
class of society. That this, besides being a
source of immense riches to individuals, and of
revenue to the government, has been highly
beneficial in improving the moral character, and

promoting the domestic habits of the nation, cannot be doubted; but notwithstanding these, and other considerations scarcely less interesting and important, we are still in a great measure unacquainted with the inhabitants of China, and comparatively uninterested in their circumstances.

Some objects attract attention by the number and diversity of their several parts,—the rarities and excellences they exhibit,—the skill and power by which they are combined,—and the character and extent of their influence; others attract attention from the remoteness of their situation,—their number and magnitude,—the dignity they assume, —the power with which they are invested,—the antiquity they claim, — the changes they have undergone, or of which they may yet be susceptible,—and the subjects of strong and lasting interest which they supply. All these combine to invite our attention to China, and some of them exist in a degree far surpassing that in which they are found in any other nation of the earth.

Whatever interest may be derived from remoteness of situation, belongs to China. This is heightened, in some measure, by the repulsive policy of its government, which has peremptorily and steadily interdicted all intercourse with foreigners. This studied seclusion has a

natural tendency to excite curiosity, and stimulate desire to explore a country, the remoteness
of whose situation, and the prohibitions of
whose inhabitants, render it to us comparatively
an unknown world.

No country presents greater diversities in its
physical geography and natural history than
this extensive territory, whether we regard its
verdant and cultivated plains, or its sterile
and solitary deserts — its mountains and its
valleys — its gigantic rivers — its cities teeming
with intelligent and civilized inhabitants,—or its
mountain fastnesses and its forests, the abodes
of wild beasts or marauding banditti. Its frontier
barrier, and its principal channel of inland navigation, are justly regarded, from their magnitude and
antiquity, as among the wonders of the world.
The former, their immense wall, carried across
rivers and over mountains, extending to the
amazing length of 1500 miles, has been built
about 2000 years. Its foundation consists of
large blocks of stone laid in mortar; but all the
rest is of brick. When carried over steep rocks,
where no horse can pass, it is about 15 or 20
feet high; but when running through a valley, or
crossing a river, it is about 30 feet high, with
square towers and embrasures at equal distances.

Mr. Barrow, in his account of this most astonishing production of human labour, remarks,
that if to its prodigious length of 1500 miles be
assumed as true the probable conjecture, that
its dimensions throughout are nearly the same as
where it was crossed by the British embassy, it
contains materials more than sufficient to erect
all the dwelling-houses in England and Scotland,
even admitting their number to be 1,800,000,
and each to contain 2000 feet of masonry. In
this calculation, the huge projecting masses of
stone, called towers, are not included, which
of themselves would erect a city as large as
London.

To assist the conceptions of the reader still
further respecting this singular and stupendous
fabric, it is observed, that were its materials
converted into a wall 12 feet high and 4 feet
thick, it would possess sufficient length to sur-
round the globe, at its equatorial circumference.

The great canal is on the same immense scale,
and presents an inland navigation of such extent
and magnitude, as to stand unrivalled: its vast
channel of water flows with scarcely any interruption for a space of 600 miles. According to
Dr. Morrison, 170,000 men were employed in
its construction.

The mariner's compass, the art of printing,
the manufacture of gunpowder, were in use in
China before discovered in Europe; and, according to Barrow,—"When the king of France introduced the luxury of silk stockings, the peasantry
of the middle provinces of China were clothed in
silks from head to foot; and when the nobility of
England were sleeping on straw, a peasant of
China had his mat and his pillow, and the man
in office enjoyed his silken mattress."

Its climate presents every variety of temperature, from the snows of Siberia to the heat of the
torrid zone, on its southern borders. Its population, though less varied perhaps than any inhabiting an equal extent of territory in some parts of
the globe, presents considerable diversity, from
the rude Cossack in the north, to the polished
mandarin of the centre and south; comprising
among its chief nations, the Chinese, Manchous,
Mongolians, Kalmuks, Tartars, and Thibetians.

Its history presents many who have attained
pre-eminence among their contemporaries, and
have displayed in a variety of ways a high
order of intellect;—many whose progress in
the several departments of learning, considering
them utterly excluded from the influence of
advancing literature and science in other parts

of the world, is truly astonishing. As a nation, unacquainted with those models of benevolence and kindness which the Bible presents, and those motives to peace on earth and good-will among men which it implants in the heart, they exhibit an urbanity of manners and a courtesy of behaviour, highly commendable; and in some respects a degree of refinement and civilization, beyond what has been attained by the most intelligent and powerful nations of the earth.

"The Chinese teach contempt of the rude instead of fighting with them; and the man who unreasonably insults another, has public opinion against him; whilst he who bears and despises the affront is esteemed. Even the government is at the utmost pains to make it appear to the people, that its conduct is reasonable and benevolent on all occasions. They have found, by the experience of many ages, that this is necessary. To make out the argument, they are not nice about a strict adherence to truth; nor are their reasons or premises such that Europeans would generally admit: but granting them their own premises and statement of facts, they never fail to prove that those whom they oppose are completely in the wrong. A Chinese would stand and reason with a man,

when an Englishman would knock him down, or
an Italian stab him. It is needless to say, which
is the more rational mode of proceeding."

The Chinese system of government, as singular and exclusive as it is organized and complete, has subjected to its influence, or controlled
by its power, a larger number of human beings,
during a longer period of time, than that of any
other nation. Its laws, though based, in many
respects, on maxims of wise policy, are often
despotic and sanguinary, and executed with
great harshness and cruelty. Its form is an
absolute hereditary monarchy. The supreme
power is vested solely in the emperor; by him
the viceroys of provinces are appointed and
removed at pleasure, and to him they are responsible for their conduct, though viceroyalties
sometimes include upwards of thirty millions
of inhabitants. The stability of the Chinese government, and the few changes that have been
made in its institutions for such a number of
ages; the vast extent of empire and immense
population, forming one society, guided by the
same laws, and governed by the will of a
single individual, offers, as Mr. Barrow observes, in reference to the account of the
embassy to which he belonged, " the grandest

collective object that can be presented 'for contemplation or research,'—the customs, habits, manners, religious notions, of the most ancient society and most populous empire existing amongst men, are without doubt a most interesting subject," while at least its commercial influence is felt more or less in every part of the civilized world. These are peculiarities which render China, to the philosopher, the scholar, the politician, the merchant and the traveller, an object of no common interest.

Travellers state, that there are no ancient palaces, nor other public edifices; no paintings, nor pieces of sculpture, to arrest the attention of the stranger. In travelling over the continent of Europe, and more especially on the classic ground of Italy and Greece, every city, mountain, river, and ruin, are rendered interesting, by something on record which concerns them,—the theme of some poet, the seat of some philosopher or lawgiver, or the scene of some memorable action ; and the conclusion has been drawn, that because to Europe the history of China has furnished no materials for the sensation which the classic scenes of Europe excite, the country itself is incapable of communicating such impressions. This may be in part accounted for, from the

very limited information which many are satisfied
with respecting this extensive empire.

On this subject, though the affairs of Europe are
of comparatively no importance whatever to China;
and on the other hand, the affairs of China do not
much concern Europeans, Dr. Morrison observes:
—" The Greeks and Romans were the ancestors
of Europeans. The scenes of their battles;—
the situation and antiquities of their cities;—the
birth-place of their poets, historians, legislators,
and orators,—all possess an acquired interest in
the minds of those whose education has led them
to an early acquaintance with them: but it
would be difficult for a Chinese, of the best
talents and education, to acquire in the years of
manhood a similar interest.

" The Chinese also can point out the scenes
of battles where thousands fought and died;
the situation of splendid courts; the tombs of
monarchs; the abodes of historians, moralists,
and poets, whose memory is dear to them, and
which interest their hearts in the antiquities of
their fathers. But what they look upon with
interest and pleasure can certainly have few
charms for a foreigner, who is excluded from
their families, and passed from Pekin to Canton
in a boat under military escort;—still from

this to deny that the country possesses any of the charms of Europe, does not seem a fair conclusion. If the reality of things is to be judged by the feelings of the inhabitants of a country, every region of the world, and every state of society, would in its turn assume the place of high superiority."

The antiquity of China renders it an object of great interest to the reflecting mind. Without giving the native chronologers credit for all they claim in this respect,—that nation cannot be viewed with indifference which possessed an organized government, an army, a written language, historians, and other literati, in a period so remote as to be coeval with the immediate successors of the inspired historian of Creation, and the lawgiver of the ancient people of God;—among whom the writings of sages, who lived 600 years before the Christian era, are still extant, and which, while the dynasties of Egypt and contemporary nations have ceased from among men, and others more powerful and celebrated have risen and sunk into oblivion,— has continued, extending, and consolidating its greatness and its power; and whose markets were the resorts of foreign merchants before the Romans invaded Britain.

According to Pinkerton, it may now be considered as extending from those parts of the Pacific Ocean, called the Chinese and Japanese Seas, to the river Sarason, or Sihon, in the west,—a space of eighty-one degrees, equal to 4200 geographical, or 4900 British miles. From north to south, it stretches from the Uralian mountains, in north latitude 50°, to the southern border, about latitude 21°, being twenty-nine degrees of latitude, 1740 geographical, or nearly 2300 British miles.

The written language of China, alike unique and ancient, is, from the singularity of its structure, and the extent to which it is employed, one of the most remarkable that has been used amongst mankind. The knotted cords, originally employed as the record of events by them as well as many other nations, in the first stages of their social existence, were superseded, at an early period in their history, by symbolic records. The founder of letters lived about 1100 years before the Christian era, and the art of printing has been in use among them for 800 years.

Whatever defects may attach to the Chinese character,—and their defects are of no common order,—they are not without traits of excellence, among which their general attention to education is most conspicuous. According to Nieuhoff and Kircher, quoted by Mr. Fisher, in the " Gentleman's Magazine," who states that the Chinese have evidently been for centuries in advance of the nations of Europe,—education is more general, and, in some respects, better conducted in China than it was when the account was written (1669), or is now in any other country. Means were provided, by the head of every family, for the instruction of its members in reading and writing, either by the parent, or hired itinerant teachers. Hence it has followed that the arts of reading and writing are understood and practised to a greater extent than among the inhabitants of any other country. The proportion of the educated to the uneducated men is said to be as four to one. This proportion is much larger than that given by Dr. Morrison, who states, that though there is a great number of teachers, and the rudiments of learning may be obtained at so low a rate as two dollars a year, not more than one half of the community is able to read. The government supports schoolmasters for the soldiery, but not for the children of the poor generally.* It

* Horæ Sinicæ, p. 3.

is, however, stated, that the government encourages education, not only by the bestowment of offices, but of literary rank, with badges
of distinction. Commissioners or inspectors
travel through the provinces, to inquire into
the state of education, and examine candidates
for literary honours. Besides this, there are
other examinations, held triennially, in which
the highest literary rewards are distributed.
One is held in the public halls of the cities of the
empire, and the other only in the imperial city.
This has created such a general competition for
literary distinction, that the public reading of
essays, prepared for this purpose by those by
whom they are read, is an exhibition of almost
constant occurrence, and takes place at least
twice in every month in all the principal towns
in China. All their legal inquiries are also
pursued by writing, and their decisions formed
on documentary evidence. The writings of some
of their most distinguished sages are directed to
the encouragement of the pursuit of letters;
the advantages of which are set forth, and
motives to diligence enforced, by striking ex-
amples. Among the latter, the following, from
a small book, on the utility and honour of
learning, which, though the author is not known,

is considered as ancient and excellent of its kind, will not be uninteresting :—

" Che-yin, when a boy, being poor, read his book by the light of a glow-worm, which he confined. And Sun-kang, in winter, read his book by the light reflected from the snow. Though their families were poor, they studied incessantly.

" Chu-mai-chin, though he subsisted by carrying fire-wood round the town to sell, yet carefully read his book. At last he became capable of, and filled a public office.

" Limie, whilst watching his cattle in the field, always had his book at hand, suspended to the horn of a cow.

" Sun-king suspended his head by its hair to the beam of the house, to prevent his sleeping over his books."*

The literati appear to have been, for a long time past, a numerous class in the community, and to have exercised great influence. Their writings, though inferior to that of other nations in which literature has been cultivated to any extent, and, from a peculiarity of circumstances scarcely admitting of a comparison, are, perhaps,

* Horæ Sinicæ, pp. 15, 16.

more abundant than that of any other nation.
The Chinese press, according to Dr. Morrison,
has been prolific, and the accumulation is vast.
Their historians have preserved an account, in
many respects analogous with that which Moses
has given of the general deluge. They place this
event about 2200 years before Christ; but their
tradition, of one of their ancestors, Neu-wo-che,
who melted stones, and repaired the heavens,
carries them back to a period between 3114 and
3254 before the Christian era.*

They possess also ancient and modern literature in great abundance, an unlicensed press,
and cheap books suited to their taste; with
poetry and music of elegant composition, and
native ancient classics. They have copious
histories of their own part of the world, with antiquities and topographical illustrations, dramatic
compositions, — delineations of men and manners in works of fiction, tales of battles and
of murders, and the tortuous stratagems of pro-
tracted and bloody civil wars. With all these,
and with mythological legends for the superstitious, the Chinese, and kindred nations, are
by the press most abundantly supplied. Nor

* Morrison's View of China for Philological Purposes,
pp. 58, 59.

is their literature destitute of theories of nature, and descriptions of her various productions, the processes of the pharmacopolist, and the history and practice of medicine.

There is also a large portion of the gentry of China devoted to letters, in order to qualify themselves to fill the offices of magistracy; and such learning as government has deemed proper for that end is encouraged and rewarded, either by honorary rank, or by actual office. It is also stated, that candidates for public offices are examined in poetry, on the ground that poetry leads to an acquaintance with the passions of men.

Besides these, they have what are deemed sacred writings, being a compilation of the works of ancient authors of the age of Confucius. The following is the character given of these books by Dr. Morrison:—

" These consist of the writings or compilations of the ancient moral philosophers of the age of Confucius (B. C. 500), with numerous notes and comments, and paraphrases on the original text, with controversies concerning its genuineness, the order of particular words or phrases, and the meaning of obscure passages. The text of the Woo-king, which name denotes five sacred books, and of the Sze-shoo, or four books, which are compiled by four of the disciples of Confucius, contain the doctrines or precepts which their master, Confucius, approved and communicated to them. In respect of external form, the five books (Woo-king) of the Chinese, correspond to the Pentateuch of Moses, and the four books (Sze-shoo), in respect of being a record of the sayings of a master, compiled by four disciples, have a slight resemblance to the four Gospels. But the contents—how different! With the exception of a few passages, in the most ancient part of the Woo-king, which retain seemingly something of the knowledge which Noah must have communicated to his children, the rest appears a godless system of personal, domestic, and political moralities, drawn only from the pride of the human heart, the love of fame, or present expediency. The sanctions of the Eternal and Almighty God, arrayed with every natural and moral perfection, wise and good, just and merciful, and the fears and hopes of immortality, and the grace of a Saviour, are wholly wanting in these ancient Chinese works."

The religion and mythology of the Chinese is a dark and cheerless system, blending, with

anomalous incongruity, atheism, and the lowest
kinds of polytheism; presenting one of the most
affecting spectacles in the universe, of the extent and completeness of the calamity, by which
the entrance of sin has been attended to our
race, shewing millions of mankind joined in one
social compact, passing through a long, uninter-
rupted series of ages, untaught of life to come,
unsanctified, unsaved; following the delusions of
their own vain imaginations, or " worshipping
the creature rather than the Creator," who hath
" not left himself without witness among them,
in that he did them good, gave them rain from
heaven, and fruitful seasons, filling their hearts
with food and gladness." Their creed presents
no proper object of reverence, hope, confidence,
and love; affords no balm for the troubles of the
mind; no support under the ills of life; no hope
for the future: their highest prospect is annihilation, or a change by transmigration to the
body of some other being in creation. In the
language of Dr. Morrison, China is full of dumb
idols, is estranged from the true God, and hates
and persecutes the name of Jesus; and well may
he exclaim, " China, the wonder and the pity
of Christians!"

Neither the one nor the other of these

emotions will be diminished, by a consideration of the extent to which the language in which this " atheistical, pantheistical system," is preserved, disseminated, and inculcated, is understood. In his exceedingly interesting philological work, the " Chinese Miscellany," Dr. Morrison states, that the " Chinese language is now *read* by a population of different nations, amounting to a large proportion of the human race, and over a very extensive geographical space,—from the borders of Russia on the north, throughout Chinese Tartary on the west, and in the east as far as Kamschatka; and downwards through Corea and Japan, in the Loo Choo Islands, Cochin China, and the islands of that Archipelago, on most of which are Chinese settlers, till you come down to the equinoctial line at Penang, Malacca, Singapore, and even beyond it on Java. Throughout all these regions, however dialects may differ, and oral languages be confounded, the Chinese *written* language is understood by all. The voyager and the merchant, the traveller and the Christian missionary, if he can *write* Chinese, may make himself understood throughout the whole of eastern Asia."*

* Miscellany, p. 1.

The amazing extent to which this language is understood, and is the medium through which mind operates on mind, darkening, bewildering, and destroying all that yield themselves to the influence of the impious and delusive theories, includes other nations besides those comprising China. Various estimates have been given of the amount; and we are not surprised that, to cool and reflecting minds, the numbers presented by the Chinese authorities, should appear startling, and beyond credibility; and that on these accounts many writers on statistics should have presented a total much below that claimed by the Chinese themselves. In this, however, they seem to have been misled by their own opinions, or the authorities on which they relied.

The following is a Statement of the Population of China and its Colonies, according to a census taken in the eighteenth year of the reign of Kea-king, A. D. 1813, and under the authority of his Imperial Majesty.

Provinces, &c.	No. of Individuals.	Families.
Chihle	27,990,871	—
Shantung.	28,958,764	—
Shanse	14,004,210	—
Honan	23,037,171	—
Keangsoo.	37,843,501	—
Ganhwuy.	34,168,059	—

Carried forward   166,002,576

Provinces, &c.	No. of Individuals.	Families.
Brought forward	166,002,576	
Keangse	30,426,999	—
Fuhkeen	14,777,410	—
Formosa (natives) . . .	1,748*	—
Chekeang	26,256,784	—
Hoopih	27,370,098	—
Hoonan	18,652,507	—
Shense	10,207,256	—
Kansuh	15,193,125	—
Barkoul and Oroumtsi .	161,750	—
Szechuen	21,435,678	—
Kwangtung or Canton .	19,174,030	—
Kwang-se	7,313,895	—
Yunnan	5,561,320	—
Kweichow	5,288,219	—
Shing-king, or Leaou-tung	942,003	—
Kirin	307,781	—
Kihlung - keang, or Teit-cihar, &c.	—	2,398
Tsinghae, or Kokonor, &c.	—	7,842
Foreign tribes under Kansuh	—	26,728
Ditto, ditto, Sze-chuen .	—	72,374
Thibetan colonies . . .	—	4,889
Ele and its dependencies .	—	69,644
Turfan and Lobnor . .	700*	2,551
Russian Border	—	1,900
Individuals . . .	361,693,879	188,326
		4
Individuals at 4 in each family .		753,304
Add individuals		361,693,879
Total individuals		362,447,183

---

* These are the numbers, not of individuals, but of effective men.

The above table is copied from the " Companion to the Anglo-Chinese Kalendar for 1832," edited by the son of the Rev. Dr. Morrison, John Robert Morrison, Esq., who, treading in the steps of his honoured father, is devoting his energies to the benefit of China. " This statement is contained in the last edition of the Ta-tsing Hwuy-leën, or collection of statutes of the Ta-tsing dynasty, published in 1825, and," as Mr. Morrison observes, " will probably serve to set at rest the numerous speculations concerning the real amount of population in China. We know, from several authorities, that in China the people are in the habit of diminishing, rather than increasing their numbers, in their reports to government. And it is unreasonable to suppose, that, in a work published by the government, not for the information of curious inquirers, but for the use of its own officers, the numbers so reported by the people should be more than doubled, as the statements of some European speculators would require us to believe."

Whatever view we take of China, whether we regard it in all its vastness of dimensions and amount of population, the singularity and extensive use of its written language, the varieties

of its literature, its early acquaintance with the
arts and most useful inventions of civilized life,
the stupendous monuments of its skill and power,
its high and venerable antiquity, the nations
now amalgamated in its gigantic empire, or
the important changes it has undergone,—it is
impossible to contemplate it without intense and
mingled emotions. The consideration of the
vicissitudes to which it has been subject, affords
but little satisfaction in the retrospect. " They
have been partially and completely conquered;
have delivered themselves, and have been conquered again; and the divisions of their country
have undergone a thousand different changes."

All these have produced no emancipation of
the mind of the Chinese. The debasing domi-
nation of grovelling superstition and delusive
idolatry, or the withering and blasting influence of scepticism, have introduced no just and
solid foundation for virtue and happiness, and
opened no prospect of rest and blessedness hereafter. They have left China ignorant of the
only true and living God, and of Jesus Christ,
whom he hath sent, and have only increased
the degradation of her mighty population, and
given additional power to her destroyers. It
is from the future that we derive our hopes in

regard to this country; and we are cheered by expectations, drawn from no uncertain sources, that a mighty deliverance yet awaits these spell-bound victims of fatal delusion, and that a moral renovation shall soon take place, which shall raise her to the possession of all the privileges and enjoyments comprised in the inspired declaration, " Blessed is the people whose God is the Lord."

In summing up their character, Dr. Morrison arrives at the following conclusion :—

" The good traits in the Chinese character, amongst themselves, are mildness and urbanity; a wish to shew that their conduct is reasonable, and, generally, a willingness to yield to what appears so; docility, industry, subordination of juniors; respect for the aged, and for parents; acknowledging the claims of poor kindred. These are virtues of public opinion, which, of course, are, in particular cases, often more show than reality; for, on the other hand, the Chinese are specious, but insincere; jealous, envious, and distrustful to a high degree. There is amongst them a considerable prevalence of scepticism, of a Sadducean, and rather atheistical spirit; and their conduct is very generally such as one would naturally expect from a people

whose minds feel not that sense of divine authority, nor that reverence for the divine Majesty
and goodness, which, in Sacred Scripture, is
denominated the ' fear of God.'   Conscience has
few checks but the laws of the land ; and a little
frigid ratiocination on the fitness of things, which
is not generally found effectual to restrain, when
the selfish and vicious propensities of our nature
may be indulged with present impunity.   The
Chinese are generally selfish, cold-blooded, and
inhumane."—He might, with great propriety,
have added, that in the punishment of criminals,
in the infliction of tortures, they are barbarously
cruel ; that human suffering or human life are
but rarely regarded by those in authority, when
the infliction of the one, or the destruction of the
other, can be made subservient to the acquisition of wealth or power.

The need in which China stands of the
change which the gospel only can effect, is
clearly evident, when, in addition to the oppression and violence under which the nation groans,
the fraud and lying practised by system, the
bribery and injustice which fills her courts, the
deception that characterises all her dealings,—
is added, their complicated system of false religion, presenting, as Dr. Milne observes, scarcely

any thing but darkness, confusion, and absurdity; the multitude of her idols, which, according to the expression of one of her sects, are as nume-rous as the sands of the Hang river. Her necessity in this respect appears more urgent, when we consider the moral character and habits of the millions constituting her vast population. Vice exists in all its diversified forms; crimes of the most revolting and debasing character are perpetrated with a frequency unequalled perhaps in any other part of the world; the tender sym-pathies of the heart are counteracted or destroyed by familiarity with cruelty, and selfishness. The female sex, as in every other heathen country, is subjected to the most humiliating degradation; allowed, indeed, to be human beings, but com-pared with the inferior orders of creation.

A Chinese writer, speaking of the ignorance of Chinese females, and consequent unamiable-ness of wives, exhorts husbands not to desist from teaching them, for even " monkeys may be taught to play antics; dogs may be taught to tread a mill; rats may be taught to run round a cylinder; and parrots may be taught to recite verses; since then it is manifest that even birds and beasts may be taught to understand human affairs, how much more so may young wives,

who, after all, are human beings." This is a
Chinese philosopher's defence of women.

Arising in a great measure from the degradation to which these views have reduced the
females of China, and from some of the absurd
dogmas of their mythology, female infanticide,
the most unnatural crime that prevails among
ferocious savages and cannibals, is perpetrated
among them to a degree almost beyond belief.
This practice is carried to such an extent, that it
may almost be said to be patronized by the government, which does not interfere to prevent, and
therefore may be said to give it countenance.
It is, according to Barrow, tacitly considered a
part of the duty of the police of Pekin, to employ certain persons to go their rounds at an
early hour in the morning with carts, in order
to pick up the bodies of such infants as may
have been thrown out into the streets in the
course of the night. No inquiries are made;
but the bodies are carried to a common pit
without the city walls, into which all those that
are living, as well as those that are dead, are said
to be thrown promiscuously.* The Roman
Catholic missionaries attended at the pit daily,
for the purpose of rescuing some of the victims,

* Barrow, p. 168.

and bringing them up in the Christian faith.
Mr. B. observes, that those of the missionaries
with whom he had daily conversation during a
residence of five weeks within the emperor's
palace, assured him that the scenes sometimes
exhibited were such as to make the feeling mind
shudder with horror. Dogs and swine are let
loose into the streets of the capital at an early
hour, before the police carts go round. Barrow
gives the average number as about 24 daily,
or nearly 9,000 for the capital annually, and
supposes an equal number are thus destroyed
in other parts of the empire. Those who reside
on the water throw their infants into the river,
with gourd tied round their necks. The number
given above is reduced by the fact, that in Pekin
infants who have died, or are still-born, are exposed in the streets to be carried away by the
police-carts, to avoid the expense of burying
them. This, the writer above referred to supposes, may reduce the number of murdered
infants to 4,000 in the capital.

The statement of this revolting practice is
confirmed by Mr. Gutzlaff, who more than once
refers to the subject, and who, besides, speaking
of the apathy with which they regarded the exposed body of a lovely and but recently murdered

infant, by remarking, in reply to his observation, that it was *only a female,* states, in reference to the people of Amoy, " That it is a general custom among them to drown a large portion of the new-born female children;" and continues,— " This unnatural crime is so common among them, that it is perpetrated without any feeling, and even in a laughing mood." But without proceeding to a further detail of their barbarities and sufferings, how affecting the illustration they supply of the truth of the Scripture, that " the dark places of the earth are full of the habitations of cruelty!" and how appalling the spectacle, in vastness and extent of crime and of misery, even in regard to the present life, which China presents! But when contemplated by the Christian in connexion with the truths of revelation, by which its inhabitants appear under the power of Satan, " having the understanding darkened, alienated from the life of God through the ignorance that is in them, without hope and without God in the world," it becomes increasingly impressive. And when under these deceptions, the Christian views successive generations of its mighty population, comprising one-third of our species, as having been moving onward under impious atheism or delusive idolatries, during a

greater number of centuries than any other community now numbered among the nations of the
earth has existed, he beholds an object which it
is scarcely possible, excepting in the absence of
all correct Christian sentiment and feeling, to
contemplate without pain. Could this view of
China be brought fully and distinctly before the
free and enlightened nations of Christendom, it
would not allow them to remain contented with
having begun to apply the only effectual remedy,
and could not fail to excite an interest so deep
and extensive, to inspire prayer so unremitted
and fervent, and stimulate to efforts, for the
moral and spiritual renovation of China, so
vigorous and persevering, as to bear some relation to their responsibility and resources.

The state of the nations to the south of this
empire, including Cochin-China, Cambodia, Laos
and Siam, is in no respect better than that
of China. They are all less civilized, but equally
wretched; their governments arbitrary despo-
tisms, sanguinary and rapacious; and their arrogance is equalled only by their deceitfulness and
treachery. The merciless tyranny of the inferior
officers, their extortion and bribery; the jealousy
and pride of the rulers, and the abject and
humiliating bondage of the people, are truly

affecting; while the frequent and heartless application of excruciating tortures, and the savage punishments inflicted on the unhappy wretches who are criminals, exhibit an accumulation of misery, and a destruction of human life that is truly appalling. Their ignorance is gross; for though education is encouraged, it is not calculated to promote the happiness of the people,—a motive that never influenced the mind of a despot, but is regarded as an instrument of rule, and is secured by the few for the more complete subjection of the many. They are the victims of a heartless atheism, or absurd and demoralizing superstition; vice of every order luxuriates in all the rankness of filthiness, debasement, and cruelty, while the future unfolds no brighter hope than annihilation, or the transmigration of the soul. The land is full of idols; the inhabitants, morally and spiritually regarded, are walking in darkness, sitting in the region of the shadow of death.

Next to China, the Siamese nation is most prominently brought before us in Mr. Gutzlaff's narrative, as the chief scene of his labours before undertaking the voyages which his journal describes. Siam is an important country, and in many respects an object of peculiar interest to the Christian. Its extent and population are considerable.

According to Mr. Crawford's accounts, from which the subjoined notices are chiefly selected, the present Siamese empire is composed of the following parts, viz.: Siam, or the proper country of the Siamese race; a large portion of Laos, a portion of Cambodia, and certain tributary Malay states. Its limits in this wide acceptation may be stated as follows:—Its farthest southern boundary, on the western shore of the Malayan Peninsula, is Kurao, in about the latitude of 5° north. Its boundary on the eastern shore, is Kamamang, in nearly about the same parallel. The northern boundary, in the present state of our information, is very little better than conjecture, but probably extends to about 21°; so that the dominions of Siam have a range of no less than 16° of latitude.

The extreme western limits of Siam, including some desert islands in the bay of Bengal, are nearly in 97° $50'$ east longitude. Its eastern boundary probably extends to at least 105°; so that it has a range of about 7° of longitude. Its area may be estimated at 190,000 geographical miles.

The country, though presenting occasionally

extensive and rich alluvial plains, is generally
mountainous.   The mountains stretch through
the country from north to south in ranges nearly
parallel; one chain, extending from within a
short distance of the coast on its southern
limits, in 11° to the 18° of north latitude, is said
to reach in some places an elevation of 5,000
feet.   The country appears to be well watered.
The Menam, literally, Mother of Waters, a river
of second or third rate magnitude among Asiatic
rivers, is the most important.   The proper
country of the Siamese is the valley of the
Menam, which, at its southern extremity, does
not exceed 60 miles in breadth, and is about
360 miles in length.   The present capital of
Siam is Bankok, which is situated on the banks
of the Menam, and is about two miles and a
half long, and a mile and a half in breadth.
The palace and chief part of the city is on
the left side of the river, which is, at this place,
nearly half a mile in breadth, having a large
space at the side, occupied by floating houses.
The depth close to the bank varies from six to
ten fathoms, and this appears to be its general
depth during its course for about 40 miles from
the capital to the bar, at its junction with the
ocean.   The number of boats moving to and fro

on the river, and the bustle among the Chinese mechanics and traffickers, give a lively and cheerful air to the city.

Mr. Tomlin, in his Journal of his Visit to Siam, in 1828, gives the following account of its appearance :—

" The view of the city suddenly opened upon us at two miles' distance : the scenery and dwellings on either side became more varied and beautiful, as we advanced towards the capital. In one part, a temple, resembling a village church, with some light elegant houses, half shaded by the foliage of acacias, presented a lovely and rural scene. Canals and small streams, branching off from the river, overhung by bamboos and willowy shrubs, present themselves to the eye for a considerable distance, and open beautiful vistas. There was a busy and lively scene on the river—innumerable boats and canoes passing to and from the city ; a long line of junks, most of them laid up on the left side of the river ; a little retired from the bank, Chinese smiths' and carpenters' shops ; behind these, the Episcopal Romish Chapel, surrounded by glittering pagodas."

The palace, considering the country, is a respectable building, but the habitations of the people in general are neither suited to cleanliness, comfort, nor durability. Many of them are constructed of the most combustible materials, and the inhabitants are often exposed to extensive and destructive conflagrations. Of one of these occurrences, to a European so alarming, the late excellent Mrs. Gutzlaff has given in a letter, written to a friend in the beginning of 1831, the annexed graphic description. After speaking of being awoke at midnight by the noise, and called to look out of the window of their dwelling, she continues :—

" The whole city of Bankok seemed to be one flame; but it being about a mile and a half from us, and the wind being rather light, we hoped for safety; we had, however, scarcely uttered our hopes, before the wind blew strongly towards us. The houses in and about Bankok are nothing more than a miserable pile of either wood, or bamboo and attap, so that a spark sets them on fire in a moment. The fire increased rapidly; and there seemed but little hope for the safety of the Chinese part of the city, which lies between us and Bankok. Suddenly the fire divided; one mass seemed to recede farther from us, while the other appeared to approach. We called up our people to make preparation for leaving, but the flames advanced with such swiftness, that I wrapped a blanket around me, and after praying to God for the sufferers, as well as for our safety, we ran out.   Mr. G. calmly resigned all to God, and prepared for the loss of every thing.   We perceived that the mass of fire approaching us consisted of a number of floating houses, which had been set adrift in order to prevent the fire communicating to others; four of them had not taken fire, but several were wrapt in flames, and threatened destruction to every thing they approached.   I stood outside with an old Chinaman to watch the approach of the sparks to our roof, while Mr. G. and others stood at the window ready to throw out the boxes.   The wind continued unabated; and it appears to me like a miracle, that although the sparks from the immense masses of burning bamboo, wood and attap houses, were flying around us in every direction, not one fell upon our hut; and we watched with tolerable composure the burning piles, with the Chinese in boats around, striving to extinguish the flame as the blazing mass floated down the river. As soon as it had fairly passed we fell on our knees to bless God for his protection.   The fire that had receded from us, and which seemed to be in the city itself, continued to rage, and appeared spreading against the wind. Several poor wretches have been to us this morning for medical aid ; some say that seven or eight streets in the Chinese part of the city were burnt, but that few lives were lost, owing to the dexterity of the Chinese in swimming."

Mr. Tomlin has given the following as the population of the Siamese capital in the year 1828 :—

Chinese (paying tax)	310,000
Descendants of Chinese	50,000
Cochin Chinese	1,000
Cambojans	2,500
Siamese	8,000
Peguans	5,000
Laos (lately come)	7,000
Ditto (old residents)	9,000
Burmans (or Bramas)	2,000
Tavoy	3,000
Malays	3,000
Christians	800
Total	401,300

A poll-tax, amounting to about three dollars, is levied upon every Chinaman on first entering the country, and re-collected triennially. This secures to them the privilege of exercising any craft, or following any trade they please, and exempts them from the half-yearly servitude required by the king from every other oriental stranger resident in Siam.

According to the data on which Mr. Crawford made his calculations, seven years before, the population of the Siamese empire was—

Siamese	1,260,000
Laos	840,000
Peguans	25,000
Cambojans	25,000
Malays	195,000
Chinese	440,000
Natives of Western India . .	3,500
Portuguese	2,000
Total . . .	2,790,500

Though the nations inhabiting the tropical regions between Hindostan and China differ widely in language, religion, institutions, manners, and physical character, from the inhabitants of the countries adjacent, in some respects they greatly resemble each other.

The Siamese, in stature, are shorter than the Chinese and Hindoos, but taller than the Malays. Mr. Crawford found the average height of twenty men, taken indiscriminately, to be 5 feet 3 inches. This would make them taller than the Malays, and shorter than the Chinese. Their lower limbs are well formed; contrary to what obtains among the natives of Hindostan, their hands are stout, destitute of the softness and delicacy which characterise those of the Hindoos; their persons in general are sufficiently robust and well proportioned, wanting, however, the grace and flexibility of their neighbours in the west; their complexion is a light brown, perhaps a shade lighter than that of the Malays, but many shades darker than that of the Chinese, yet never approaching to the black of the African or Hindoo.

Several writers have remarked, as the most characteristic features in the Siamese countetenance, the height and breadth of the cheekbones, which give to the face the form of a lozenge, instead of the oval of western Asia or Europe; and it is added that, though according to our ideas, beauty is not seen among them, yet we meet with many countenances not disagreeable, and they are said to be a handsomer race than the Chinese or Indian islanders. The aspect of the Siamese is, however, stated to be rather sullen and cheerless, while their gait is sluggish and ungraceful. Their dress, with the exception of the priests, is scanty, and inferior

to that worn by the Hindoos or Chinese; in
general it consists in a piece of silk or cotton
round the loins, leaving the legs and upper
parts of the body uncovered, excepting when a
narrow scarf is thrown over the shoulder. Their
dress is usually dark, white being the colour of
the habiliments of mourning. No turban or
other covering is worn on the head by either
sex, excepting on occasions of formal court
ceremonies, when a singular conical cap is used
by the chiefs.

The Siamese, like the Chinese and other
nations of the farther east, permit the nails of
their hands to grow to an unnatural and inconvenient length, sometimes to the extent of two
inches, presenting, as cleanliness is not a national virtue, a very offensive appearance to an
European.

Notwithstanding the fertility, abundance, and
value of the natural resources of the country,
and the antiquity of the nation, the Siamese
have made but little progress in civilization.
A gloomy superstition and an ignorant despotism are alike opposed to all culture of the
intellect and increase of knowledge. With the
sciences of astronomy, geography, navigation and
medicine, they are unacquainted. The Siamese

are fond of music. Loubere, who visited them in 1688, speaks of their admiration of the trumpets of the French, as so much better than their own; and most writers bear testimony to their superiority in this respect as compared with that of other oriental nations. Their melodies are often wild and plaintive, but more frequently brisk and lively, resembling Scotch and Irish airs, and pleasant to an European ear. Mr. Gutzlaff, however, in his journal, speaking of the music of the Laos, describes their organ made of reeds as among the sweetest instruments to be met with in Asia; and adds, " Under the hand of an European master it would become one of the most perfect instruments in existence."

The habits of the Siamese are described as filthy and indolent. Of any knowledge of the useful arts they appear to be almost wholly destitute; those that are found among them being practised chiefly by the enterprising and industrious Chinese settlers.

The government is absolute and rapacious; imperious and vain, in proportion to its ignorance and impotence. Titles and homage, scarcely less impious than those claimed by the sovereign of the celestial empire, are assumed and required by its rulers, and rendered by the

people. When he is spoken of, it is as " Sacred
Lord of Heads," "Sacred Lord of Lives," " The
Owner of all ;" and other epithets, equally
impious and absurd. He is also designated
the " lord of the white elephant ;" this animal
being regarded as one of the greatest treasures of the kingdom, the banner of the
nation is a white elephant on a crimson field.
The government is administered by four chief
officers ; these, as well as every other public
functionary, take the oath of allegiance, which is
repeated every succeeding year. The ceremony
takes place at the palace, and in administering
the oath, the king plunges his sword, the appropriate sceptre of Siam, into a jar of water, of
which every one taking the oath must drink; to
the officers at a distance a portion of this water
is sent. The servility of the people is abject,
and the exactions of the government oppressive ; their use of torture truly barbarous,
and their punishments sanguinary. Of the
former, the late Mrs. Gutzlaff has recorded the
following affecting instance, as inflicted on a
poor unhappy lunatic :—

" About four months ago, one of the princesses
died. In a neighbouring province there dwelt
a young female, who fell into a trance, and who,

on recovering, after having remained in that state above two days and nights, declared herself the identical princess who had died. To prove her assertion, she maintained that she could mention every article which the princess had possessed during her lifetime. It is reported that her enumeration of these was correct, although she had never known the princess. The governor of the province thought this fact so extraordinary, that he sent the poor creature to the king of Siam. One of the princes was appointed to examine her. She persisted in the fact that she was the princess, his sister, and again recounted the possessions of the aforesaid princess, adding that a mighty power had transformed her; stating, that previously to her trance she was very dark, but that since that period she had become fair. Both the king and prince were so indignant, that they ordered her to receive thirty lashes, and have the instruments of torture applied to her hands and head. That used for the head consists of two flat pieces of wood; the head being placed between these pieces, the ends are gradually drawn together, so tightly as to force the eye-balls from their sockets, and cause an effusion of blood from the ears. Smaller pieces of wood are placed between the fingers and drawn together, so as to cause blood to start from the finger-nails. These tortures were applied, the thirty lashes given, and borne in the presence of hundreds, without a sigh or a groan. Two days afterwards, she was re-examined; and persisting in the same assertions, was sentenced to receive fifty lashes and again to submit to tortures; such was the quiet fortitude with which she bore it, that the people declared that she must be superhuman. At the end of each punishment she mildly said, ' I have told you, and do tell you again, I *am* the princess.' To render the situation of this wretched individual still more distressing, one of the king's telepoys (priests) told his majesty that the sacred books contained a prophecy, that whenever such a person should arise, the kingdom of Siam would pass to another nation. This raised the king's wrath to despair: a grave council was summoned to devise fresh punishment; decapitation, with the extermination of her family, was proposed; but instead of this she was sentenced to receive ninety lashes, which last she bore with the same fortitude as before. It was then decreed that she should be seated on a raft of bamboo, and turned adrift on the open sea. But the above-mentioned telepoy, touched with compassion, interposed in her behalf, saying, ' Who could tell whether this were the very person of whom the book spoke ?' This allayed the wrath of the king, and the poor woman was sentenced to grind rice in the king's kitchen during the remainder of her life !"

The horrible barbarities practised in their iniquitous war with Laos,—their treatment of the king and his family, who were basely betrayed into their hands, afford a melancholy exhibition of their ferocity. The situation of the captives is thus described by Mr. Tomlin, who was residing as a missionary at Bankok when they were brought in :—

" The king of Laos and his family when taken prisoners, were brought here in chains, and exposed to public view for a fortnight *in a large iron cage !* The news of their arrival caused great joy; the Prah Klang and other high personages were long busied in devising the best mode of torturing and putting them to death." Mr. Tomlin, who went to see them, observes, " We were disappointed in not seeing the king. Nine of his sons and grandsons were in the cage; most of them grown up, but two were mere children, who deeply affected us by their wretched condition, all having chains round their necks and legs; one particularly, of an open cheerful countenance, sat like an innocent lamb, alike unconscious of having done any wrong, and of the miserable fate which awaited him. Two or three, however, hung their heads, and were apparently sunk into a melancholy stupor. Now and then they raised them, and cast a momentary glance upon us, their countenances displaying a wild and cheerless aspect. The sad spectacle they exhibited was heightened rather than alleviated by the laughter and playfulness of the Siamese boys who went to see them. Close by are the various instruments of torture in terrific array. A large iron boiler for heating oil, to be poured on the body of the king, after being cut and mangled with knives! On the right of the cage a large gallows is erected, having a chain suspended from the top beam, with a large hook at the end of it. The king, after being tortured, will be hung upon this hook. In the front there is a long row of triangular gibbets, formed by three poles joined at the top, and extended at the bottom. A spear rises up from the joining of the poles a foot or more above them. The king's two principal wives, and his sons, grandsons, &c., amounting in all to fourteen, are to be fixed on these as upon a seat.

On the right of the cage is a wooden mortar and pestle, to pound the king's children in. Such are the means these unsophisticated children of nature employ to maintain their superiority over one another,—such the engines of power despotism employs to secure its prerogative,—and such the worse than fiendish cruelty of man towards his fellow-man, when left to the unsoftened dictates of his own depraved heart. Shortly afterwards, the old Laos king expired, and thus escaped the hands of his tormentors. He is said to have gradually pined away, and died broken-hearted. His corpse was removed to the place of execution, decapitated, and hung on a gibbet by the river side, a little below the city, exposed to the gaze of every one passing by, and left a prey to the birds. His son afterwards escaped, but on being pursued, put an end to his existence. Of the fate of the others we have not heard."

The use of letters has long prevailed in Siam; the knowledge of reading and writing, a most important fact in connexion with missionary efforts, is generally diffused. But their literature is comparatively worse than useless. It contains no treasures of valuable knowledge; nothing to invigorate and expand the faculties of the mind, or to improve the heart. It consists of the trifling amusements of mental imbecility and indolence, or comments on the tenets of Budhism, the national religion of Siam, as well as the adjacent countries. The deadly influence of this atheistical system, combined with the tyranny of the government, completes the mental and spiritual wretchedness of the people. Such is the power of this system, that most of the male population at one period or other during life belong to the priesthood. According to the information received by Mr. Crawford, the telepoys or priests in the capital, amounted to 5,000, and in the whole of the kingdom to 50,000; nearly one-fortieth of the Budhist population. The influence of so large a portion of idle mendicants must operate with prodigiously destructive force on the industry of the people; and their maintenance must be an intolerable burden, while their ignorance seals and perpetuates the mental weakness of the nation.

In morals, the Siamese appear scarcely more advanced than in civilization. Debauchery appears to exist in its most odious forms; gaming, and intoxication from the use of opium, augment the misery, while fraud and falsehood appear as universal as they are offensive. " I regret," observes Mr. Gutzlaff, "not to have found one honest man; sordid oppression, priestcraft, allied with wretchedness and filth, are everywhere to be met with."

Such are some of the principal features in the character and circumstances of the Siamese,— next to China, one of the most important of the ultra-Gangetic nations. These are probably applicable, with slight variations, to the inhabitants of the adjacent countries; and while they present a number of points deeply interesting, the world exhibits few objects more worthy of the prayers, solicitude, and exertions of the enlightened and christian portions of mankind.

Although the countries beyond the Ganges have not received a measure of attention equal to that which has been given to some parts of the world, they have not been overlooked by the communities professing Christianity. Scarcely had the Portuguese, in that spirit of adventurous discovery and commerce by which they were characterised in the sixteenth century, opened an intercourse with these countries, than the Catholics of Europe sent forth a host of ecclesiastics to convert the nations of the East to the Romish faith. In the enterprise they manifested an enthusiasm, in some respects resembling that which, a few centuries before, had induced them to send forth the rabble of their zealots and the flower of their chivalry for the recovery of Palestine. The learning, talents, address, and unwearied assiduity of many of the missionaries, secured a degree of success that drew upon them a large measure of the attention of their respective countries, and the civilized world. Ecclesiastical history preserves the record of their perseverance and their triumph. But though Protestants have in these parts of the world engaged with avidity and zeal in the pursuits of commerce for nearly two centuries, as our first intercourse with Siam appears to have taken place in 1612, there is no memorial of their efforts to communicate the gospel to the nations of the East, for more than an equal period after they had emerged from the darkness of Popery, and had obtained free access to the oracles of truth. This renders it, as one of our own prelates* has observed, no small reproach to the Protestant religion, that to our unwearied endeavours to promote the interest of trade in foreign parts, there hath not been joined a like zeal and industry for propagating the christian religion. It is only recently, and within the

* Tillotson.

present century, that British churches have endeavoured to communicate to the millions inhabiting south-eastern Asia, the knowledge of the living God.

The first effort of Protestant Europe to communicate the gospel to the millions of China, was made by the Christians of England united in a voluntary association, designated THE MISSIONARY SOCIETY. This institution was formed in the year 1795, by the union of clergymen and laymen of the Episcopal and other denominations of Christians; and its sole object was to spread the knowledge of Christ among heathen and other unenlightened nations. Some distinct appellation having since been found necessary, without the slightest change of constitution, principle, or object, the original designation has been altered to that of *The London Missionary Society.*

Soon after the establishment of this Institution, its attention was directed to China; but the vastness of the work here presented, the difficulties and perils of every order which attended any endeavour to gain access to the people, acquire their language, and introduce the doctrines of the gospel, were such as to repel rather than invite to the attempt. The barriers to

success, from the principles and policy of the
government, and other sources, appeared also
to be such as to prove, in the absence of
the direct and visible manifestation of Divine
power, almost insurmountable. It was, however, deemed a solemn duty to make the attempt. Mr. Robert Morrison, then a student,
was selected as an individual to whom the important trust could be confided, and all the means
available in preparing for the work were made
use of prior to his departure. The sending
forth of several individuals was at first contemplated, and Dr. W. Brown, the present
Secretary of the Scottish Missionary Society,
was chosen as one of the associates of Mr.
Morrison; but this intention was afterwards
relinquished, and ultimately the latter embarked
alone.

Uncertain where his lot would be cast;
whether jealousy and bigotry would permit him
to remain in China, or force him to remove;
whether he should be cast among friends and
Christians, or strangers and enemies, he went
forth relying on the faithfulness and power of
Him who had said, " Lo, I am with you always,
even unto the end." Referring to their chief
design, and to their hopes in sending him forth,

the Directors of the Society, in their letter of
instructions, observe:—" We trust that no objection will be made to your continuing in
Canton, till you have accomplished your great
object of acquiring the language; when this is
done, you may probably soon afterwards begin
to turn this attainment into a direction which
may be of extensive use to the world. Perhaps
you may have the honour of forming a Chinese
Dictionary, more comprehensive and correct than
any preceding one; or, the still greater honour
of translating the Sacred Scriptures into a language spoken by a third part of the human
race." How satisfactorily, by the Divine blessing, these works have been accomplished, will be
shewn hereafter.

In the month of January, 1807, Mr. Morrison
left his native land, and was viewed by some,
probably by many, as a weak, infatuated enthusiast, but regarded by others as bound on
an errand the most benevolent and important
that had ever been undertaken. He was followed by the warm affection and the fervent
prayers of many of the most pious and devoted
ministers and members of the British churches.
The following is the record he has preserved
of his feelings on taking his leave of the

shores of Britain:—"This is in all probability (but God alone knows) the closing prospect of a land I shall visit no more. O may the blessing of God rest upon it! The land that gave me birth!—the land that till this hour has nourished me!—the land of my fathers' sepulchres!—a land I esteem most precious, because there I trust I was born again, and there the saints in numbers dwell! Happy land! May the light of the gospel never be removed from thee. The prayers of a departing missionary are ended. Amen and Amen." Mr. Morrison sailed by way of America, and the sympathy, kindness, and attention he received from devoted christian friends, during the period of his short sojourn there, were of the greatest service to him in the early period of his residence at Canton.

By the care of a gracious Providence he reached the shores of China, in September, 1807. Here an unexplored field, an untrodden path, and a work, the vastness and perplexities of which would have been appalling to an ordinary mind, appeared before him. He had difficulties to contend with that no future missionary will meet; and labour to perform, which, once achieved, will serve for all who may follow in

his train. Keeping his eye steadily fixed on
the great object of his mission, as soon as he
reached his destination he pursued, under circumstances of great privation, the study of the
language, which he had commenced, with the
best assistance he could procure, before leaving
his native country. He was favoured with the
blessing of health, and in dependence on the
Divine blessing, he grappled with the difficulties
of his work. By a circumspection the most careful and unremitted, he escaped interruption from
the suspicious jealousy of his enemies; and by
persevering labour, unrelaxed and undiverted, he
finally overcame the difficulties of his task. The
self-denial which he imposed, and the earnestness
with which he sought to make every thing bear
upon the object of his mission, will appear
from the fact of his spending the day with his
teacher, studying, eating, and sleeping, in a room
underground,—adopting the Chinese costume—
foregoing the pleasure of intercourse with his
countrymen, and taking his meal with the Chinese
who taught him the language. As Mr. Milne
remarks, " He felt a zeal which bore up his
mind, and enabled him, by the blessing of God,
to persevere. So desirous was he to acquire the
language, that even his secret prayers to the

Almighty were offered in broken Chinese. The place of retirement is often fresh in his memory, and he always feels a sort of regard for it as being the childhood of his Chinese existence.

" At this time, so strong was his sense of the necessity of caution, so unwilling was he to obtrude himself on the notice of the people of Macao, that he never ventured out of his house. He carried this precaution further than was necessary; but it seemed better to err on the safe side. His health began to suffer from it, so that he could scarcely walk across the room with ease to himself. The first time he ventured out in the fields adjoining the town of Macao, was in a moon-light night, under the escort of two Chinese."

The friendly regard of the Americans resident at Canton has been already noticed. The gentlemen connected with the East-India Company were many of them not less attentive. In the close of the year 1808, Mr. Morrison received an appointment in the Honourable Company's factory, which he has held to the present time, with credit to himself, satisfaction to the Company, and without neglecting the great object of his mission,—the communication of the gospel to the Chinese. Intent on this, as soon as he

was sufficiently acquainted with Chinese, his
endeavours were directed to the communication
of divine knowledge, to those who taught him
the language of their country. The religious
instruction given on the Sabbath to the few
Chinese who could be induced to attend, has,
excepting under unavoidable interruptions, been
continued to the present time. The labours to
which all who devote themselves to the service
of Christ among the heathen, look forward with
strong anticipations of pleasure, were pursued
under very different circumstances from those
which have attended the efforts of the christian
missionary in other parts of the world. The
latter has generally, when master of the language
of the people, been permitted, as often as his
strength and other means would admit, to repair
to the highways, the markets, the festivals and
temples of idolatry, and lifting up his voice
amidst the crowds gathered around him, declare
unto them the unsearchable riches of Christ.
" Instead of this," as Dr. Milne observes, in his
Retrospect of the Mission, " all that the missionaries to China could frequently do, was to
address an individual or two with fear and trem-
bling, in an inner apartment, with the doors
securely locked." To persevere under such

discouragements required no common strength of principle, no faint and wavering love to Christ and love to souls, and no mere transient impulse of desire for their salvation.

After this experiment had been continued nearly three years, this devoted missionary tried the practicability of printing part of the Scriptures. The Acts of the Apostles,—the translation of which had been the work of some Roman Catholic missionary,—a copy of which he had obtained in England; and had, as his knowledge of Chinese increased, revised it for printing, was his first undertaking. The effort was successful, and encouraged him to persevere. A Grammar was next prepared.

In 1811, within four years after his arrival in the country, the translation of the Gospel of Luke was finished and printed; and other smaller works, of the catechetical and devotional kind, were prepared. Directing, however, his attention chiefly to the translation of the Sacred Scriptures, this great work was carried forward with diligence and care.

In the early part of 1813, another portion of the Sacred Scriptures was finished and printed, and a few copies forwarded to the Directors of the London Missionary Society. On their presenting a copy to the British and Foreign Bible Society, that Institution, with a degree of liberality which has characterised all its proceedings, voted 500*l.* towards the printing and circulation of portions of the Scriptures in China.

Hitherto Mr. Morrison had pursued his arduous labours alone, a circumstance which adds to the difficulties, and diminishes the facilities for usefulness in any mission. But even under these disadvantages he had proved that the difficulties were not insurmountable, and had shown the practicability of the object proposed by its establishment. He had solicited assistance, and in 1812, the Rev. W. Milne, who had been preparing for missionary service, under the able tuition of the late Rev. Dr. Bogue, was appointed to be his companion. Accompanied by Mrs. Milne, he reached Macao in July of the following year (1813), was welcomed by Mr. Morrison with sincere and ardent joy; but within two or three days after his landing, the jealousy and intolerance of the Papists prohibited his remaining in the place, and a peremptory order from the Portuguese governor of Macao required him to embark in a vessel then leaving the harbour. Remonstrance and entreaty were useless; he was under the necessity, in about a fortnight afterwards, of separating from his wife, and proceeding to Canton, where, as he expresses it in his Retrospect of the Mission, he found among the heathen that hospitality which had been denied him in a Christian colony. For perils among pagans he had endeavoured to prepare himself, but this was a trial which he did not expect. Deprived of the encouragement, counsel, and assistance of his predecessor, at a period when his experience, his acquaintance with the genius and character of the Chinese, and his instruction in the language appeared so indispensable, he pursued alone, with the few aids within his reach, the study of the language, until he was joined by his predecessor at Canton. For three months he enjoyed every advantage which the instruction and guidance of Mr. Morrison could afford; and while employed in the laborious task of acquiring the language, every other kind of mental employment was suspended, and the energy of all his faculties devoted exclusively to this great object.

The season during which the gentlemen connected with the East India Company remain at Canton was closed, and Mr. Morrison was about to return with them to Macao. The jealous suspicion of the Chinese authorities rendered it unsafe for him to remain at Canton during the whole year, and the Portuguese refused him admittance to Macao. Under these circumstances, it was agreed between his fellow-labourer and himself that he should undertake a voyage to Java, and other principal Chinese settlements in the straits, to distribute the Holy Scriptures, and select a spot on which the objects of the Chinese mission might be pursued under more favourable auspices.

By the close of 1813, the translation of the whole of the New Testament was finished and revised. This was the most important work that had yet been achieved in behalf of China. With great circumspection and many fears from the jealousy of the Chinese government, an edition of 2,000 copies was printed, also 10,000 of a tract, and 5,000 of a catechism. With the greater part of the edition under his care, Mr. Milne embarked for Java in February, 1814. Between 400 and 500 Chinese emigrants to Banca sailed in the same ship, and among them this enterprising missionary had the pleasure of distributing many tracts, and a number of copies of the New Testament, probably the first complete New Testament in the Chinese language ever put into circulation.

On reaching Java, Mr. M. received the greatest attention and kindness from that enlightened and distinguished philanthropist, the late Sir Stamford Raffles, Lieut.-Governor of Java, and from a number of respectable residents in the place. Encouraged by the facilities afforded, he travelled over great part of Java, visiting the most important places, ascertaining the circumstances and disposition of the Chinese, and distributing liberally among them copies of the New Testament and other religious publications. He also visited, for the same purpose, the adjacent island of Madura. At Malacca, he was cordially welcomed by the resident and commandant, Major W. Farquhar; and having accomplished the object of his visit, returned to China in the autumn of 1814.

Seven years had now passed away, since the first Protestant missionary landed on the shores of China. During this period he had laboured in hope, breaking up, with unremitting toil, the fallow ground, and scattering, as opportunity offered, the incorruptible seed of the divine word. Much useful and important instruction had been communicated, and received by many with attention and seriousness; yet hitherto no decisive result had appeared. But while the hearts of

the devoted servants of the Redeemer were
cheered by the facilities afforded for the wider
diffusion of the knowledge of Christ, it was
their happiness to behold it made, they had
reason to believe, the power of God unto salvation. The concealed, though extreme vigilance
of the government, their known hostility to the
Christian religion, the severe and intimidating
edict of the emperor, in 1812, had, it was presumed, deterred some from making a profession
of their faith, who were convinced of the truth
of Christianity, and desirous to place themselves under its influence. In this year, Tsae-
a-ko, a Chinese, in the vigour of life, being
twenty-seven years of age, after becoming acquainted with the doctrines of the gospel, made
known his desires to be admitted to share the
privileges of the people of God; and, after what
was deemed satisfactory evidence, received the
ordinance of Christian baptism.

After copying his confession of faith, and
accompanying it with an outline of his character,
Mr. Morrison, in forwarding the account of this
interesting event, continues:—" At a spring of
water, issuing from the foot of a lofty hill by the
sea-side, away from human observation, I bap-
tized, in the name of the Father, Son, and Holy

Spirit, Tsae-a-ko, whose character and confession have been given above. O that the Lord may cleanse him from all sin in the blood of Jesus, and purify his heart by the influences of his Holy Spirit! May he be the first-fruits of a great harvest; one of millions, who shall believe and be saved from the wrath to come!" Four years afterwards he was removed by death, but maintained until that period, so far as it was known, a holy, blameless, and consistent life.

Besides the Grammar already noticed, Mr. Morrison prepared, as he proceeded in the study of the language, materials for a Chinese and English Dictionary. The East India Company, on its having been recommended to their notice, were so deeply impressed with the importance and value of this work, that they readily undertook its publication; and in September, 1814, printing presses, types, &c., arrived at Macao for this purpose. Besides thus defraying the entire charge of printing, the Honourable Company generously gave to the able compiler 500 copies of the work for his own use.

The chief part of the first edition of the New Testament having been distributed, it was deemed requisite to prepare for a second, in a smaller size. Blocks were accordingly cut for an edition in 12mo., and liberal grants for defraying the expense were made by the British and Foreign Bible Society. A generous individual* had also bequeathed to Mr. Morrison 1000 dollars, to diffuse the knowledge of our blessed religion. This sum was appropriated chiefly to the printing this smaller edition of the New Testament.

It has been already stated, that one of the objects of Mr. Milne's visit to the Chinese settlements in the Malayan Archipelago, was to ascertain in what spot the chief seat of the Chinese mission could be placed, so as to be exempt from the constant alarm and peril to which its members were exposed, and to prosecute its objects with more facility. Malacca was selected, on account of the comparative salubrity of its climate, its proximity to China, and the facilities it afforded for the extensive distribution of the Sacred Scriptures.

In the month of April, 1815, after having experienced great hospitality from friends in Canton, Mr. and Mrs. Milne removed to Malacca, where they were cordially welcomed by the resident, Major Farquhar, who, on every occasion, manifested the utmost regard to Mr. Milne, and to the objects of his mission. Besides performing

---

* W. Parry, Esq., one of the East India Company's factory.

the duties of chaplain at the station, Mr. Milne's first efforts were directed to the establishment of a free-school for the Chinese. Some idea of the difficulties attending missionary operations in a new station among this people, may be gathered from the fact, that, for a year, many kept their children away, from suspicion that the offer to teach originated in some improper motive. At length two gave in their names, and ultimately fifteen were on the list. The school was opened in August, 1815, with five scholars, but the number was afterwards increased. The difficulties attending it were less formidable than had been apprehended. Christian books were introduced. The master and scholars were induced to attend daily the worship of the true God. The missionary was cheered by the encouragement and liberality of Christian friends, by whom the expense of the school was amply provided for, and went forward with gratitude and hope. The education of the Chinese youth in Malacca, thus commenced, was afterwards extended by the formation of other schools, and has been continued unto the present time. Other departments of labour received a share of his attention proportioned to their importance and utility.

In the month of September, of this year, he was joined by Mr. Thomsen, who directed his attention to the acquisition of the Malay language, with a view of communicating the gospel to the Malays. He is still labouring, and has attained a proficiency in writing the language rarely exceeded by one not a native of the country.

In 1816, Mr. Milne visited Penang, where he was treated with the greatest hospitality and kindness by the members of the government, and the European residents. He obtained from the government a grant of land for the Malay mission, and thus secured the means of uninterruptedly pursuing its great objects.

While thus engaged, Mr. Milne had the satisfaction of beholding the Divine blessing attending his labours in the conversion of a Chinese, who had accompanied him from Canton, and been diligent in attending the duties of his station, but whose heart the Lord appeared to have opened to receive the truth in love, and to yield himself up to Christ. Satisfied of his sincerity, and his just views of the ordinance he now desired, Mr. Milne admitted into the visible church, the first-fruits of his labours among the Chinese, by the rite which was designed to be a formal renunciation of heathenism, and an avowal of Christian discipleship. This interesting event took place on the 3d of November, in a private room in the mission-house, and according to the wish of the convert, precisely at mid-day. The ordinance, Mr. M. observes, was dispensed with mingled affection, joy, hope, and fear. Those who have not been placed in similar circumstances, can form no adequate idea of the deep, but varied feelings, such an event is adapted to excite. The joys it imparts are peculiarly a missionary's own; and the hopes it inspires can only be duly estimated by those by whom they are experienced.

Eighteen years have now passed away since this event took place. The devoted servant of Christ, who was honoured to turn this deluded idolater from darkness to light, has been removed to his rest and his reward, but his son in the faith still survives, and has maintained his profession of discipleship unsullied and unimpaired. His life has been devoted to the service of his Redeemer in the instruction of his countrymen. The beneficial effects of his example and labours, in writing and distributing religious books, and copies of the Scriptures, and teaching, though for the most part probably unknown to himself, have been frequently manifest in those who have renounced their idols, and yielded themselves to God. He has several times written to the friends of the Society, through the instrumentality of whose missionary he was made acquainted with the gospel; and his letters evince, in a remarkable degree, the correctness of his views of divine truth, the simplicity and sincerity of his piety, and the animating hope of future blessedness which the gospel has inspired. The following is a copy of the last letter received from him; it is dated, and is addressed to the Treasurer of the London Missionary Society:—

" Leangafa, with a respectful obeisance, presents this letter before the honoured presence of the venerable Mr. Wilson, wishing him a golden tranquillity.

" For several years past, I have had to be grateful for our Lord and Saviour's gracious protection, and bestowment of the Holy Spirit to open my heart and form my will.

" I have always received great kindness from Dr. Morrison, in giving me instruction, by which I have attained to some knowledge of the mysteries of the gospel. I have also preached the gospel, and exhorted for several years the people of my native place; and have had the happiness

of receiving the Lord and Saviour's great grace
in saving some out of the hands of the devil,
turning them from depravity to righteousness,
casting away their idols, and serving the living
and true God, obeying and believing in the Lord
and Saviour, and hoping for the salvation of
their souls.

"During this year, several persons have obeyed,
and believed in the Saviour, and entered the
general church of the reformed holy religion.
There are upwards of ten of us who, with one
heart and united minds, continually serve the
Lord, and learn and practise the holy doctrines
of the gospel. Every holy Sabbath-day we
assemble together to praise the Saviour for the
mighty grace of redemption.

"Happily, the Lord most high has graciously
granted us protection, so that we have enjoyed
hearts at peace and in tranquil joy; therefore I
respectfully prepare this slip of paper, with
writing on it, to inform you, venerable Sir, of
these things, and to pray that you would, as is
right, joyfully praise our heavenly Father for
converting us by his great grace.

"Further, I look up and hope that you,
venerable Sir, will pray to our Lord and Saviour
for us, that he will confer the Holy Spirit's

secret aid, to influence and rouse our hearts, that
from first to last we may, with one mind, and
persevering intention, cultivate virtue, and persuade the men of the world every year to come
in greater numbers to serve the Lord, that we
may together ascend to the heavenly regions,
and assemble with the vast multitude who, in his
presence, shall praise the self-existent and ever-
living God, throughout never to be exhausted,
never ending ages.

" Just as in 1 Cor. xiii. 12, holy Paul says, ' For
now we see through a glass darkly, but then face to
face :' we who in this world reverently believe in
our Lord and Saviour, although we cannot, with
fleshly eyes, see the honoured countenance of our
heavenly Father, still in the life that is to come
we shall be able to view, face to face, the majesty
of our heavenly Father. Though you and I
are separated as far as one boundary of the sky
to its extreme opposite, and cannot see each
other in our own proper persons, still we hope to
meet and see each other in the presence of our
heavenly Father, and praise his great power
for ever.

" My special wish, Sir, is, that in this life you
may leap with joy and delight to assist in the
concerns of our high Lord ; then, in that day, the

Lord of general judgment will bestow a crown of righteousness on those who love our Lord and Saviour's appearing.   (See 2 Tim. iv. 8.)

" This letter is respectfully presented on the right side of the chair of the venerable Mr. Wilson."

Messrs. Morrison and Milne pursued the work with unabated ardour and activity, and were greatly encouraged by the liberal aid afforded by other institutions, as well as the Society with which they were connected; especially the generous grants of the British and Foreign Bible and the Religious Tract Societies.   Early in 1817, the operations of the missionary press were commenced.   In the month of June, in the same year, Mr. Medhurst, who had been appointed to co-operate with Mr. Milne, arrived at Malacca, where he was cordially welcomed by the founder of the mission, whom the affliction of his beloved wife, and the failure of his own health, obliged to visit China in the end of the year.   On the 24th of Dec. 1817, the Senatus Academicus of Glasgow unanimously conferred the title of Doctor in Divinity on Mr. Morrison, in token of their approbation of his philological labours; and in 1820, the same was presented to his

colleague, Mr. Milne. In 1818, Mr. and Mrs.
Milne returned to Malacca, where they found
Mr. Thomsen, who had been, on account of
Mrs. Thomsen's illness, obliged to visit Europe.
On his return, he had been accompanied by
another missionary; and in the month of Sep-
tember the mission was farther strengthened by
the arrival of Messrs. Milton, Beighton, and
Ince.

Mr. Milne's visit to China had enabled him
to confer with his colleague, Dr. Morrison, on a
number of subjects connected with the mission;
and among the comprehensive views they entertained of the best means of giving stability,
efficiency, and permanence, to their labours,
was the establishment of the ANGLO-CHINESE
COLLEGE, for the purpose of blending the
culture of Chinese and European literature,
and rendering its advantages subservient to the
advancement of the cause of Christ in China.
Towards this noble object, of which he was at
once the projector and the founder, Dr. Morrison
contributed 1000*l.* with an annual subscription
of 100*l.* for five years. Though the generous
contributions of the friends of this important
institution have been equal to the operations
hitherto carried on, they have been altogether

inadequate to the extent of those contemplated, and the managers are exceedingly anxious to extend its benefits as soon as more ample means shall enable them to do so. The foundation stone of the College was laid on the 11th of November, 1818.

The nature and design of the Institution, the necessity for its establishment, and the benefits that may be expected ultimately to result from its influence, are stated with great ability and force by the late Dr. Milne, in an address, delivered in the presence of the English and Dutch authorities, and a numerous assemblage of friends, on the occasion of laying the foundation-stone of the building. After speaking of the want, in Europe, of enlarged information respecting the nations beyond the Ganges, and the extreme ignorance of even the accomplished scholars of China respecting christian nations, as shewn by the sentiments of a grave Chinese author, profoundly skilled in the literature of his own nation, congratulating himself that he was not born in our barbarous countries of the West; and who observes, "for then I must have lived in a cave under ground,—eaten the bark and roots of trees,—worn leaves and long grass for my covering, and been really a beast, though in the shape of a man:" Dr. Milne points out the desirableness of introducing the Chinese to the ample stores of western knowledge, and shews that this knowledge is chiefly valuable, as it " points upward to the Deity, and forward to eternity. It is intended to conduct man to God, and to make him happy for ever. Most of those things about which our thoughts are now engrossed, our talents employed, our property expended, and our time exhausted, are destined to perish :

" MORTALIA FACTA PERIBUNT.

" We can look forward to a period when the most magnificent works of art, on which the skill and wealth of nations have been exhausted, shall be destroyed, and not a single vestige of human greatness or human science left about them ; and when the richest and most extensive collections of books, and curiosities, and apparatus, which literary, philosophical, and antiquarian industry has heaped together, through a long succession of ages, shall be melted down in the flames of the dissolving universe, and no longer distinguishable from the confused mass of its ashes !"

The number of students in the college has

varied at different periods, and when the last accounts were forwarded, amounted to thirty. The advantages for obtaining general knowledge afforded to a number of Chinese youths by the college have been highly important; and the Institution on this account, as well as others, entitled to the approval and liberal support of all who are concerned for the welfare of China, and a more extensive and beneficial intercourse between its inhabitants and those of Europe. Mr. Marjoribanks, in describing what he saw when on a visit to the Institution, observes,— "The son of a Malacca peasant derives an enlightened education denied to the son of the emperor of China." Besides these and other minor benefits, all favourable to the accomplishment of the great object, several instances have occurred in which the inmates of the college have attained that knowledge which has made them wise for eternity. It was in the college that the devoted Afä first professed his attachment to Christ. Le, a native teacher, who recently returned to China, avowed himself a Christian, so far as education is considered. A devoted Chinese teacher is labouring with the American missionaries in Burmah, who was formerly a pupil in the college, and has since

professed his faith in Christ; and five Chinese
Christians, from the college, are now actively
employed in diffusing the knowledge of Christ
among their countrymen.

In 1816, Dr. Milne visited Penang, with
a view to ultimate exertions for the spiritual
benefit of its inhabitants. In 1819, Mr. Medhurst
visited the island, and succeeded in establishing
two Chinese schools, for the support of which
a grant was made by the government, and in
the same year missionary operations were commenced among the Malays by Mr. Beighton,
and the Chinese by Mr. Ince.   After a short
but faithful career of devotedness to the Saviour,
Mr. Ince was removed by death, in April, 1825.
Mr. Dyer has since laboured with great diligence in the Chinese department.   The mission
has been continued, and has rendered important
and effective aid in diffusing the knowledge of
the gospel among the heathen residents and
traders visiting this land.

Besides the efforts that have been made at
Canton, Malacca, and Penang, in 1814 missionary
operations were commenced by the Rev. J. C.
Supper, at Batavia, in the populous island of
Java, under the protection, and favoured by the
sanction of the governor, the late enlightened

and excellent Sir Stamford Raffles. Mr. Supper was removed by death in 1817. In 1822 the station was occupied by the Rev. W. H. Medhurst, who has continued to labour with diligence and fidelity. Although his efforts have not been attended with that visible success which he has so earnestly desired and sought, he is not without evidence that they have been highly serviceable. Between 100,000 and 200,000 books and tracts in different languages, many of them printed at the Mission press at Batavia, have been circulated, besides numerous copies of portions of the Scriptures, in Malay and Chinese. In addition to his other labours, Mr. Medhurst has prepared a Japanese and English Vocabulary, a Fokeen-Chinese and English Dictionary; the latter work, in testimony of their approval, the Honourable East India Company have printed at their press in Canton. In October, 1819, a mission was commenced at Singapore, by the Rev. C. H. Thomsen, whose labours have been chiefly among the Malays, and whose intimate acquaintance with their language has eminently qualified him for the translation or preparation of books for the use of the people, in which department of labour he has, through the medium of the press at Singapore, rendered important services. When the mission commenced, the population of Singapore was about 5,000, half of whom were Chinese; in 1830 it was estimated at between 16,000 and 17,000, of whom 6,500 were Chinese, 5,000 Malays, and the rest natives of the adjacent islands.

In 1823 the attention of the Directors of the London Missionary Society was turned towards Siam, and they decided, in dependence on Divine Providence, to attempt a translation of the Scriptures into the language of its inhabitants as soon as practicable. About this time Mr. Milton, then one of the missionaries at Singapore, commenced the translation of portions of the Scriptures, and also the compilation of a Siamese dictionary, towards which 13,000 words were alphabetically arranged.

In 1826 Mr. Medhurst proposed a visit to Siam for the distribution of copies of the Scriptures, and Tracts, &c., but was prevented, and it was not until August 1828, that Mr. Tomlin, one of the missionaries of the Society, and Mr. Gutzlaff, formerly connected with the Netherlands Missionary Society, embarked from Singapore for Siam, and arrived in safety at Bankok, the capital, after a voyage of seventeen days. They were kindly received by the Phrah Klang,

or minister of his Siamese Majesty, and
were treated with great attention and kindness
by the Portuguese consul. After remaining
actively and usefully employed in this important
field six months, they returned to Singapore.
An interesting account of their proceedings,
written by Mr. Tomlin, is already before the
public. In February, 1830, Mr. Gutzlaff returned to Siam, and pursued with unwearied
devotedness his delightful work, until the spring
of the following year, when he undertook a
voyage to China. He has prefixed an interesting
account of these labours to the narrative of his
voyages.

Mr. Gutzlaff is a native of Stettin, in Prussia.
In early life he gave indications of a spirit
of adventurous enterprise, which was the
means of procuring royal favour and patronage,
which opened before him the fairest prospects in his native land ; but these were to him
less attractive than the privilege of preaching Christ to the heathen. Before proceeding
to his distant field of labour, he visited England,
became acquainted with many friends and sup-
porters of missions, and among them, Dr. Morrison, then on a visit to his native land, and
displayed the most commendable diligence in

seeking information likely to be useful in his future labours. The great Head of the Church appears to have endowed him with qualifications peculiarly suited to the important work to which his life is devoted. To a good constitution, and a frame capable of enduring great privations and fatigue, he unites a readiness in the acquisition of language, a frankness of manner, and a freedom in communicating with the people, a facility in accommodating himself to his circumstances, blending so much of what appeared natural to the Chinese, with what was entirely new, that, while they hailed him in some parts of the coast as "the child of the western ocean," they professed to recognize him as a descendant of one of their countrymen, who had moved with the tide of emigration to some distant settlement. His knowledge of the healing art gave him access to all classes, and his steadiness of aim has enabled him to render all subservient to the communication to the Chinese of the unsearchable riches of Christ.

On his return to Singapore, after his first visit to Siam, he entered into the marriage relation with Miss Newell, who had been employed under the London Missionary Society, in the superintendence of female schools. She was like-minded with himself, and every way suited to be the companion of his joys and toils. She accompanied him to Siam, and during the twelve interesting months they were permitted to cooperate in labour there, she united cordially and successfully in all his pursuits, studying the languages of the people around them, administering to the sick, translating the Scriptures, and teaching both the rich and poor who came for instruction. After the labours of the day, they were accustomed in the evening to pursue their literary engagements. Many tracts have been written, a Siamese and Cochin Chinese dictionary framed, and the Scriptures partially or wholly translated into five dialects. On the 16th of February, 1831, Mrs. Gutzlaff was summoned by death from the church militant to the church triumphant. The memory of the just is blessed; and her works of faith and labour of love will not be forgotten, especially by the people who were accustomed to call her "the woman amongst ten thousand." Shortly after this afflictive event, to which he more than once makes a touching allusion, Mr. Gutzlaff commenced those attempts to introduce the gospel to China, of which the following journals contain valuable and instructive accounts.

Soon after the departure of Mr. Gutzlaff for China, Mr. Tomlin, and Mr. Abell, a missionary from America, arrived, and prosecuted the work until the former returned to Singapore, and the latter was under the necessity of seeking the restoration of health by a voyage to a more temperate climate.

In 1831, the Directors of the London Missionary Society appointed two missionaries to Siam; but the afflictive bereavements by death which the missionaries in Bengal experienced, rendering it necessary to reinforce the latter, their destination was altered, and no subsequent appointment was made until June, 1833, when two missionaries were sent out by the American Board of Commissioners for Foreign Missions, to commence a permanent mission in this important part of south-eastern Asia.

Since the termination of the first voyage from Siam to China, and the second in the ship *Lord Amherst*, Mr. Gutzlaff has made a third visit to the northern ports of China, and it is ardently to be hoped that his enterprise and perseverance will be ultimately, in the course of Divine Providence, rewarded by the privilege of entering the country in his proper character,— as a christian missionary, — and proclaiming among its inhabitants the glad tidings of salvation.

The churches of Christendom are under lasting obligations to this devoted missionary, for the exertions he has made to enter the empire of China, and to facilitate the more direct and extended communication of the gospel to its inhabitants. The enterprise was perilous in the highest degree; — danger, not imaginary, but actual and imminent, threatened; he embarked alone, amidst cold-blooded, treacherous barbarians; he went, emphatically, with his life in his hand;—but his aim was noble; his object, in its magnitude and importance, was worthy of the risk; and its results will only be fully realized in eternity. No Christian will read the account of his feelings and views, when entering and pursuing his first voyage, without becoming sensible of the efficacy and the value of the motives which could impel him onward in such a career, and the principles which could support him amidst the trials it imposed. Happy would it be for China were a hundred such men now hovering around her coasts, not to convey opium, or ardent spirits, or other means of demoralization and crime,—too frequently the chief traffic of foreign visitors,—

but the knowledge of the true God, and the only Saviour!

The comparative indifference with which the moral and spiritual necessities of the Chinese, and the solemn obligations of a nation professing Christianity, to attempt the alleviation of those wants, have been regarded, is as unjustifiable in us, as it has been injurious to them. It is a humiliating fact, that were our commercial relations with China now to cease, after having traded with this singular nation for nearly two centuries, (to such an extent, that the duties on the imports, in one single article, have exceeded 3,000,000 annually,) we should, but for the labours of men whom other motives and objects than those of buying and selling, and getting gain, have led to this distant country, leave the inhabitants of China as ignorant of all the verities of Christianity, as if no Christian had ever visited their shores. The labours of Drs. Morrison and Milne, and their companions, especially in the translation of the Holy Scriptures, though often regarded with ridicule or contempt, will remain the most honourable and imperishable memorials of British intercourse with China. They have, as far as their limited numbers admitted, redeemed the character of their country from the charge of a practical declaration that it was destitute of all religion, or regarded religion, in comparison with the emoluments of commerce or the trophies of war, as unimportant to itself and useless to others. They have also rendered the path of all future missionaries to the nations by whom the Chinese language is spoken (and missionaries from America are now entering the field) comparatively easy;—and the Chinese will continue to derive benefit from their labours, even to the latest generations.

Should the changes in our trade facilitate more direct intercourse with the people, China will be one of the most imposing and commanding objects ever presented to the attention of christian nations. While the commercial world is all activity and enterprise, in the expectation of securing, from the changes, speedy and abundant wealth, may the churches of Christendom be equally vigilant and active to secure more important ends;—May the colleges of our land send forth her pious and devoted sons; the merchants facilitate their passage to the vast and important field; the churches support them by their offerings, and follow them with their prayers;—may the Lord open before them a wide door, and effectual; and the influence of the Holy Spirit make the preaching of the gospel a means of spiritual benefit to thousands!

That the inhabitants of China will ultimately become a christian people, no one who believes the Bible can entertain a doubt; and in effecting this we have no reason to believe that any other order of means will be employed besides those now applied; viz. the distribution of the Sacred Scriptures, and the instruction of christian teachers. What results might have followed, had these been more vigorously and extensively employed, it is not easy to say. The labour hitherto performed, though vast in itself, and essential to all stability and efficiency, has been chiefly preparatory; and the labourer may yet be called to much toil and self-denial, and patience and peril, before any great results become generally visible, although, ultimately, this is certain. China has been the frequent scene of foreign invasion, and violent revolutions, and has changed its masters, without altering the chief feature of its policy—its determined refusal of intercourse with other nations. The science, learning, and genius of the West have unfolded their attainments and excellences;—select and

splendid embassies, from the most distinguished
sovereigns of the civilized world, have been sent
to its imperial court, charged with the strongest
declarations of amity and good-will; commerce
has applied its enterprise and perseverance to
the task, and has disclosed the advantages of its
honourable pursuit;—but all have failed to form
those relations, and secure that intercommuni-
cation, and the recognition of that reciprocity
of interests, which bind civilized nations to each
other.   China still proclaims her proud and un-
approachable supremacy, and disdainfully rejects
all pretensions in any other nation to be considered as her equal. This feeling of contemptible
vanity Christianity alone will, in all probability,
be able to destroy. Where other means have failed,
the gospel will triumph; this will fraternize the
Chinese with the rest of mankind; and will teach
them, that while there is one true God—God
hath made of one blood all nations of men for
to dwell on the face of the earth. The gospel,
while it will unfold to them that they are one in
circumstances and in destiny, will link them in
sympathy with other portions of their species,
and thus add to the triumphs it has achieved,
and the glory of Him who is its author and its
end, — who regards the human race as his

family, and is hastening on the period, when all its varied tribes shall, through the Redeemer, acknowledge him as their Father and their God.

Since the greater part of the following sheets were printed, the Journal of Mr. Gutzlaff's third voyage to the eastern coast of China, and the ports of Mantchou-Tartary to the north, has been received in this country;* and the publication of the work has been delayed that it might include this account.

The narrative of the third visit to the east and northern parts of China is not less replete with interest than the account of his voyages in the Chinese junk and the *Lord Amherst*; while the additional information it supplies, in reference to the disposition of the Chinese towards foreigners, the hopes it is adapted to

* This Account appeared originally in the "Canton Register," a truly valuable Monthly Journal, published at Canton, but which may be obtained at Messrs. Parbury, Allen, and Co.'s, Leadenhall-street. This excellent periodical will be found exceedingly interesting to those who are concerned for the welfare of China, and highly valuable to every one who is desirous to obtain accurate and useful information respecting the country and the people.

inspire of more unrestricted and friendly intercourse with China, and a wide and rapid diffusion of the Gospel among the millions of its inhabitants, is valuable and encouraging.

Any slight inconvenience that may have been occasioned by the delay of the issuing of these interesting Journals, will, it is presumed, be amply compensated by the complete form in which the narrative of the proceedings, and the observations of this intelligent missionary, are now given to the British public.

THE

JOURNAL OF THREE VOYAGES

ALONG

The Coast of China,

IN

1831, 1832, & 1833.

INTRODUCTION.

INTERCOURSE WITH CHINA.

THE system of excluding foreigners from all intercourse with China, has often been extolled as the greatest proof of wisdom in her rulers; but, upon a nearer investigation, it will be found that nothing is more at variance with sound policy than this unnatural law of restriction.

All mankind are created and upheld by the same God, descended from the same parents, subject to the same changes, are living under the same canopy of heaven, upon the same planet, and therefore have a natural right to claim fellowship.* The refusal of it is a transgression of

* An emperor of China, in 1300, before the Tartar Conquest, sent an embassy to Japan for the sake of cultivating an amicable intercourse. In his letter he said, " The sages considered the whole world as *one family;* but if all the members have not a friendly intercourse, how can it be said, that the principle of one family is maintained?"

the divine law of benevolence, which is equally
binding upon all the nations of the earth. Savages
might better be excused for secluding themselves
from other nations, since the loss must be chiefly
their own; but a people, like the Chinese, acquainted with letters, endowed with intelligence,
and boasting of a civilization superior to that of
any other nation, cannot do the same without
injury to others, as well as themselves.

The most deplorable consequence of this un-
social system is, that the worship of the only
living and true God has been thereby excluded
from this vast empire. Whilst all nature proclaims an Almighty Creator and Preserver, the
sons of China worship the work of their own
hands. Peace is proclaimed between God and
men, through the mediation of Jesus Christ, the
Saviour, not of any favoured nation, but ' of the
world;' but China has not welcomed these 'glad
tidings.' Although she once despatched ambassadors to India to inquire into the doctrines of
Budhism, she has never been equally anxious to
possess the divine revelation, or to examine it
when brought to her doors. It may perhaps be
said in excuse for the Chinese, that the true
Gospel was formerly purposely withheld from
them, whilst they were offered, in its stead, only

the frivolous legends of a spurious Christianity.
Protestant Christians are indeed chargeable with
guilt in having so long neglected to send the
Gospel to them; but we confidently hope, that,
when an opportunity is offered to introduce it,
and they are found willing to receive it, Christians will no longer be slow to give them the
word of life.

Perhaps it will be said, that all attempts to
remove the barriers to intercourse with China
have hitherto proved abortive, and will be so in
future. The former is partly true, the latter
remains to be proved. It may be interesting
to inquire, what causes have operated so powerfully as to defeat all past attempts to establish
mutual intercourse?

It is remarkable that all the nations which use
the Chinese written character, harbour the same
prejudices against foreigners. By means of this
written language they have been united for ages
under similar laws, institutions, and religion.
Hence they have formed one great family, quite
distinct from other nations, in all points of national
peculiarity. As they enjoyed the privileges
of civilization at an early period, while the adjoining nations were living in barbarism, they
learned to look down upon them with contempt,

and in all collisions with them, to treat them, if
inferior, as vanquished enemies, or if superior,
as savage intruders. By sedulously shunning
any intercourse with the 'barbarians,' the opinion
of their ferocity and depravity, which the Chinese
had first imbibed, continued to be cherished
through ignorance of its objects and settled prejudice. This general contempt was increased
also by the consciousness that they were the
most numerous of the nations of the world.
The fact is certainly true, but not so the conclusion which they derive from it, that their country
was the most extensive of all. Fancying the
earth to be a square, they assumed to themselves
the main land in the centre, and allowed to the
other nations the small and remote clusters of
islands, in various directions around themselves.
How could they look upon the poor inhabitants
of those scattered lands otherwise than with the
utmost contempt! The sovereign of so great a
nation, also, regarding himself as the sole potentate of earth and the vicegerent of heaven, claimed
the universal dominion over all the lands and
the four seas. Their princes, he considered his
vassals and tributaries. He slighted them when
he pleased, viewing them merely as the petty
chiefs of barbarous tribes; yet, with much com-

passion, he occasionally condescended to receive
their embassies. Though the modern improve-
ments in navigation, the progress in the science
of geography and in general information, have
partially rectified their opinions on this subject,
yet they are too proud to confess the fact of their
national ignorance; to this moment they claim
the title of "the flowery middle kingdom," and
would have all the princes of the earth humbly
do them homage. We still hear the same old
stories about the "four seas" repeated, and maps
of the world may be met with, which so represent
it still. So long as the public opinion is swayed
by such notions, we cannot expect foreigners to
be held in any just estimation among them.
Those petty nations which use the Chinese
written character, and acknowledge their vassalage
to the Celestial Empire, imitate them also in all
the arrogance of national vanity.

Another cause operating to favour the same
system of restriction, exists in their literature.
The Chinese are much attached to their own
literature, and are therefore prepared highly to
value any degree of eminence in this department. But foreigners are not often acquainted
with their literary productions, and having
scarcely any thing else which, in the estimation

of a Chinese, entitles them to rank among the
" literati," they are together regarded as ignorant
barbarians.   Proud of their own observance of
the rules of propriety and justice, the Chinese
are also taught by their classical authors to look
down upon these barbarians as rude and fraudu-
lent, and to esteem any friendly intercourse contaminating.   " These barbarians," they are told,
" have never felt the transforming influence of
the Celestial Empire, and though they may
therefore be pitied, yet much more do they call
for our contempt.   Drive them away, banish
them from the empire."   This is true Chinese
policy.

To increase and perpetuate this contempt of
foreigners, various methods have been adopted
by the government, and with various degrees of
success.   They know, though reluctant to admit
it, that some barbarians are more warlike than
themselves, that they have made extensive conquests in their vicinity, and that in the event of
a war with them, they themselves would be an
unequal match for them.   This has led them to
regard these nations with constant suspicion.
But to conceal from the people their fear of the
superiority of Europeans, they are accustomed
to stigmatize their characters as infamous, and in

their intercourse with them, to substitute violence and cunning for principle and candour. I am firmly persuaded that government would, were it possible, reduce all European residents and visitants to the same state of humiliation which the Dutch endure at Japan.

It must, however, be acknowledged, that Europeans have frequently, by petty aggressions, provoked the Chinese to carry their laws of exclusion into the most rigorous execution. We have cause to regret that they have never been so successful in re-establishing friendly intercourse, as unfortunate in giving occasion for stopping it.

As in the instances where actual force was used to decide disputed claims, the Chinese have generally proved inferior, they have become desirous to avoid any recourse to physical strength. Instead of spilling blood, they prefer to spill ink, and have proved to the world that China is invincible in a paper war. Like the anathemas of the Papal See, fulminating edicts have been invariably issued on such occasions against intruding foreigners. These edicts are in general very specious, and would persuade a European unacquainted with the case, to believe that the Chinese have justice on their side.

Their threats are intimidating, and their commands almost irresistible, but here they stop: for the intruder either yields and retraces his steps, or if not, the Chinese is too wise to let matters come to the extremity of force, where he is as sure of defeat, as he is certain of victory in a pitched battle of words.

The continual collision of the foreign mercantile establishments at Canton, with the Chinese authorities, has occasioned great surprise to persons but slightly acquainted with the native character. The most severe animadversions also have been called forth from capitalists who have suffered loss, and who have not been on the ground to judge of the case. But so long as the prejudice against foreigners is cherished, there must be contests; on the one part, to maintain old privileges, ameliorate their present condition, and extend the trade, and on the other, to retrench the liberties and enforce the exclusion of strangers. The experience of centuries has taught Europeans that the Chinese authorities will heap insult on insult upon them, when it can be done with impunity to themselves and their interests. But when an opponent supports his argument with physical force, or their interest demands it, they can be crouching, gentle, and even kind. This peculiarity of national character, so very unlike our own, has been prolific in mutual evils.

It has exhibited the measures taken by the European residents to redress their grievances, in a light the most unfavourable by contrast with their own plausible and forbearing deportment. While we do not forget the long catalogue of petty annoyances from the Chinese authorities, which the Europeans have suffered from the first arrival of the Portuguese to this day; we regret that the possession of the gospel has not taught Europeans more forbearance and long-suffering. Had these been oftener practised on suitable occasions, we should have had fewer causes of complaint against the Chinese. But it is not strange, that Europeans, destitute of the spirit of Christian meekness, on coming to this country, and finding themselves treated as barbarians by a nation so evidently below them in civilization, should feel their indignation roused, and should retaliate insolence for insolence and dislike for hatred. Thus the line of separation became broader and broader. Governmental proclamations, detailing the infamous conduct of barbarians, have been repeatedly posted up at Canton. Foreigners have wisely taken no notice of them, but the minds of the people have been thus imbued with strong antipathy against such worthless barbarians. Thus the authorities gained their point, for the aversion to foreigners thus excited and cherished, was the best precaution against forming too close a friendship with them. The writer has often heard the natives rehearse these accusations with self-gratulation at their own superiority.

Thus every event has contributed to widen the breach between foreign nations and the Chinese. In vain have embassies been tried to conciliate their favour; no presents have been withheld, no trouble spared, in order to bring about a friendly intercourse. An explanation of these failures will be found in the above remarks on the general spirit of the nation and the policy of its rulers. The Portuguese, who were the first of the European nations to lead the way to China, had frequent opportunities and causes to solicit the imperial favour. In 1520, a Portuguese ambassador to the Court of Peking, was sent back without having gained any advantage, and eventually, on account of the jealousy caused by their conquests in India, imprisoned and slain.* In 1667, they sent an ambassador to Kang-he, the reigning emperor: this was repeated during the reign of Yung-Ching. They were treated as Chinese vassals, but enjoyed more liberty than any natives during their residence at Peking. The Dutch, from the first, had attempted negotiation with China; but only their conquests in its neighbourhood effected the opening of their trade. To establish it on a permanent basis they sent an embassy to Kang-he, in 1655. This was very graciously received by the young sovereign, who had a clear conviction of European superiority; yet he was unable to stem the torrent of opposing prejudice against foreigners, and could therefore only grant a few inconsiderable privileges, which by no means effected a reciprocal intercourse.

The present relations of the British with China, make a definite treaty of trade highly desirable. Much might have been accomplished by a well-conducted embassy to Peking, near the close of the last century, and with a sovereign like Keen-lung, had not the old custom of national exclusion operated too strongly against them. The Dutch, supposing the failure of

* Chinese Repository.

this English embassy in 1793, chiefly ascribable to the unyielding spirit of the ambassador, enjoined upon the deputation which they soon afterwards sent, implicit submission to every prescribed ceremony, however humiliating. The consequence was, that while the former had been dismissed honourably, the latter were despised. For it is a Chinese maxim to trample on the voluntary submissive and abject, while they respect firmness and decision. A second ambassador from his British Majesty, in 1816, encountered still greater difficulties, and had less success than the first. These fruitless embassies will teach the sovereigns either to attempt no negotiations at all, or to propose them in a different state of affairs. For there are two grand obstacles: the pretension of China to supremacy over all the nations of the world, and her dread of every superior power. Add to this the want of veracity prevalent in all the departments of her government, the ignorance on subjects of general knowledge, and their bigoted adherence to unfounded opinions; and we shall the less blame the ambassadors for the failure of missions, in which there was scarcely a possibility of success.

That class of persons who form their opinions

from the Chinese writings, and regard the nation with that obsolete admiration which was once so fashionable, will rejoice that the government has persevered in the exclusion of strangers, or has so circumscribed their intercourse as to render it harmless. " This wise policy," they say, " has preserved from ruin and change, the excellent laws and customs of this ancient empire: the patriarchal institutions which have the sanction of ages are still existing there: and while the other countries of the world are agitated by war, China enjoys the enviable blessings of peace and plenty. The unwarrantable attempts of foreigners first to gain an intercourse, and then to subvert the existing laws, the Chinese have justly repelled. These strangers should be thankful for the privileges granted them merely by Chinese humanity; they should praise and obey those laws which secure the happiness of more than three hundred millions of people. All attempts at changes should be promptly repelled; otherwise China would soon be in the present servile condition of Hindostan: internal wars, fermented by foreign influence, would desolate the country, and destroy the industrious inhabitants, or reduce them to star-vation."

These reasonings are as specious as the Chinese writings on national prosperity: for the sake of suffering humanity, we wish they were verified by facts.

Notwithstanding their utmost precautions, the Chinese have repeatedly fallen under a foreign power. And even at the present time, they are subject to the chief of a Tartar horde. Had Europeans designed their conquest, and had they succeeded in their design, still the condition of China would not have been so abject a slavery as at present. Look at the civil and religious rights enjoyed in Hindostan, the rapid progress there made in science, and the knowledge of divine truth, and then see China; China! never in advance, but always in retrograde movement, groaning under arbitrary rule, doomed to perpetual seclusion from the world, from its interests, its sympathies, and its progressive illumination.

We fully accord to many political institutions and laws of the " Celestial Empire," the praise of high excellence in theory, and of practical utility during ages of trial. We grant·that the government which has kept so many millions of subjects comparatively quiet, cannot be devoid of some principles of sound policy. At the same time, many of their laws are far from being praiseworthy ; some impracticable, because not adapted to the actual state of human nature : so numerous also and strict, that it is impossible to be a subject and not a transgressor. Hence the relaxation of punishment, hence the introduction of bribery with all its concomitant evils.

The patriarchal institutions exist only on paper, and the paternal exhortations are similar to the addresses of the inquisitors to the temporal judges, when delivering them a victim. Happily there are a few exceptions to this mode of administering "justice;" but they are very rare. To talk of the constant peace of an empire where rebellion is frequently breaking forth, is denying facts, to establish a theory. Of the "plenty" said to abound in China, we will only say that no where else have we seen so much want as here, though we do not charge upon the government the entire amount of the prevailing misery. Those persons who form their opinion from Du Halde alone, will be ready to consider the Chinese a most virtuous nation. Surely there are amiable qualities in the Chinese character, but their vices are also very repulsive. Without enumerating them, we may confidently aver, that their manners cannot be very much deteriorated by foreign intercourse.   In their morals there is, unhappily, not too much good theory, and very little practice of it.   Every point of etiquette is rigorously observed, while the claims of mercy and justice are forgotten.

Extortion seems universally prevalent; where it cannot be effected directly, it is done indirectly. To escape these numerous impositions there is one mode, often recommended and even enforced by the Chinese authorities; namely, to leave the country.

No class of strangers have submitted to so great indignities as the Catholic missionaries. Their zeal to enter China was stronger than any travellers to reach Timbuctoo.   Francis Xavier died in sight of this beloved land, and prayed with his expiring breath for its conversion. Alexander Valignano, general of the India Missions, who resided at Macao, often turned his face towards the coast of China and exclaimed, "O rock! O rock! when wilt thou open!" Difficulties abated not their zeal; they overcame them all by perseverance, and Matthew Ricci actually entered the Celestial Empire in 1582. Had they then spread the pure Gospel instead of the doctrines of the Romish Church, China would have been numbered among the

social nations, for true Christianity seeks to
unite all the inhabitants of the world together.
Many of them were men of superior talents,
of insinuating address, and matchless patience.
Amongst so great a variety of character, some
must have been men of true piety, whose anxiety
to advance the Redeemer's kingdom would free
their religion from much of human invention.
We admire the uprightness and intrepidity which
many showed in defence of the Gospel; while
we detest the servility by which a great number
conciliated the favour of the Chinese autocrat.
Men like Schaal, Verbiest, Gerbillon, Bremarre
and Bouvet, would have shone in Europe by
the lustre of their genius.   In China they inspired the emperor with a very high opinion of
European science, but failed to gain his sincere
love of the Gospel.   Their successors could
never gain the same ascendancy over his mind,
and though willing to endure, as they actually
did, all the hardships of their predecessors, they
never rose so high into favour.   After the aboli-
tion of the order of Jesuits, the missions of the
various orders of monks sunk down to comparative insignificance.   Yet their professed converts are numerous even to this day.   The most
severe prohibitions have not prevented their

entering the forbidden ground. Ridicule and contempt, persecution and martyrdom, have been directed against their religion and its votaries, yet they still continue their attachment to it, and their efforts to promote it.*

When love to our Saviour shall transcend all minor and selfish passions, and fully possessing the heart, shall prompt to the utmost exertions to glorify his name, we humbly believe that all the barriers of Chinese misanthropy will fall. There is something irresistible in that holy ardour which counts all things nothing for Christ, and which is prepared for any sacrifices to exalt his glorious name. The prince of darkness, with all his infernal array, can never prevail against the men who rely upon their Redeemer's strength, who walk in his spirit, and who live and die in his service. As he is the ruler of the universe, and the sole potentate, upholding the world by his almighty hand, the removal of obstacles insurmountable to man is to him an easy work. A simple, steady faith in him, exalts its possessor above impediments and repeated disappointments: he knows that his Saviour will

* In 1815, the late emperor, Kea-King, encouraged a persecution against the Christians. The present emperor, Taou-Kwang, has never persecuted them.

triumph over all his enemies, and under all difficulties in the path of duty, will uphold him. In
the divine promise, surer than any human cove-
nant, that all the nations of the earth shall be
given to his Lord, he reads the certain conversion
of China. Armed with this faith, he is confident
that the day, though remote, is yet sure, and
that small efforts, in the day of small things, will
subserve the cause of God. The translation and
circulation of the Holy Scriptures, the composition and distribution of tracts, with occasional
oral addresses to the people, are the means he
would employ to promulgate the Gospel of
Christ. Many thousands may read, and hear,
and not understand; yet, if a few among these
thousands embrace the word of eternal life, the
salvation of that few is an abundant reward: for
to save one soul is far more valuable than to
conquer the world. While quoting this divine
truth, I am convinced that individual Christians,
thoroughly penetrated with such sentiments,
could accomplish more for the benefit of
China, than the greatest statesmen as mere
politicians. Of the former there have been few
to consecrate their lives to this great object,
and still fewer who have been successful in
their attempts; but more will arise so soon

as the enterprise shall cease to be regarded as hopeless.

After the total or partial failure of so many endeavours to open an intercourse, a very general doubt of the success of any future attempt seems to exist.   Yet exertions, prompted solely by a desire for the glory of God and the good of men, and executed with a single eye to the Almighty for guidance and strength, can never be wholly useless.   The divine promise, the experience of past ages, and the present dispensations of Providence, are in our favour.

When we express our confident hope of success through the Invisible One, it is not meant to deny the difficulties of spreading the Gospel in China, but only that the successful result is foreseen through them all by the believer.   The outcry against the Gospel will doubtless be very great.   It must subvert a system of atheism, superstition, and self-righteous morality.   The Gospel of peace will be accused of a rebellious tendency, and its preachers will undergo a persecution more severe than did their predecessors, the Roman Catholics.   But whatever may befal its champions, the final overthrow of the kingdom of darkness is sure, and the ultimate result will be glorious.

While representing Christianity as the only effectual means of establishing a friendly intercourse, I would not reject the efforts of commercial enterprise to open a trade with the maritime provinces, but rather regard them as the probable means of introducing that Gospel into a country to which the only access is by sea.

JOURNAL

A RESIDENCE IN SIAM, &c.

CHAPTER I.

MAY, 1831. During a residence of almost three years in Siam, I had the high gratification of seeing the prejudices of the natives vanish; and perceived with delight, that a large field amongst the different people who inhabit Siam, was opening. As long as the junks from China stayed, most of the time was taken up by administering to the spiritual and bodily wants of large numbers of Chinese. We experienced this year the peculiar blessings of our divine Saviour. The demand for books, the inquiries after the truth, the friendship shown, were most favourable tokens of divine approbation upon our feeble endeavours. The work of translation proceeded rapidly; we were enabled to illustrate the rudiments of languages hitherto unknown to Europeans; and to embody the substance of our philological researches in small volumes, which will remain in manuscript, presuming that they may be of some advantage to other missionaries. Some individuals, either prompted by curiosity, or drawn by an interest for their own eternal welfare, applied for instruction, and one of them made an open profession of Christianity.

When we first arrived, our appearance spread a general panic. It was well known by the predictions of the Bali books, that a certain religion of the west would vanquish Budhism; and, as the votaries of a western religion had conquered Burmah, people presumed, that their religious principles would prove equally victorious in Siam. By and by, fears subsided; but were, on a sudden, again roused, when there were brought to Bankok, Burman tracts, written by Mr. Judson, in which it was stated that the Gospel would soon triumph over all false religions. Constant inquiries were made about the *certain* time when this should take place; the passages of holy

writ, which we quoted in confirmation of the
grand triumph of Christ's kingdom, were duly
weighed, and only few objections started. At
this time the Siamese looked with great anxiety
upon the part which the English would take, in
the war between Quedah and themselves. When
the king first heard of their neutrality, he exclaimed: " I behold, finally, that there is some
truth in Christianity, which formerly I considered very doubtful." This favorable opinion
influenced the people to become friendly with us.
The consequence was, that we gained access to
persons of all ranks and of both sexes. Under
such circumstances, it would have been folly to
leave the country, if Providence had not ordered
otherwise, in disabling me by sickness, from further labour there. A pain in my left side, accompanied by headache, great weakness, and want of
appetite, threw me upon my couch. Though I
endeavoured to rally my robust constitution, I
could readily perceive, that I was verging, daily,
with quick strides, towards the grave ; and a burial
place was actually engaged.

Bright as the prospects were, there were also
great obstacles in the way, to retard the achieve-
ment of our endeavours, the salvation of souls.
The Siamese are very fickle, and will often be

very anxious to embrace an opinion to-day, which
to-morrow they will entirely reject. Their friendship is unsteady; the attachment which many of
them professed to the Gospel, as the word of
eternal life, has never been very sincere; neither
could we fully succeed in fixing their minds on
the Saviour. Though all religions are tolerated
in Siam, yet Budhism is the religion of the state,
and all the public institutions are for the promotion of this superstition. This system of the
grossest lies, which can find champions only in
the biased minds of some scholars in Europe,
engrosses, theoretically as well as practically, the
minds of its votaries, and renders every step
towards improvement most difficult. We were
allowed to preach in the temples of Budha; and
the numerous priests were anxious to engage with
us in conversation; yet their hearts were, generally, steeled against divine truth.

Budhism is atheism, according to the creed
which one of the Siamese high-priests gave me;
the highest degree of happiness consists in annihilation; the greatest enjoyment is in indolence; and their sole hope is founded upon endless
transmigration. We may very easily conclude
what an effect these doctrines must have upon the
morals of both priests and laymen, especially if

we keep in mind that they are duly inculcated,
and almost every male in Siam, for a certain time,
becomes a priest, in order to study them. From
the king to the meanest of his subjects, self-
sufficiency is characteristic; the former prides
himself on account of having acquired so high a
dignity for his virtuous deeds in a former life; the
latter is firmly assured, that by degrees, in the
course of some thousands of years, he will come
to the same honour. I regret not to have found
one honest man; many have the reputation of
being such, but upon nearer inspection they are
equally void of this standard virtue. Sordid oppression, priestcraft, allied to wretchedness and
filth, are every where to be met. Notwithstanding, the Siamese are superior in morality to
the Malays. They are neither sanguinary nor
bigoted, and are not entirely shut against persuasion.

Favoured by an over-ruling Providence, I had
equal access to the palace and to the cottage;
and was frequently, against my inclination, called
to the former. Chow-fa-nooi, the younger brother of the late king, and the rightful heir of the
crown, is a youth of about twenty-three, possessing some abilities, which are however swallowed
up in childishness. He speaks English; can

write a little; can imitate works of European
artisans; and is a decided friend of European
sciences, and of Christianity. He courts the
friendship of every European; holds free conversation with him, and is anxious to learn whatever he can. He is beloved by the whole nation,
which is wearied out by heavy taxes; but his.
elder brother, Chow-fa-yay, who is just now a
priest, is still more beloved. If they ascend the
throne, the changes in all the institutions of the
country will be great, but perhaps too sudden.
The son of the Phra Klang, or minister of foreign
affairs, is of superior intelligence, but has a spirit
for intrigue, which renders him formidable at
court, and dangerous to foreigners. He looks with
contempt upon his whole nation; but crouches
before every individual, by means of whom he
may gain any influence. Chow-nin, the step-
brother of the king, is a young man of good
talents, which are however spoiled by his habit
of smoking opium. Kroma-sun-ton, late brother
of the king, and chief justice of the kingdom, was
the person by whom I could communicate my
sentiments to the king. Officially invited, I spent
hours with him in conversation, principally upon
Christianity, and often upon the character of the
British nation. Though himself a most dissolute

person, he requested me to educate his son, (a
stupid boy), and seemed the best medium for
communicating Christian truth to the highest
personages of the kingdom. At his request, I
wrote a work upon Christianity, but he did not live
to read it; for he was burnt in his palace in the
beginning of 1831. Kroma-khun, brother-in-law
to the former king, a stern old man, called in my
medical help, and I took occasion to converse
with him on religious subjects. He greatly approved of Christian principles, but did not apply
to the fountain of all virtue, Jesus Christ. In
consequence of an ulcer in his left side, he again
called in my aid; yet his proud son despised the
assistance of a barbarian; neither would the royal
physicians accept of my advice; and the man soon
died. Even a disaster of this description served
to recommend me to his majesty the present king,
who is naturally fond of Europeans; and he en-
treated me not to leave the kingdom on any
account; but rather to become an officer, in the
capacity of a physician. Paya-meh-tap, the commander in chief of the Siamese army in the war
against the Laos or Chans, otherwise written
Shans, returning from his victorious exploits,
was honoured with royal favour, and loaded with
the spoils of an oppressed nation, near the brink

of destruction. A severe disease prompted him
to call me near his person. He promised gold,
which he never intended to pay, as a reward
for my services. And when restored, he condescended so far as to make me sit down by his
side, and converse with him upon various important subjects. Paya-rak, a man hated by all
the Siamese nobility, on account of his mean,
intriguing spirit, and sent as a spy to the frontiers
of Cochin-China, urged me to explain to him the
nature of the Gospel; and as he found my discourse reasonable, he gave me a present of dried
fish for the trouble I had taken. The mother of
prince Kroma-zorin, one of the wives of the late
king, contrasted evangelical truth with Budhis-
tical nonsense, when she made me meet one of
her most favourite priests, of whom she is a decided patron. Though she had built a temple
for the accommodation of the priests of Budha,
that mass might be constantly performed in behalf of her son, who lately died, she thought it
necessary to hear, with all her retinue, the new
doctrine, of which so much had been said at
court of late. The sister of Paya-meh-tap invited me, on purpose to hear me explain the
doctrine of the Gospel, which she, according
to her own expression, believed to be the

same with the wondrous stories of the Virgin
Mary.

In relating these facts, I would only remark,
that I maintained intercourse with the individuals here mentioned, against my inclination;
for it is burdensome and disgusting to cultivate
friendship with the Siamese nobles. They used
to call at midnight at our cottage, and would frequently send for me at whatever time it might
suit their foolish fancies. At the same time, it
must be acknowledged that, in this manner Providence opened a way to speak to their hearts,
and also to vindicate the character of Europeans,
which is so insidiously misrepresented to the
king.

I will mention also a few individuals in the
humbler spheres of life; but who profited more
by our instructions than any of the nobles. Two
priests—one of them the favourite chaplain of his
majesty, the other a young man of good parts,
but without experience—were anxious to be fully
instructed in the doctrines of the Gospel. They
came during the night, and persevered in their
application, even to the neglect of the study of
Bali, the sacred language, and of their usual
services in Budhism. The elder, a most intelligent man, about twenty years of age, continued

for months to repair with the Bible to a forest, boldly incurring the displeasure of the king. He also urged his younger brother to leave his native country, in order to acquire a full knowledge of Christianity and European sciences, so as afterwards to become the instructor of his benighted fellow-citizens; a Cambojan priest was willing to embark for the same purpose. Finally, a company of friends invited me to preach to them, that they might know what was the religion of the Pharangs, or Europeans.

Siam has never received, so much as it ought, the attention of European philanthropists and merchants. It is one of the most fertile countries in Asia. Under a good government it might be superior to Bengal, and Bankok would outweigh Calcutta. But Europeans have always been treated there with distrust, and even insolence, if it could be done with impunity. They have been liable to every sort of petty annoyance, which would weary out the most patient spirit; and have been subjected to the most unheard-of oppression. Some of them proposed to introduce some useful arts, which might increase power and riches; for instance, steam engines, saw mills, cannon foundries, cultivation of indigo and coffee; but with the exception of one French-

man, their offers were all refused; and the latter
had to leave the country in disgrace, after having
commenced the construction of an engine for
boring guns. When works for their benefit were
accomplished, their value was depreciated, in
order to dispense with the necessity of rewarding
European industry, and of thereby acknowledging
the superiority of European genius.

The general idea hitherto entertained by the
majority of the nation as to the European character, was derived from a small number of Christians, so styled, who, born in the country, and
partly descended from Portuguese, crouch before
their nobles as dogs, and are employed in all
menial services, and occasionally suffered to enlist
as soldiers or surgeons. All reproaches heaped
upon them are eventually realized; and their
character as faithful children to the Romish
church, has been fairly exhibited by drunkenness
and cockfighting. No industry, no genius, no
honesty is found amongst them, with the exception of one individual, who indeed has a right to
claim the latter virtue as his own. From this
misconception has emanated all the disgraceful
treatment of Europeans up to the time of the war
between Burmah and the Company. When the
first British envoy arrived, he was treated with

contempt, because the extent of English power was not known. When the English had taken Rangoon, it was not believed by the king, until he had sent a trustworthy person to ascertain the fact. Still, doubts agitated the royal breast as to the issue of the war with the invincible Burmans. Reluctantly did the Siamese hear of the victories of their British allies, though they were protected thereby from the ravages of the Burmans, who surely would have turned the edge of their swords against them, if the British had not conquered these, their inveterate enemies. Notwithstanding, the Siamese government could gladly hail the emissaries of Burmah, who privately arrived with despatches, the sole object of which was to prevail upon the king of Siam not to assist the English, in case of a breach, upon the plea of common religion and usages. But the national childish vanity of the Siamese in thinking themselves superior to all nations, except the Chinese and Burmans, has vanished; and the more the English are feared, the better is the treatment which is experienced during their residence in this country. The more the ascendency of their genius is acknowledged, the more their friendship as individuals is courted, their customs imitated, and their language studied.

His majesty has decked a few straggling wretches in the uniform of Sepoys, and considers them as brave and well-disciplined as their patterns. Chow-fa-nooi, desirous of imitating foreigners, has built a ship, on a small scale, and intends doing the same on a larger one, as soon as his funds will admit. English, as well as Americans, are disencumbered in their intercourse, and enjoy at present privileges of which even the favoured Chinese cannot boast.

The natives of China come in great numbers from Chaou-chow-foo, the most eastern part of Canton Province. They are mostly agriculturists; while another Canton tribe, called the Kih or Ka, consists chiefly of artisans. Emigrants from Tang-an (or Tung-an) district, in Fuhkeen province, are few; mostly sailors or merchants. Those from Hai-nan are chiefly pedlars and fishermen, and form perhaps the poorest, yet the most cheerful class. Language, as well as customs, derived from the Chaou-chow Chinese, are prevalent throughout the country. They delight to live in wretchedness and filth, and are very anxious to conform to the vile habits of the Siamese. In some cases when they enter into matrimonial alliances with these latter, they even throw away their jackets and trowsers, and become Siamese in their very dress. As the lax, indifferent religious principles of the Chinese do not differ essentially from those of the Siamese, the former are very prone to conform entirely to the religious rites of the latter. And if they have children, these frequently cut off their queues, and become for a certain time Siamese priests. Within two or three generations, all the distinguishing marks of the Chinese character dwindle entirely away; and a nation which adheres so obstinately to its national customs becomes wholly changed to Siamese. These people usually neglect their own literature, and apply themselves to the Siamese. To them nothing is so welcome as the being presented, by the king, with an honorary title; and this generally takes place when they have acquired great riches, or have betrayed some of their own countrymen. From that moment they become slaves of the king; the more so if they are made his officers. No service is then so menial, so expensive, so difficult, but they are forced to perform it. And in case of disobedience, they are severely punished, and, perhaps, put into chains for their whole lives. Nothing, therefore, exceeds the fear of the Chinese,—they pay the highest respect to their oppressors, and cringe when addressed by them.   Notwithstanding the heavy taxes laid upon their industry, they labour patiently from morning to night, to feed their insolent and indolent tyrants, who think it below their dignity to gain their daily bread by their own exertions. With the exception of the Hwuy Hwuy, or Triad society, implicit obedience is paid to their most exorbitant demands, by every Chinese settler.

Some years back, this society formed a conspiracy, seized upon some native craft at Bamplasoi, a place near the mouth of the Meinam, and began to revenge themselves upon their tyrants; but falling short of provisions, they were forced to put to sea.   Followed by a small Siamese squadron they were compelled to flee; till contrary winds, and utter want of the necessaries of life, obliged them to surrender.   The ringleader escaped to Cochin-China, but most of his followers were either massacred or sent to prison for life.   From that time all hope of recovering the nation from abject bondage disappeared; though there are a great many individuals, who trust that the English (according to their own expression) will extend their benevolent government as far as Siam.   Every arrival of a ship enlivens their expectations,—every departure damps their joy.

Great numbers of the agriculturists in Siam are Peguans, or Mons (as they call themselves). This nation was formerly governed by a king of its own, who waged war againt the Burmans and Siamese, and proved successful. But having, eventually, been overwhelmed, alternately, by Burman and Siamese armies, the Peguans are now the slaves of both. They are a strong race of people, very industrious in their habits, open in their conversation, and cheerful in their intercourse. The new palace which the king of Siam has built, was principally erected by their labour, in token of the homage paid by them to the " lord of the white elephant." Their religion is the same with that of the Siamese. In their dress, the males conform to their masters; but the females let their hair grow, and dress differently from the Siamese women. Few nations are so well prepared for the reception of the Gospel as this; but, alas! few nations have less drawn the attention of European philanthropists.

The Siamese are in the habit of stealing Burmans and making them their slaves. Though the English have of late interposed with some effect, they nevertheless delight in exercising this nefarious practice. There are several thousand Burmans living, who have been enslaved in this

way, and who are compelled to work harder
than any other of his majesty's subjects. They
are held in the utmost contempt, treated barbarously, and are scarcely able to get the necessaries
of life.

Perhaps no nation has been benefited, by
coming under the Siamese dominion, with the
exception of the Malays. These Malays, also,
are principally slaves or tenants of large tracts
of land, which they cultivate with great care.
They generally lose, as almost every nation does
in Siam, their national character, become industrious, conform to Siamese customs, and often
gain a little property. With the exception of
a few Hadjis, they have no priests; but these
exercise an uncontrolled sway over their votaries,
and know the art of enriching themselves without
injury to their character as saints. These Hadjis
teach also the Koran, and have generally a great
many scholars, of whom, however, few make any
progress, choosing rather to yield to paganism,
even so far as to throw off their turbans, than to
follow their spiritual guides.

There are also some Moors resident in the
country, who are styled emphatically by the Siamese, *Kah*, strangers, and are mostly country-
born. Their chief and his son, Rasitty, enjoy

the highest honours with his majesty; the former
being the medium of speech, whereby persons of
inferior rank convey their ideas to the royal ear.
As it is considered below the dignity of so high
a potentate as his Siamese majesty to speak the
same language as his subjects have adopted, the
above mentioned Moor-man's office consists in
moulding the simplest expressions into nonsen-
sical bombast, in order that the speech addressed
to so mighty a ruler may be equal to the eulogiums bestowed upon Budha. Yet by being
made the medium of speech, this Moor has it in
his power to represent matters according to his
own interest, and he never fails to make ample
use of this prerogative. Hence no individual is
so much hated or feared by the nobles, and
scarcely any one wields so imperious a sway
over the royal resolutions. Being averse to an
extensive trade with Europeans, he avails himself
of every opportunity to shackle it, and to promote
intercourse with his own countrymen, whom he
nevertheless squeezes whenever it is in his power.
All the other Moor-men are either his vassals or
in his immediate employ, and may be said to be
an organized body of wily constituents. They
do not wear the turban, and they dispense with
the wide oriental dress: nor do they scruple

even to attend at pagan festivals and rites, merely to conciliate the favour of their masters, and to indulge in the unrestrained habits of the Siamese.

In the capacity of missionary and physician, I came in contact with the Laos or Chans, a nation scarcely known to Europeans. I learnt their language, which is very similar to Siamese, though the written character, used in their common as well as sacred books, differs from that of the Siamese. This nation, which occupies a great part of the eastern peninsula, from the northern frontiers of Siam, along Camboja and Cochin-China on the one side, and Burmah on the other, up to the borders of China and Tonquin, is divided by the Laos into Lau-pung-kau (white Laos.) and Lau-pung-dam (black or dark Laos,) owing partly to the colour of their skin. These people inhabit mostly mountainous regions, cultivate the ground, or hunt; and live under the government of many petty princes, who are dependent on Siam, Burmah, Cochin-China, and China. Though their country abounds in many precious articles, and among them a considerable quantity of gold, yet the people are poor, and live even more wretchedly than the Siamese, with the exception of those who are under the jurisdiction of the Chinese. Though they have a national literature, they are not very anxious to study it; nor does it afford them a fountain of knowledge. Their best books are relations of the common occurrences of life, in prose; or contemptible tales of giants and fairies. Their religious books, in the Bali language, are very little understood by their priests, who differ from the Siamese priests only in their stupidity. Although their country may be considered as the cradle of Budhism in these parts, because most of the vestiges of Samo Nakodum, apparently the first missionary of paganism, are to be met with in their precincts; yet the temples built in honour of Budha are by no means equal to those in Siam, nor are the Laos as superstitious as their neighbours. Their language is very soft and melodious, and sufficiently capacious to express their ideas.

The Laos are dirty in their habits, sportful in their temper, careless in their actions, and lovers of music and dancing in their diversions. Their organ, made of reeds, in a peculiar manner, is among the sweetest instruments to be met with in Asia. Under the hand of an European master, it would become one of the most perfect instruments in existence. Every noble maintains a number of dancing boys, who amuse their masters

with the most awkward gestures, while music is
playing in accordance with their twistings and
turnings.

The southern districts carry on a very brisk
trade with Siam, whither the natives come in long
narrow boats, covered with grass; importing the
productions of their own country, such as ivory,
gold, tiger skins, aromatics, &c.; and exporting
European and Indian manufactures, and some
articles of Siamese industry. This trade gave
rise, in 1827, to a war with the Siamese, who
used every stratagem to oppress the subjects of
one of the Laos tributary chiefs, Chow-vin-chan.
This prince, who was formerly so high in favour
with the late king of Siam, as to be received, at
his last visit, in a gilded boat, and to be carried
in a gilded sedan chair, found the exorbitant exactions of the Siamese governor on the frontier
injurious to the trade of his subjects and to his
own revenues. He applied, repeatedly, to the
Court at Bankok for redress: and being unsuccessful, he then addressed the governor himself:
but no attention was paid to his grievances. He
finally had recourse to arms, to punish the governor, without any intention of waging war with
the king, an event for which he was wholly
unprepared. His rising, however, transfused so

general a panic among the Siamese, that they very soon marched *en masse* against him, and met with immediate success. From that moment the country became the scene of bloodshed and devastation. Paya - meh - tap, the Siamese commander-in-chief, not only endeavoured to enrich himself with immense spoils, but committed the most horrible acts of cruelty, butchering all, without regard to sex or age. And whenever this was found too tedious, he shut up a number of victims together, and then either set fire to the house, or blew it up with gunpowder. The number of captives, generally country people, was very great. They were brought down the Meinam on rafts; and were so short of provision, that the major part died from starvation: the remainder were distributed among the nobles as slaves, and were treated more inhumanly than the most inveterate enemies; while many of the fair sex were placed in the harems of the king and his nobles.

Forsaken by all his subjects, Chow-vin-chan fled with his family to one of the neighbouring Laos chiefs; in the mean time, the Cochin-Chinese sent an envoy to interpose with the Siamese commander-in-chief on his behalf. The envoy was treacherously murdered by the Siamese,

together with his whole retinue, consisting
of one hundred men, of whom one only was
suffered to return to give an account of the tragedy. Enraged at such a breach of the law of
nations, but feeling themselves too weak to
revenge cruelty by cruelty, the Cochin-Chinese
then sent an ambassador to Bankok, demanding
that the author of the murder should be delivered
up; and, at the same time, declaring Cochin-
China the mother of the Laos people, while to
Siam was given the title of father. Nothing
could be more conciliatory than the letter addressed, on the occasion, to the king of Siam;
but the latter, refusing to give any decisive answer to this and other messages repeatedly sent
to him, himself despatched a wily politician to
Hue,* who, however, was plainly refused admittance, and given to understand that the kings of
Siam and Cochin-China ceased henceforth to be
friends. The king of Siam, who was rather intimidated by such a blunt reply, ordered his
principal nobles and Chinese subjects to build
some hundred war boats, after the model made
by the governor of Ligore.

But while those war boats, or as they might

* The capital city of Cochin-China.

be more appropriately called, pleasure boats, were building, Chow-vin-chan, with his whole family, was betrayed into the hands of the Siamese. Being confined in cages, within sight of the instruments of torture, the old man, worn out by fatigue and hard treatment, died; while his son and heir to the crown effected his escape. Great rewards were offered for the latter, and he was found out, and would have been instantly murdered, but climbing up to the roof of a pagoda, he remained there till all means of escape failed, when he threw himself down upon a rock, and perished. The royal race of this Laos tribe, Chan-Pung-dam, synonymous with Lau-Pung-dam, (black or dark Laos), is now extinct; the country is laid waste; the peasants, to the number of 100,000, have been dispersed over different parts of Siam; and the whole territory has been brought, notwithstanding the remonstrances of the court of Hue, under the immediate control of the Siamese, who are anxious to have it peopled by other tribes. Those Laos nobles who yielded to the Siamese at the first onset, are at present kept confined in the spacious buildings of the Samplung pagoda, a temple erected by the father of Paya-meh-tap, on the banks of the Meinam, near the city of Bankok. I paid them a visit there, and found them exceedingly dejected, but open and polite in their conversation. They cherish the hope that they shall be sent back to their native country, relying on the compassion of his Siamese majesty, who forgives even when no offence has been given.

Although the Laos, generally, are in a low state of civilization, yet there are some tribes, amongst their most inaccessible mountains, inferior even to the rest of the nation. One of the most peaceful of these are the Kahs. The Laos, imitating the Siamese, are in the habit of stealing individuals of this tribe, and bringing them to Bankok for sale. Hence I have been able to converse with some of the Kahs, who stated to me, that their countrymen live peaceably and without wants, on their mountains, cultivating just so much rice as is sufficient for their own use ; and that they are without religion or laws, in a state of society not far superior to that of herding elephants. Nevertheless, they seem capable of great improvement, and, under the hand of a patient minister of Christ, may be as much benefited by the divine Gospel, as have been the lately so savage inhabitants of Tahiti or Hawaii.

Some Laos, who were sent by their chiefs, a

few years ago, with a Chinese mandarin from the frontiers of China, appeared a superior class of people, though speaking the same language as the other tribes. They have been greatly improved by their intercourse with the Chinese, to whose emperor they are accustomed to send regular tribute, by the hands of an ambassador.

Amongst the various races of people who inhabit Siam, there are also Kamehs or natives of Camboja. This country, situated to the southeast of Siam, is doubtless of higher antiquity than any of the surrounding states. The name Camboja occurs in the Ramayan and other ancient Hindoo poems; and in the earliest accounts of the country, Hindostan is mentioned as the cradle of Budhism. The language of the Cambojans differs materially from the Siamese, and is more harsh, but at the same time also more copious. Their literature is very extensive, and their books are written in a character called *Khom*, which is used by the Siamese only in writing their sacred Bali books. Most of their books,—and, with the exception of the national laws and history, perhaps all,—are in poetry. They treat generally on very trivial subjects, abound in repetitions, and are often extremely childish. I have seen a geographical work,

written some centuries ago, which is more correct
than Chinese works of the same kind.

Camboja was very long ruled by its own
princes; but lately, disunion induced two brothers
to take up arms against each other. Cochin-
China and Siam both profited by this discord,
and divided the country between themselves,
while one of the princes fled to Cochin-China,
and three to Siam. I was acquainted with two
of the latter, the third having died. They entertain the hope that their country will yet be
restored to them, since they did nothing to for-
feit it. The younger of the two is a man of
genius, and ready to improve his mind, but too
childish to take advantage of any opportunity
which may offer to him. The Cambojans are a
cringing, coarse people, narrow-minded, insolent,
and officious, as circumstances require. They
are, however, open to conviction, and capable of
improvement. The males are many of them
well formed, but the females are very vulgar in
their appearance. They are on equality with
their neighbours, in regard to filth and wretchedness, and are by no means inferior to them in
laziness. They carry on scarcely any trade except
in silk stuffs, which they fabricate themselves,
although to do so is contrary to the institutes of

Budha, because the life of the silk-worm is endangered during the process. To spend hours before their nobles in the posture of crouching dogs, to chew betel-nut, and to converse in their harsh language, are the most agreeable amusements of this people.

Camboja is watered by the Meinam kom, a large river, which takes its rise in Thibet. Like the southern part of Siam, the land is low and fertile, and even well inhabited. The principal emporium is Luknooi (so called by the natives), the Saigon of Europeans. This place has many Chinese settlers within its precincts, and carries on, under the jurisdiction of the Cochin-Chinese, a very brisk trade (principally in betel-nut and silk), both with Singapore and the northern ports of China. The capital of Camboja is surrounded by a wall, erected in high antiquity. The country itself is highly cultivated, though not to the extent that it might be; for, as the people are satisfied with a little rice and dry fish, they are not anxious to improve their condition by industry.

Hitherto Camboja has been the cause of much hostility between Siam and Cochin-China; each nation being anxious to extend its own jurisdiction over the whole country, Even so late as

1818, a Cochin-Chinese squadron, collected at
Kuknooi, was about to put out to sea in order
to defend the Cambojan coast against an expected
descent of the Siamese; while, at the same time,
the Cambojans are anxious to regain their
liberty, and to expel the Cochin-Chinese, their
oppressors.

Cochin-China or Annam, united by the last
revolution with Tonquin, has always viewed
Siam with the greatest distrust. Formerly the
country was divided by civil contests; but when
a French bishop had organized the kingdom,
and amplified its resources under the reign of
Kaung Shung, Annam could defy the prowess
of Siam. Even when the French influence had
ceased, and the country had relapsed into its
former weakness, the Cochin-Chinese continued
to keep a jealous eye on Siam. The Siamese,
conscious of their own inferiority, burnt, on one
occasion, a large quantity of timber collected for
ships of war, which were to have been built in a
Cochin-Chinese harbour; they have also been
successful in kidnapping some of the subjects of
Annam: and the captives have mostly settled at
Bankok, and are very able tradesmen. If the
character of the Cochin-Chinese were not deteriorated by the government, the people would

hold a superior rank in the scale of nations.
They are lively, intelligent, inquisitive, and
docile, though uncleanly and rather indolent.
This indolence, however, results from the tyranny
of government, which compels the people to
work most of the time for its benefit. The
Cochin-Chinese pay great regard to persons
acquainted with Chinese literature. Their
written language differs materially from their
oral; the latter is like the Cambojan, while the
former is similar to the dialect spoken on the
island of Hainan.

It remains now to make some remarks on
the introduction of Christianity into Siam.
When the Portugese first came to this country,
in 1622, they immediately propagated their
own religious tenets. The French missionaries
came to the country some time afterward, by
land. They had high anticipations of success
from the assistance of Cephalonian Phaulkon;
and as soon as the French embassy arrived,
and French influence gained the ascendency,
they increased the number of able labourers.
Two of them even shaved their heads, and
conformed to the customs of the Siamese talapoys
or priests, under pretence of learning the
Bali language. But, when the treachery of

Phaulkon had been discovered, he himself
killed, and the French expelled, the influence
of the priests vanished; the number of their
converts, instead of increasing, rapidly diminished; and the two individuals, who went to
live with the Siamese priests, were never more
heard of. Though the French missionaries
have maintained their station here to this day,
yet at times they have been driven to great
straits, and subjected to frequent imprisonments.

It is astonishing that, while in all other countries where Romanists have entered, their converts have been numerous, there have never been
but a few in Siam. At present, only a small
number,—mostly the descendants of the Portuguese, who speak the Cambojan and Siamese
languages,—constitute their flock; they have at
Bankok, four churches; at Chantibun, one; and
lately, a small one has been built at Jutaya, the
ancient capital. Yet all this would be of little
consequence, if even a few individuals had been
converted to their Saviour, by the influence of
the Holy Spirit. But, to effect this change of
heart and life, seems, alas! never to have been
the intention of the spiritual guides, or the endeavour of their followers. I lament the degradation
of people who so disgrace the name of Christians;

and would earnestly wish that never any convert of such a description was made.

The labours of the protestant mission have hitherto only been preparatory, and are in their incipient state. However, the attention of all the different races of people who inhabit Siam has been universally roused; and we may predict the approach of the happy time, when even Siam shall stretch forth its hands to the Saviour of the world.

A country so rich in productions as Siam, offers a large field for mercantile enterprise. Sugar, sapan-wood, beche-de-mar, birds' nests, sharks' fins, gamboge, indigo, cotton, ivory, and other articles, attract the notice of a great number of Chinese traders, whose junks every year, in February, March, and the beginning of April, arrive from Hainan, Canton, Soakah (or Shan-keo, in Chaou-chow-Foo,) Amoy, Ningpo, Seang-hae, (or Shang-hea-heen, in Keang-nan,) and other places. Their principal imports consist of various articles for the consumption of the Chinese, and a considerable amount of bullion. They select their export cargo according to the different places of destination, and leave Siam in the last of May, in June, and July. These vessels are about eighty in number. Those

which go up to the Yellow sea take, mostly,
sugar, sapan-wood, and betel-nut. They are
called Pak-tow-sun, (or Pih-tow-chuen, white
headed vessels,) are usually built in Siam, and
are of about 290 or 300 tons, manned by Chaou-
chow-men, from the eastern district of Canton
province. The major part of these junks are
owned either by Chinese settlers at Bankok or
by Siamese nobles. The former put on board,
as supercargo, some relative of their own, generally a young man, who has married one of their
daughters; the latter take surety of the relatives
of the person whom they appoint supercargo.
If any thing happens to the junk, the individuals
who secured her are held responsible, and are
often, very unjustly, thrown into prison. Though
the trade to the Indian archipelago is not so
important, yet about thirty or forty vessels are
annually despatched thither from Siam.

Chinese vessels have generally a captain, who
might more properly be styled a supercargo.
Whether the owner or not, he has charge of the
whole of the cargo, buys and sells as circumstances require; but has no command whatever
over the sailing of the ship. This is the business
of the Ho-chang or pilot. During the whole
voyage, to observe the shores and promontories

are the principal objects which occupy his attention, day and night. He sits steadily on the
side of the ship, and sleeps when standing, just
as it suits his convenience. Though he has,
nominally, the command over the sailors, yet
they obey him only when they find it agreeable
to their own wishes; and they scold and brave
him, just as if he belonged to their own company. Next to the pilot (or mate) is the To-
kung (helmsman), who manages the sailing of
the ship; there are a few men under his immediate command. There are, besides, two clerks;
one to keep the accounts, and the other to superintend the cargo that is put on board. Also,
a comprador, to purchase provisions; and a
Heang-kung, (or priest), who attends the idols,
and burns, every morning, a certain quantity of
incense, and of gold and silver paper. The
sailors are divided into two classes; a few, called
Tow-muh (or head men), have charge of the
anchor, sails, &c.; and the rest, called Ho-ke,
(or comrades), perform the menial work, such as
pulling ropes, and heaving the anchor. A cook and
some barbers make up the remainder of the crew.

All these personages, except the second class
of sailors, have cabins; long, narrow holes, in
which one may stretch himself, but cannot stand

erect. If any person wishes to go as a passenger, he must apply to the Tow-muh, in order to hire one of their cabins, which they let on such conditions as they please. In fact, the sailors exercise full control over the vessel, and oppose every measure which they think may prove injurious to their own interest; so that even the captain and pilot are frequently obliged, when wearied out with their insolent behaviour, to crave their kind assistance, and to request them to show a better temper.

The several individuals of the crew form one whole, whose principal object in going to sea is trade, the working of the junk being only a secondary object. Every one is a shareholder, having the liberty of putting a certain quantity of goods on board; with which he trades, wheresoever the vessel may touch, caring very little about how soon she may arrive at the port of destination.

The common sailors receive from the captain nothing but dry rice, and have to provide for themselves their other fare, which is usually very slender. These sailors are not, usually, men who have been trained up to their occupation; but wretches, who were obliged to flee from their homes; and they frequently engage for a voyage, before they have ever been on board a junk. All of them, however stupid, are commanders; and if any thing of importance is to be done, they will bawl out their commands to each other, till all is utter confusion. There is no subordination, no cleanliness, no mutual regard or interest.

The navigation of junks is performed without the aid of charts, or any other helps, except the compass; it is mere coasting, and the whole art of the pilot consists in directing the course according to the promontories in sight. In time of danger, the men immediately lose all their courage; and their indecision frequently proves the destruction of their vessel. Although they consider our mode of sailing as somewhat better than their own, still they cannot but allow the palm of superiority to the ancient craft of the "Celestial Empire." When any alteration for improvement is proposed, they will readily answer,—If we adopt this measure we shall justly fall under the suspicion of barbarism.

The most disgusting thing on board a junk is idolatry, the rites of which are performed with the greatest punctuality. The goddess of the sea is Ma-tsoo-po, called also Teen-how, "queen of heaven." She is said to have been a virgin, who lived some centuries ago in Fuhkeen, near the district of Fuhchow. On account of having, with great fortitude, and by a kind miracle, saved her brother who was on the point of drowning, she was deified, and loaded with titles, not dissimilar to those bestowed on the Virgin Mary. Every vessel is furnished with an image of this goddess, before which a lamp is kept burning. Some satellites, in hideous shape, stand round the portly queen, who is always represented in a sitting posture. Cups of tea are placed before her, and some tinsel adorns her shrine.

When a vessel is about to proceed on a voyage, she is taken in procession to a temple, where many offerings are displayed before her. The priest recites some prayers, the mate makes several prostrations, and the captain usually honours her by appearing in a full dress before her image. Then an entertainment is given, and the food presented to the idol is greedily devoured. Afterwards the good mother, who does not partake of the gross earthly substance, is carried in front of a stage, to behold the minstrels, and to admire the dexterity of the actors; thence she is brought back, with music, to the junk, where the merry peals of the gong receive the venerable old inmate, and the jolly sailors anxiously strive to seize whatever may happen to remain of her banquet.

The care of the goddess is intrusted to the priest, who never dares to appear before her with his face unwashed. Every morning he puts sticks of burning incense into the censer, and repeats his ceremonies in every part of the ship, not excepting even the cook's room. When the junk reaches any promontory, or when contrary winds prevail, the priest makes an offering to the spirits of the mountains, or of the air. On such occasions, (and only on such,) pigs and fowls are killed. When the offering is duly arranged, the priest adds to it some spirits and fruits, burns gilt paper, makes several prostrations, and then cries out to the sailors,—"Follow the spirits!"— who suddenly rise and devour most of the sacrifice. When sailing out of a river, offerings of paper are constantly thrown out near the rudder. But to no part of the junk are so many offerings made as to the compass. Some red cloth, which is also tied to the rudder and cable, is put over it; incense-sticks in great quantities are kindled; and gilt paper, made into the shape of a junk, is burnt before it. Near the compass, some tobacco, a pipe, and a burning lamp are placed,

the joint property of all; and hither they all
crowd to enjoy themselves. When there is a
calm, the sailors generally contribute a certain
quantity of gilt paper, which, pasted into the
form of a junk, is set adrift. If no wind follows,
the goddess is thought to be out of humour, and
recourse is had to the demons of the air. When
all endeavours prove unsuccessful, the offerings
cease, and the sailors wait with indifference.

Such are the idolatrous principles of the Chinese, that they never spread a sail without
having conciliated the favour of the demons, nor
return from a voyage without showing their
gratitude to their tutelar deity. Christians are
the servants of the living God, who has created
the heavens and the earth; at whose command
the winds and the waves rise or are still; in
whose mercy is salvation, and in whose wrath
is destruction; how much more, then, should
they endeavour to conciliate the favour of the
Almighty, and to be grateful to the Author of
all good! If idolaters feel dependent on superior beings; if they look up to them for protection and success; if they are punctual in
paying their vows; what should be the conduct
of nations who acknowledge Christ to be their
Saviour? Reverence before the name of the

Most High; reliance on his gracious protection;
submission to his just dispensations; and devout
prayers, humble thanksgiving, glorious praise of
the Lord of the earth and of the sea, ought to
be habitual on board our vessels; and if this is
not the case, the heathen will rise up against us
in the judgment, for having paid more attention
to their dumb idols, than we have to the worship of the living and true God.

The Chinese sailors are, generally, as intimated above, from the most debased class of
people. The major part of them are opium-
smokers, gamblers, thieves, and fornicators.
They will indulge in the drug till all their wages
are squandered; they will gamble as long as a
farthing remains; they will put off their only
jacket and give it to a prostitute. They are
poor and in debt; they cheat, and are cheated
by one another, whenever it is possible; and
when they have entered a harbour, they have no
wish to depart till all they have is wasted,
although their families at home may be in the
utmost want and distress. Their curses and
imprecations are most horrible, their language
most filthy and obscene; yet they never condemn themselves to eternal destruction. A
person who has lived among these men, would

be best qualified to give a description of Sodom and Gomorrah, as well as to appreciate the blessings of Christianity ; which, even in its most degenerate state, proves a greater check on human depravity than the best arranged maxims of men.

The whole coast of China is very well known to the Chinese themselves. As their navigation is only coasting, they discover, at a great distance, promontories and islands, and are seldom wrong in their conjectures. They have a directory, which, being the result of centuries of experience, is pretty correct in pointing out the shoals, the entrances of harbours, rocks, &c. As they keep no dead reckoning, nor take observations, they judge of the distance they have made by the promontories they have passed. They reckon by divisions, ten of which are about equal to a degree. Their compass differs materially from that of Europeans. It has several concentric circles ; one is divided into four, and another into eight parts, somewhat similar to our divisions of the compass ; a third is divided into twenty-four parts, in conformity to the horary division of twenty-four hours, which are distinguished by the same number of characters or signs ; according to these divisions, and with these signs, the courses are marked in their directory, and the vessel steered.

China has, for centuries, presented to the Romanists a great sphere for action. Latterly, the individuals belonging to the mission have not been so eminent for talents as their predecessors, and their influence has greatly decreased. Although the tenets of their religion are proscribed, some individuals belonging to their mission have always found their way into China; at the present time they enter principally by the way of Fuhkeen. It would have been well, at the time they exercised a great influence over the mind of Kang-he, if,—by representing the European character in its true light, and showing the advantages to be derived from an open intercourse with western nations,—they had endeavoured to destroy the wall of separation, which has hitherto debarred the Chinese from marching on in the line of national improvement. Their policy did not admit of this; the only thing they were desirous of, was to secure the trade to the faithful children of the mother church, and the possession of Macao to the Portuguese. In the latter they succeeded; in the former all their exertions have been baffled by the superior enterprising spirit of protestant

nations; and their own system of narrow policy
has tended, not only to exclude themselves from
what they once occupied, but to excite the antipathy of the Chinese government against every
stranger.

Protestant missionaries, it is to be hoped, will
adopt a more liberal policy: while they preach
the glorious Gospel of Christ, they will have to
show that the spread of divine truth opens the
door for every useful art and science; that un-
shackled commercial relations will be of mutual
benefit; and that foreigners and Chinese, as inhabitants of the same globe, and children of the
same Creator, have an equal claim to an amicable
intercourse, and a free reciprocal communication.
Great obstacles are in the way, and have hitherto
prevented the attainment of these objects; but,
nevertheless, some preparatory steps have been
taken; such as the completion of a Chinese and
English dictionary, by one of the most distinguished members of the protestant mission;
the translation of the Bible; the publication of
tracts on a great variety of subjects; the establishment of the Anglo-Chinese college, and
numerous schools; and other different proceedings, all for the same purpose.

One of the greatest inconveniences in our

operations has been, that most of our labours, with the exception of those of Drs. Morrison and Milne, were confined to Chinese from the Canton and Fuhkeen provinces, who annually visit the ports of the Indian archipelago, and of whom many become permanent residents abroad. When the junks arrived in those ports, we were in the habit of supplying them with books, which found their way to most of the emporiums of the Chinese empire. As no place, south of China, is the rendezvous of so many Chinese junks as Siam, that country has been the most important station for the distribution of Christian and scientific books. And, moreover, a missionary residing there, and coming in contact with a great many people from the different provinces, may render himself endeared to them, and so gain an opportunity of entering China without incurring any great personal risk.

All these advantages had long ago determined the minds of Mr. Tomlin and of myself, to make an attempt to enter China in this unobtruding way; but indisposition snatched from my side a worthy fellow-labourer, and peculiar circumstances prolonged my stay in Siam, till a great loss in the death of a beloved partner, and a severe illness, made me anxious to proceed on

my intended voyage. Although I had been
frequently invited to become a passenger, yet my
first application to the captain of a junk, destined
to Teen-tsin, the commercial emporium of the
capital, met with a repulse. This junk afterwards left Siam in company with us, and was
never more heard of. The refusal of Jin, the
captain, was re-echoed by several others; till,
unexpectedly, the Siamese ambassador, who had
to go to Peking this year, promised to take me
gratis to the capital, in the character of his physician. He had great reason to desire the latter
stipulation, because several of his predecessors
had died for want of medical assistance. I
gladly hailed this opportunity of an immediate
entrance into the country, with a desire of doing
every thing that Providence should put in my
way, and enable me to accomplish. But I was
sorely disappointed; for by the intervention of a
gentleman, who wished to detain me in Siam,
the ambassador did not fulfil his proposals.

CHAPTER II.

DURING this interval of uncertainty, my indis-position had increased to an alarming degree; when I was surprised by the arrival of one of my mercantile Chinese friends, a native of the eastern part of Canton province, who felt himself interested in taking me to China. He used every argument to prevail on me to embark; but, as I was verging so fast to the grave, I was reluctant to comply. Nevertheless Lin-jung (for this was the man's name) succeeded, for his arguments were imperious; and I agreed with Captain Sin-shun, the owner of the junk Shunle, to embark in his vessel for Teen-tsin. This junk was of about two hundred and fifty tons burden, built in Siam, but holding its license from Canton; it was loaded with sapan-wood, sugar, pepper, feathers, calicoes, &c., and was manned by about fifty sailors.

The 3d of June was the day appointed for our departure. Mr. Hunter, Capt. Dawson, and Mr. Mac Dalnac, had the kindness to accompany me on board the junk. I am under

very great obligations to the first of these gentlemen, for his frequent and ready support, to the
utmost of his power, of any measures that could
tend towards the civilization of the natives.
When I got on board, my cabin in the steerage
was pointed out to me; it was a hole, only large
enough for a person to lie down in, and to receive a small box. I had six fellow-passengers.
One of them, a captain sixty years of age, was
obliged to become a passenger, because his own
junk was unseaworthy, having sprung a leak
whilst moored in the Meinam. He was my declared enemy; a master in opium-smoking
(using the drug to the amount of about one dollar per day); a man thoroughly versed in all
sorts of villany; and averse to the instruction of
his countrymen; though, at the same time, he
was well aware of the superiority of Europeans,
and knew the value of their arts. His son was
an insolent youth, well trained for mercantile
transactions, and anxious to amass wealth; he
became my friend and neighbour. My mercantile friend, already mentioned, had a cabin
beneath mine. He was remarkable for deceitfulness, loquacity, childish pride, and unnatural
crime. His companion in trade was wealthy,
self-sufficient, and debauched, but polite. In

the practice of wickedness and deceit, no one
was superior to captain Fo, another of my fellow-
passengers. This man had formerly been in
command of a Siamese junk, bearing tribute to
China, and was shipwrecked on the coast of
Pulo Way. On his release from that island, he
returned to Bankok. Being skilful in various
sorts of workmanship, especially in painting and
mechanics, he at length gained so much property,
that he was able, this year, to put some hundred
peculs of goods on board a junk, and to proceed
to China, where he had two wives still living.
He was devoted to opium, and prone to lying;
but according to his own declaration, my best
friend.

Our captain, Sin-shun, was a friendly man,
well versed in the art of Chinese navigation; but,
unhappily, long habituated to opium smoking.
His younger brother showed himself to be a man
of truth; he was my private friend and associate
in every sort of trouble. One of the captain's
brothers-in-law was the clerk; he denominated
himself (from the moment I stepped on board)
my younger brother; paid attention to the instructions of the Gospel; and abstained from
every sort of idolatry. The pilot claimed
cousinship with me, being (as he said) of the

same clan. He was little versed in the art of
navigation, but had never been so unlucky as to
sail his junk on shore. He was a man of a
peaceful temper, a yielding disposition, and a
constant object of raillery to the sailors. To all
his good qualities, he added that of opium-smoking, in which art he had made considerable
proficiency. His assistant was quarrelsome, but
more attentive to the navigation than any other
individual on board; and he also, as is the case
with almost all the pilots, was trained up to the
use of the drug; after having inspired the delicious
fumes, he would often, against his inclination,
sleep at his watch. All the principal persons,
on whom depended the management of the
vessel, partook freely of this intoxicating luxury;
by which they were alternately, and sometimes
simultaneously, rendered unfit for service.

When I embarked, though in a very feeble
state of body, I cherished the hope, that God,
in his mercy, would restore me again to health,
if it were his good pleasure to employ in his service a being so unworthy as myself—the least,
doubtless, of all my fellow-labourers in the Chinese mission. I took with me a large quantity
of Christian books, and a small stock of medicines,—the remnant of a large remittance, made,

not long before, by some kind English friends.
I was also provided with some charts, a quadrant,
and other instruments to be used in case of
emergency. Long before leaving Siam I became
a naturalized subject of the Celestial Empire, by
adoption into the clan or family of Kwo, from
the Tung-an district in Fuhkeen. I took, also,
the name Shih-lee, — wore, occasionally, the
Chinese dress,—and was recognized (by those
among whom I lived) as a member of the great
nation. *Now*, I had to conform entirely to the
customs of the Chinese, and even to dispense
with the use of European books. I gladly met
all their propositions, being only anxious to prepare myself for death; and was joyful in the
hope of acceptance before God, by the mediatorial office of Jesus Christ. My wish to depart
from this life was very fervent, yet I had a sincere desire of becoming subservient to the cause
of the Redeemer, among the Chinese; and only
on this account I prayed to God for the prolongation of my life.

In three days after embarking, we passed
down the serpentine Meinam, suffering greatly
from the swarms of musquitoes, which are a
better defence to the country than the miserable
forts built at the mouth of the river. Such was

my debility that I could scarcely walk; I could
swallow no food; and for some time river-water
alone served to keep me alive. During the
night of the 8th of June, I seemed to be near my
end; my breath almost failed, and I lay stretched
out in my berth, without the assistance of a
single individual; for my servant Yu, a Fuhkeen
man, thought and acted like all his countrymen,
who give a man up and leave him to his fate, as
soon as he is unable to eat rice. While in this
exceedingly depressed state, so much consciousness remained, that I was able, at length, to
rally a little strength, and leave my cabin;
scarcely had I reached the steerage, when a
strong vomiting fit freed me from the danger of
suffocation.

On the 9th day of June, we reached the bar,
where there is very little depth of water : here
we were detained for some time. Every vessel
built in Siam has a Siamese noble for its patron;
the patron of ours was the highest officer in the
kingdom, who sent one of his clerks on board to
see us safe out to sea. This man was greatly
astonished at seeing me on board a Chinese junk,
and expressed some doubts in regard to my
safety. In fact, all my friends expressed their
fears for my life, which might fall a prey, either

to the rapacity of the sailors, or to the villany of the mandarins. Many fearful dangers were predicted concerning me; there was not one individual who approved of my course; and I had no other consolation than looking up to God, under the consideration that I was in the path of duty.

In three days we were able to pass the bar, but it was effected with much difficulty. When the tide was in our favour, a cable was thrown out, by means of which the vessel was moved forward, in a manner which did high credit to the sailors.

The people treated me with great kindness; regretted the loss of my wife, whom most of them had seen and knew; and endeavoured to alleviate my sufferings in a way which was very irksome. The poor fellows, notwithstanding their scanty fare of salt, vegetables, and dried rice, and rags hardly sufficient to cover their nakedness, were healthy and cheerful, and some of them even strong. They highly congratulated me, that at length I had left the regions of barbarians, to enter the Celestial Empire. Though most of them were of mean birth, the major part could read, and took pleasure in perusing such books as they possessed. In the libraries of

E

some of them I was delighted to find our tracts. It has always afforded me the greatest pleasure to observe the extensive circulation of christian books; this gives me the confident hope, that God, in his great mercy, will make the written word the means of bringing multitudes of those who read it to the knowledge and enjoyment of eternal life.

On the 14th of June, some Siamese came on board to search for me; not knowing their intentions, I withdrew. If, at this moment, the message they brought had been delivered to me, my feeble frame would perhaps have fallen; but it was not till long afterwards that I heard, that my dearest infant daughter had died soon after I embarked. The mournful tidings excited the deepest grief. After this, I passed several days alone in my cabin, which was constantly filled with the vile smell of opium fumigation. As soon as the men laid down their pipes, they would indulge in the most obscene and abominable language; thus adding offence to offence. All this I had to bear patiently, till I acquired sufficient strength to talk with them; I then admonished them, in the plainest terms; and, contrary to my expectations, received from some apologies for their ill conduct towards me.

At length our passengers had all come on
board, and the men were beginning to heave the
anchor, when it was discovered that the junk
was overloaded: a circumstance which very frequently occurs, as every individual takes as
many goods on board as he pleases. The captain had now to go back to Bankok; immediately on his return, some of the cargo was
discharged; and on June the 18th we finally
got under weigh. But we moved very slowly
along the coast of the Siamese territory, attempting to sail only when the tide was in our favour.
Proceeding eastward, we anchored near the promontory and city of Bamplasoi, which is principally inhabited by Chinese, and is celebrated for
its fisheries and salt works. Here the Siamese
have some salt inspectors, and keep the country
in complete subjection. On the 19th, we espied Ko-Kram, formerly the resort of pirates;
it is an island with a temple on its summit, in
which is a representation of Budha in a sleeping
posture. On arriving at this place, the Chinese
generally make an offering to this indolent idol.
Those on board the richly-laden junks make
an offering of a pig; poor people are satisfied
with a fowl or duck; both which offerings are
duly consumed by the sailors after having been

exposed a short time to the air. Concerning this practice, so repugnant to common sense, I made some satirical remarks, which met with the approbation of the sailors, who, however, were not very anxious to part with the offerings.

I now began to cherish the hope that my health was recovering, and turned my attention to Chinese books; but great weakness soon compelled me to abandon the pursuit, and to pass my time in idleness. My fellow-passengers, meantime, endeavoured, by various means, to keep up my spirits, and to amuse me with sundry tales about the beauty of the Celestial Empire. My thoughts were now more than ever directed to my heavenly abode; I longed to be with Christ, while I felt strong compassion for these poor beings, who have no other home to hope for than an earthly one.

After having passed Cape Liant, which in most charts is placed too far west by two degrees, we approached Chantibun, a place of considerable trade, and inhabited by Siamese, Chinese, and Cochin-Chinese. Pepper, rice, and betel-nut, are found here in great abundance; and several junks, principally from Canton, are annually loaded with these articles. Ships proceeding to

China might occasionally touch here and trade to advantage.

When my strength was somewhat regained, I took observations regularly, and was requested, by the captain and others, to explain the method of finding the latitude and longitude. When I had fully explained the theory, the captain wondered that I brought the sun upon a level with the horizon of the sea, and remarked, " If you can do this, you can also tell the depth of the water." But as I was unable to give him the soundings, he told me plainly, that observations were entirely useless, and truly barbarian. So I lost his confidence; which, however, was soon recovered, when I told him that in a few hours we should see Pulo Way. On this island, one hundred years ago, a British fort was erected; but it was afterwards abandoned, on account of the treachery of some Bugees troops who murdered the English garrison. During the civil wars in Cochin-China, near the close of the last century, Kaung-Shung, the late king, took refuge here, where he lived for several years in a most wretched condition. In the year 1790, he made a descent upon his own territory, gained over a party, expelled the usurpers, conquered Tonquin, and, by the assistance of Adran, a

French missionary, improved the condition of his whole empire. Some time back, the island was the retreat of Malay pirates; but at present it is the resort only of a few fishermen, and is wholly covered with jungle.

With the utmost difficulty we arrived at the mouth of the Kang-kau river, in Camboja, where there is a city, which carries on considerable trade with Singapore, principally in rice and mats. The Cochin-Chinese, pursuing a very narrow policy, shut the door against improvement, and hinder, as far as they can, the trade of the Chinese. They think it their highest policy to keep the Cambojans in utter poverty, that they may remain their slaves for ever. Among the several junks at this place, we saw the "tribute bearer," having on board the Siamese ambassador. Though the Siamese acknowledge, nominally, the sovereignty of China, and show their vassalage by sending to Peking tribute of all the productions of their own country, yet the reason of their paying homage so regularly is gain. The vessels sent on these expeditions are exempt from duty, and being very large, are consequently very profitable; but the management of them is entrusted to Chinese, who take care to secure to themselves a good share of the gains. Within a few years several of these junks have been wrecked.

On July 4th, we reached Pulo Condore, called by the Chinese Kwun-lun. This island is inhabited by Cochin-Chinese fishermen. The low coast of Camboja presents nothing to attract attention; but the country seems well adapted for the caltivation of rice. When we passed this place, the Cochin-Chinese squadron, fearful of a descent of the Siamese on Luknooi, were ready to repel any attack. Of eight junks loaded with betel-nut this year at Luknooi, and destined to Teen-tsin, only four reached that harbour; and of these, one was wrecked on her return voyage.

At this time, though I was suffering much from fear and sickness, I found rich consolation in the firm belief, that the gospel of God would be carried into China, whatever might be the result of the first attempts. The perusal of John's Gospel, which details the Saviour's transcendent love, was encouraging and consoling, though as yet I could not see that peculiar love extended to China; but God will send the word of eternal life to a nation hitherto unvisited by the life-giving influences of the Holy Ghost. In these meditations I tasted the powers of the world to come, and lost myself in the adoration

of that glorious name, the only one given under
heaven whereby we must be saved. Under such
circumstances, it was easy to bear all the contempt that was heaped on me; neither did the
kindness of some individuals make me forget
that there were dishonest men around me, and
that I owed my preservation solely to the divine
protection.

The coast of Tsiompa is picturesque, the
country itself closely overgrown with jungle, and
thinly inhabited by the aborigines, and by Cochin-Chinese and Malays. I could gain very
little information of this region; even the Chinese
do not often trade thither; but it appears, that
the natives are in the habit of sending their articles to some of the neighbouring harbours
visited by the Chinese.

Here we saw large quantities of fish in every
direction, and good supplies of them were readily
caught. By chance, some very large ones were
taken; and a person who had always much influence in the deliberations of the company, advised that such should be offered to the mother
of heaven, Ma-tsoo-po. The propriety of this
measure I disputed strongly, and prevailed on
the sailors not to enhance their guilt by conse-
crating the creatures of God to idols.

From Pulo Condore the wind was in our favour, and in five days we passed the coast of Cochin-China. The islands and promontories of this coast have a very romantic appearance; particularly Padaran, Varela, and San-ho. Many rivers and rivulets disembogue themselves along the coast; and the sea abounds with fish, which seem to be a principal article of food with the natives. Hundreds of boats are seen cruising in every direction. The Cochin-Chinese are a very poor people, and their condition has been made more abject by the late revolution. Hence they are very economical in their diet, and sparing in their apparel. The king is well aware of his own poverty and that of his subjects, but is averse to opening a trade with Europeans, which might remedy this evil. The natives themselves are open and frank, and anxious to conciliate the favour of strangers.

On the 10th of July we saw Teen-fung, a high and rugged rock. The joy of the sailors was extreme, this being the first object of their native country which they espied. Teen-fung is about three or four leagues from Hainan. This island is wholly surrounded by mountains, while the interior has many level districts, where rice and sugar are cultivated. There are aborigines, not unlike the inhabitants of Manilla, who live in the forests and mountains; but the principal inhabitants are the descendants of people, who, some centuries back, came from Fuhkeen; and who, though they have changed in their external appearance, still bear traces of their origin preserved in their language. They are a most friendly people, always cheerful, always kind. In their habits they are industrious, clean, and very persevering. To a naturally inquisitive mind they join love of truth, which, however, they are slow in understanding. The Roman Catholic missionaries very early perceived the amiableness of this people, and were successful in their endeavours to convert them; and to this day many of the people profess to be Christians, and seem anxious to prove themselves such.

Hainan is, on the whole, a barren country; and, with the exception of timber, rice, and sugar, (the latter of which is principally carried to the north of China,) there are no articles of export. The inhabitants carry on some trade abroad; they visit Tonquin, Cochin-China, Siam, and also Singapore. On their voyages to Siam, they cut timber along the coasts of Tsiompa and Camboja; and when they arrive at Bankok, buy an additional quantity, with which they build

junks. In two months a junk is finished—the
sails, ropes, anchor, and all the other work, being
done by their own hands. These junks are then
loaded with cargoes, saleable at Canton or on
their native island ; and both junks and cargoes
being sold, the profits are divided among the
builders. Other junks, loaded with rice, and bones
for manure, are usually despatched for Hainan.

During my residence in Siam, I had an extensive intercourse with this people. They took
a particular delight in perusing christian books,
and conversing on the precepts of the gospel.
And almost all of those, who came annually to
Bankok, took away books, as valuable presents
to their friends at home. Others spoke of the
good effects produced by the books, and invited
me to visit their country. Humbly trusting in
the mercies of our God and Redeemer, that he
will accomplish, in his own time, the good work
which has been commenced, I would invite
some of my brethren to make this island the
sphere of their exertions, and to bring the
joyful tidings of the gospel to a people anxious
to receive its precious contents.

As soon as the first promontory of the Chinese continent was in sight, the captain was
prompt and liberal in making sacrifices, and

the sailors were not backward in feasting upon them. Great numbers of boats appeared in all directions, and made the scene very lively. We were becalmed in sight of the Lema islands, and suffered much from the intense heat. While there was not wind enough to ruffle the dazzling surface of the sea, we were driven on by the current to the place of our destination, Soakah,* in Chaou-chow-foo, the most eastern department of Canton province, bordering on Fuhkeen. This district is extensive, and closely peopled. The inhabitants occupy every portion of it; and must amount, at a moderate calculation, to three or four millions. Its principal ports are Ting-hae (the chief emporium,) Ampoh, Hae-eo, Kit-eo, and Jeao-ping. The people are, in general, mean, uncleanly, avaricious, but affable and fond of strangers. Necessity urges them to leave their native soil, and more than 5000 of them go every year

---

* The Chinese characters, and, consequently, the mandarin pronunciation, of this and several other names in the following pages, we are unable to ascertain; Mr. G. having only inserted in the MS. he left with us the names of the places, according to their Fuhkeen pronunciation. *Ting-hae* is Ching-hae-heen, and *Jeao-ping* is Jaou-ping-heen. *Hae-eo*, and *Kit-eo*, we believe to be Hae-yang-heen, and Kee-yang-heen. *Soakah* (or Shan-keo,) is a small port near the mouth of the Jaou-ping river. Ampoh is the same as Gan-po.

to the various settlements of the Indian archipelago, to Cochin-China, and to Hainan, or
gain their livelihood as sailors. Being neighbours to the inhabitants of Fuhkeen, the dialects of the two people are very similar, but in
their manners there is a great difference. This
dissimilarity in their customs, joined to the simi-
larity of their pursuits, has given rise to considerable rivalry, which frequently results in
open hostility. But the Fuhkeen men have
gained the ascendency, and use all their influence
to destroy the trade of their competitors.

Our sailors were natives of this district, and
anxious to see their families after a year's absence. As, however, our junk had no permit,
we could not enter the river of Soakah, but
had to anchor in the harbour of Nan-aou, (or
Namoh,) whilst passage - boats came in all
directions to carry the men to their homes. Rice
being very cheap in Siam, every sailor had
provided a bag or two, as a present to his
family. In fact, the chief thing they wish and
work for, is rice; their domestic accounts are
regulated by the quantity of rice consumed;
their meals according to the number of bowls
of it boiled; and their exertions, according to
the quantity wanted. Every substitute for this

delicious food is considered meagre, and indicative of the greatest wretchedness. When they cannot obtain a sufficient quantity to satisfy their appetites, they supply the deficiency of rice with an equal weight of water. Inquiring whether the western barbarians eat rice, and finding me slow to give them an answer, they exclaimed; " O, the sterile regions of barbarians, which produce not the necessaries of life! Strange, that the inhabitants have not, long ago, died of hunger!" I endeavoured to show them that we had substitutes for rice, which were equal, if not superior to it. But all to no purpose; and they still maintained, that it is only rice which can properly sustain the life of a human being.

When most of the sailors had left the junk, I was led to reflect on their miserable condition. Almost entirely destitute of clothes and money, they return home, and in a few days hurry away —again to encounter new dangers and new perils. But, however wretched their present condition may be, their prospects for eternity are far more deplorable. Reprobates in this life, they tremble to enter into eternity, of which they have very confused ideas. They defy God, who rules over the seas; they curse their parents, who gave them life; they are enemies to each other, and seem entirely regardless of the future; they glory in their shame; and do not startle when convicted of being the servants of Satan.

It was the 17th of July when we anchored in the harbour of Namoh. The island, from which this harbour takes its name, is mostly barren rock, consisting of two mountains connected by a narrow isthmus, in lat. 26 deg. 28 min. N.; long. 116 deg. 39 min. E. It is a military station; it has a fort; and is a place of considerable trade, which is carried on between the people of Fuhkeen and Canton. The harbour is spacious and deep, but the entrance is difficult and dangerous.

The entrance of the Soakah river is very shallow; but numerous small craft, principally from Ting-hae, are seen here. The duties, as well as the permit to enter the river, are very high; but the people know how to elude the mandarins, as the mandarins do the emperor. Ting-hae is a large place, tolerably well built, and inhabited principally by merchants, fishermen, and sailors. The productions of the surrounding country are not sufficient to maintain the inhabitants, who contrive various ways and means to gain a livelihood. There is no want of capital or merchants, but a great lack of honesty and upright dealing.

As soon as we had anchored, numerous boats surrounded us, with females on board, some of them brought by their parents, husbands, or brothers. I addressed the sailors who remained in the junk, and hoped that I had prevailed on them, in some degree, to curb their evil passions. But, alas! no sooner had I left the deck, than they threw off all restraint; and the disgusting scene which ensued, might well have entitled our vessel to the name of Sodom. The sailors, un-mindful of their starving families at home, and dis-tracted, blinded, stupified by sensuality, seemed willing to give up aught and every thing they possessed, rather than abstain from that crime which entails misery, disease, and death. Having exhausted all their previous earnings, they became a prey to reckless remorse and gloomy despair. As their vicious partners were opium-smokers by habit, and drunkards by custom, it was necessary that strong drink and opium should be provided; and the retailers of these articles were soon present to lend a helping hand. Thus, all these circumstances conspired to nourish vice, to squander property, and to render the votaries of crime most unhappy.

When all their resources failed, the men became furious, and watched for an opportunity to reimburse their loss, either by deceit or force. Observing my trunks well secured, it was surmised by the sailors that they contained silver and gold; and a conspiracy was formed to cleave my head with a hatchet, and to seize the trunks, and divide the money among themselves. In favour of this scheme it was stated, that I did not understand the use of money, and that they themselves could appropriate it to the very best advantage. All the persons who formed this plot were *opium-smokers;* the leader was an old sailor, and, nominally, my friend. Just as they were about to execute their plan, an old man came forward and declared to them, that a few days before he had seen the trunks opened, and that they contained nothing but books, which they might obtain without cleaving my head. Witnesses were then called, and it being satisfactorily ascertained that such was the fact, in regard to the trunks, they all agreed to desist from the execution of their plot.

In the midst of such abominations, the feeble voice of exhortation was not entirely disregarded. Some individuals willingly followed my advice. A young man, who had repeatedly heard the gospel, and anxiously inquired about his eternal destinies, was reclaimed; and, covered with shame, and penetrated with a sense of guilt, he acknowledged the insufficiency of all moral precepts, if no heavenly principle influenced the heart.

My visitors were very numerous; they generally thought me to be a pilot or mate, and behaved very politely. In the long conversations I held with them, they seemed attentive, and not entirely ignorant of the doctrines of Christianity; and they frequently noticed, as a proof of its power, the mere circumstance, that one of its votaries stood unmoved, while the stream of vice carried away every thing around him. To these visitors I distributed the word of life; expressing my earnest wish, that it might prove the means of their salvation. There was one old man, who stated that he had two sons, literary graduates, whom, as he himself was hastening to the grave, he wished to see reading the exhortations to the world, (so they call our Christian books.) I enjoyed myself in the company of some other individuals, to whom it was intimated that we should endeavour to establish a mission at this place, since so many millions of their countrymen were without the means of knowing the way of salvation.

The return of the captain, who had been on shore, checked the progress of vice. Being a man of firm principle, he drove out the prostitutes, and brought the men to order;—his vigilance, however, was in some instances eluded; but when those wretched beings had obtained their money, (their great object,) they generally, of their own accord, abandoned the junk. I had now full scope to speak to those around me of the folly and misery of such conduct; and I was successful in applying the discourse to themselves. The Chinese, generally, will bear with just reproof, and even heap eulogiums on those who administer it.

Here I saw many natives famishing for want of food; they would greedily seize, and were very thankful for, the smallest quantities of rice thrown out to them. Though healthy, and strong, and able to work, they complained of want of employment, and the scarcity of the means of subsistence.* Urged on by poverty,

* In the department of Chaou-chow-foo, to which these remarks apply, as also in the neighbouring province of Fuhkeen, and in the adjoining department of Hwuy-chow-foo in this province, famine has very generally prevailed during the last few months. Pirates, consequently, abound, and insurrections have in several cases occurred ; numbers of peasants also are induced, by hunger and want of employment, to join the secret

some of them become pirates, and in the night time surprise and plunder the junks in the harbour. When fourteen days had elapsed, all were anxious to depart, because their treasure was exhausted, and the opportunities for farther expenditures were only the means of tantalizing and annoying them. As we were getting under weigh, an old man predicted that we should have to encounter storms; but this did not deter us from proceeding. Many junks, loaded with sugar for the north of China, left the harbour in company with us.

On July 30th, we passed Amoy, the principal emporium of Fuhkeen province, and the residence of numerous merchants, who are the owners of more than 300 large junks, and who carry on an extensive commerce, not only to all the ports of China, but to many also in the Indian archipelago. Notwithstanding the heavy duties levied on exports and imports, these merchants maintain their trade, and baffle the efforts of the mandarins. They would hail with joy any opportunity of opening a trade with Europeans, and would, doubtless, improve upon that of Canton.

associations of banditti which infest China, particularly its southern provinces.

On the following day, favourable winds continued till we reached the channel of Formosa (or Tea-wan.) This island has flourished greatly since it has been in the possession of the Chinese, who go thither, generally, from Tung-an in Fuhkeen, as colonists, and who gain a livelihood by trade, and the cultivation of rice, sugar, and camphor. Formosa has several deep and spacious harbours, but all the entrances are extremely shallow. The trade is carried on in small junks belonging to Amoy; they go to all the western ports of the island, and either return loaded with rice, or go up to the north of China with sugar. The rapidity with which this island has been colonized, and the advantages it affords for the colonists to throw off their allegiance, have induced the Chinese government to adopt restrictive measures, and no person can now emigrate without a permit. The colonists are wealthy and unruly; and hence there are numerous revolts, which are repressed with great difficulty, because the leaders, withdrawing to the mountains, stand out against the government to the very uttermost. In no part of China are executions so frequent as they are here; and in no place do they produce a less salutary influence. The literati are very successful; and people in Fuhkeen sometimes send their sons to Formosa to obtain literary degrees.

Northerly winds, with a high sea, are very frequent in the channel of Formosa. When we had reached Ting-hae, in the department of Fuh-chow-foo, the wind, becoming more and more adverse, compelled us to change our course; and fearing that stormy weather would overtake us, we came to anchor near the island of Ma-oh, (or Ma-aou,) on which the goddess Ma-tsoo-po is said to have lived. Here we were detained some time. The houses on the coast are well built; the people seemed poor, but honest; and are principally employed in fishing, and in rearing gourds. Their country is very rocky.

A few miles in the interior are the tea hills, where thousands of people find employment. The city of Fuh-chow-foo, the residence of the governor of Fuhkeen and Chekeang, is large and well built. Small vessels can enter the river; the harbour of Ting-hae is deep, and very spacious. We saw there numerous junks laden with salt, also some fishing craft.

When we were preparing to leave the harbour, another gale came on, and forced us to anchor; but instead of choosing an excellent anchorage which was near to us, a station was selected in the neighbourhood of rocks, where our lives were placed in great danger. The next day the storm increased, and the gale became a tornado, which threatened to whelm us in the foaming billows. The junk was exposed to the united fury of the winds and waves, and we expected every moment that she would be dashed in pieces. The rain soon began to descend in torrents, and every part of the vessel was thoroughly drenched.

For several days Egyptian darkness hung over us : with composure I could look up to God our Saviour, could rejoice in his promises, and was fully confident, that he would neither leave nor forsake us. I was almost the only person who ventured on deck ; for it is customary with the Chinese, in bad weather, to take shelter and repose in their cabins till the tempest is over. At the present juncture, they were dispelling their cares by sleeping and opium-smoking.

Notwithstanding all this they formed a plot, principally on account of the riches which they supposed me to possess, to sink the junk, to seize on the money, and then to flee in a small boat to the neighbouring shore. Having gained some information of their designs, I left my cabin and walked near them with my wonted cheerfulness. The ringleaders seeing this, and observing the approach of a Canton junk at the same time, desisted from their treacherous scheme.

It was most evident that these heroes in wickedness were cowards; they trembled, and their courage failed them, in the hour of approaching death. For ten days we were in suspense between life and death; when at length, God in his mercy sent again his sun to shine, and clothed the firmament with brightness. I could now feel with Noah, and render praise to God our great benefactor. While I was thus engaged, some of our fellow-passengers went on shore; unconscious of the object of their visit, I was rather puzzled when I saw them returning in their state dress; but soon suspected, (what was true,) that they had been to the temple of Ma-tsoo-po, to render homage to their protectress. At such an act of defiance, after such a signal deliverance, I was highly indignant, and rebuked them sharply. One of them held his peace; the other acknowledged his guilt, and promised, in future, to be more thankful to the Supreme Ruler of all things. He remarked, that it was only a pilgrimage to the birth-place of the goddess, and that he had only thrice prostrated himself before her image. I told him, that on account of such conduct he had great reason to fear the wrath of God would overtake him; when he heard that, he kept a solemn silence.

The temple of Ma-tsoo-po is not very splendid, though it has been built at a great expense. The priests are numerous and well maintained, the number of pilgrims being very great. When we were about to sail, a priest came on board with some candlesticks and incense, which, being sacred to the goddess, had power, it was supposed, to secure the vessel against imminent dangers. He held up in his hand a biography of the goddess, and was eloquent in trying to persuade the people to make large offerings. The priest belonging to our junk replied to him, "We are already sanctified, and need no additional goodness;—go to others who are wanting in devotion." I improved this opportunity to remark on the sinfulness of paying homage to their goddess; and reminded them how, during the storm, the idol shook and would have fallen into the sea, if they had not caught it with their own hands. The priest, anxious to maintain his ground, said, "Ah! she was angry." I replied, "She is weak—away with an image that cannot protect itself — cast it into the ocean, and let us see if it has power to rescue itself."

The people from the tea plantations, who came

F

on board our junk, were civil and characterised
by a simplicity of manner which was very commendable.   I conversed much with them, asked
them many questions, and was pleased with the
propriety and correctness of their answers.

Before we left Namoh, our captain, the owner
of the junk, attracted by the pleasures of domestic
life, had charged his uncle with the management
of the vessel, and left us.   This new captain was
an elderly man, who had read a great deal, and
who could write with readiness, and was quite
conversant with the character of Europeans.
These good qualities, however, were clouded by
his ignorance of navigation, and by his habitual
roguishness.   His younger brother, a proud man
and without experience, was a mere drone.   He
had a bad cough, and was covered with the itch;
and being my messmate, he was exceedingly
annoying, and often spoiled our best meals.   Our
daily food was rather sparing—it consisted principally of rice, and of salted and dried vegetables.
When any thing extra was obtained, it was seized
so greedily, that my gleanings were scanty indeed; yet I trusted in the Lord, who sweetened
the most meagre meals, and made me cheerful
and happy under every privation.

A large party was, at one time, formed against

me, who disapproved of my proceedings as a missionary. My books, they said, were not wanted at Teen-tsin; there were priests enough already, and they had long ago made every needful provision for the people. And as for medical aid, there were hundreds of doctors, who, rather than allow me to do it, would gladly take charge of the poor and the sick. Moreover, they all expressed their fears that I should become a prey to rogues, who are very numerous throughout China. But when I told them that I proceeded as the servant of Shang-te (the supreme Ruler), and did not fear the wrath of man in a good cause, they held their peace. By a reference to the immorality of their lives, I could easily silence all their objections;—"If you are really under the influence of the transforming laws of the Celestial Empire, as you all affirm, why do those rules prove so weak a restraint on your vicious practices, whilst the gospel of Christ preserves its votaries from wickedness and crime?" They replied, "We are indeed sinners, and are lost irremediably."—"But," I inquired, "have you never read the books I gave you, which assure us that Jesus died for the world?"—"Yes, we have; but we find that they contain much which does not accord with the truth." To show them that they were wrong, I took one of the books of Scripture and went through it, sentence by sentence, shewing them that the gospel was not only profitable for this life, but also for the life to come. This procedure put them to shame; and from that time they ceased to offer their objections, and admitted the correctness of the principles of the gospel, and their happy tendency on the human heart.

As soon as we had come in sight of the Chusan (or Chow-shan) islands, which are in lat. 29 deg. 22 min. N., we were again becalmed. The sailors, anxious to proceed, collected among themselves some gilt paper, and formed it into the shape of a junk; and, after marching a while in procession to the peal of the gong, launched the paper junk into the sea, but obtained no change of weather in consequence of this superstitious rite; the calm still continued, and was even more oppressive than before.

The city of Chu-san (or Chow-shan), situated in lat. 30 deg. 26 min. N., has fallen into decay since it has ceased to be visited by European vessels; its harbour, however, is the rendezvous of a few native junks. Ning-po, which is situated a short distance westward of Chusan, is the principal emporium of Che-keang province. Native vessels belonging to this place are generally of about two hundred tons burden, and have four oblong sails, which are made of cloth. These vessels, which are similar to those of Keangnan province, trade mostly to the north of China: copper cash, reduced to about one half the value of the currency, is their principal article of export.

About the 20th of August we reached the mouth of the river Yang-tsze-keang, on the banks of which stands the city of Seanghae (Shang-hae-heen), the emporium of Nanking, and of the whole of Keangnan province; and as far as the native trade is concerned, perhaps the principal commercial city in the empire. It is laid out with great taste ; the temples are very numerous ; the houses neat and comfortable; and the inhabitants polite, though rather servile in their manners. Here, as at Ning-po, the trade is chiefly carried on by Fuhkeen men. More than a thousand small vessels go up to the north, several times annually, exporting silk and other Keangnan manufactures, and importing peas and medical drugs. Some few junks, owned by Fuhkeen men, go to the Indian archipelago, and return with very rich cargoes.

It was with great difficulty that we reached the

extremity of the Shantung promontory, in lat. 37 deg. 23 min. N.; and when we did so, the wind continuing unfavourable, we cast anchor at Leto (Letaou, an island in the bay of Sang-kow), where there is a spacious and deep harbour, surrounded by rocks, with great shoals on the left side. This was on the 23d of August. There were several vessels in the harbour, driven thither by the severity of the weather. At one extremity of Leto harbour a small town is situated. The surrounding country is rocky, and productive of scarcely any thing, except a few fruits. The houses are built of granite, and covered with sea-weeds; within they were very poorly furnished. The people themselves were rather neat in their appearance, and polite in their manners, but not of high attainments. Though very little conversant with their written character, they nevertheless spoke the mandarin dialect better than I had ever before heard. They seemed very poor, and had few means of subsistence; but they appeared industrious, and laboured hard to gain a livelihood. I visited them in their cottages, and was treated with much kindness—even invited to a dinner, where the principal men of the place were present. As their attention was much attracted towards me, being a stranger, I took occasion to explain the reason of my visiting their country, and amply gratified their curiosity. They paid me visits in return; some of them called me Seyang-tsze, "child of the western ocean;" and others a foreign-born Chinese; but the major part of them seemed to care little about the place of my nativity.

Apples, grapes, and some other fruits we found here in abundance; and such refreshments was very acceptable after having lived for a long time on dry rice and salt vegetables. Fish also was plentiful and cheap. The common food of the inhabitants is the Barbadoes millet, called *kaou-leang;* they grind it in a mill, which is worked by asses, and eat it like rice. There are several kinds of the *leang* grain, which differ considerably in taste as well as in size.

Some sales were made here, but the people were too poor to trade to any considerable extent. It is worthy of remark, that, in the very neighbourhood of the place where Confucius was born, the moral precepts of that sage are (as I had opportunity to witness) trampled upon, and even when referred to are treated with scorn. Here our sailors, especially those who went to visit the temple of Ma-tsoo-po, were again ensnared by

wretched women—the most degraded beings I
ever beheld. But the poor fellows soon felt the
consequences of their wicked conduct; for some
of them had not only to sell their little stock of
merchandise, but were also visited with loathsome
disease. Often did they lament their folly; and
as often did they remark, that they had no power
to become better men. Some of my fellow-passengers, when they had recovered their senses,
felt keenly the stings of conscience. Captain Eo
was among this number;— " I am a forlorn
wretch," said he; " in vain I strive against vice,
every day brings me nearer eternal destruction."
Though he endeavoured to stifle remorse, by
placing an idol in his cabin, and by repeating
his " O-me-to-Fuh," (*i. e.* Amida Budha, an expression which commences most prayers to that
deity,) yet all his efforts were in vain; his heart
became more depraved, his superstitions more
strong, and he seemed utterly incorrigible. He
would often remark, as I sat with him in his
cabin, talking about the gospel of Christ,—" I
have no friend; all my vicious companions for-
sook me when I was wrecked on Pulo Way; the
little property I now have is only sufficient to
support myself alone; but I have a family at
home, who are looking to me for support, while

I am giving myself up to folly and vice." The body of this poor man was emaciated, and he passed most of his time in sleep. Occasionally he would enter into conversation with Captain Hae, his neighbour, who was a great proficient in iniquitous schemes and practices. In conversation, during the night-time, they would relate to each other the particulars of their feats; it was painful to hear their narrations, especially when I remembered that, in the case of Eo, they proceeded from the lips of a hoary-headed man, who, after a wicked life of more than sixty years, was fast verging to the grave. O what must be the company of hell, where all the heroes of wickedness meet, and hold eternal intercourse, making daily progress in sin!

Although my sentiments were entirely at variance with those of Eo, he frequently showed me marks of real kindness, lamented my lonely state, and feared that I should fall a prey to wicked men, because I was over righteous. He would sometimes give me accounts of geography, according to the popular notions of the Chinese, which he considered as the only correct ones, and ours as altogether erroneous. As he was a painter, he drew a map; in which Africa was placed near Siberia, and Corea in the neighbourhood of some unknown country, which he thought might be America. Though his ideas were ridiculous, he possessed a good understanding; and had he not been debased by idolatry and crime, he might have formed a talented and useful member of society. But, alas! Satan first debars God's creatures from improvement, and then reduces them to the level of brutes.

The vessels of the last English embassy touched, it seems, at Leto, and their stay there was still fresh in the recollection of the natives. They frequently referred to those majestic ships, which might have spread destruction in every direction; and to this day they are over-awed and tremble, even at the mention of the Kea-pan* ships, as European vessels are denominated. I was closely questioned on this subject, but as I was not well informed respecting the expedition, I could give them no satisfactory answers; I was able, however, by describing the character of Europeans, in some degree, to quiet their minds. " If," said I, " they had come to injure you, they would have done so immediately; but as they came and went away peaceably, they ought

---

* We are unable to ascertain the meaning of this term *Kea-pan*. It may perhaps be derived from *Captain*, or some other foreign word.

to be considered as the friends of the Chinese."
My reasoning, however, was of little avail;—
" They were not traders," they replied; " if they
had been, we should have hailed them as friends;
but they came with guns, and as men never do
any thing without design, they must have had
some object, and that object must have been conquest. Those mandarins who did not inform the
emperor of their arrival were severely punished;
and how could this have been done, if he had not
perceived an ultra design?"

Europe is supposed, by a great majority of the
Chinese, to be a small country, inhabited by a
few merchants, who speak different languages,
and who maintain themselves principally by their
commerce with China. With a view to correct
their ideas, I gave them some account of the different nations who inhabit Europe, but all to no
purpose; the popular belief, that it is merely a
small island, containing only a few thousands of
inhabitants, was too strong to be removed.

They were anxious, however, to know from
whence all the dollars came, which are brought
to China; and when I told them more of the
western world, they expressed a wish to go
thither, because they thought gold and silver
must be as abundant there as granite is in China;

but when I told them that in going thither they could see no land for many days, they became unwilling to engage for such a voyage;—" For where," they earnestly inquired, " shall we take shelter and come to anchor, when storms overtake us? And whither shall we find refuge when once we are wrecked?"

Though they soon abandoned the idea of visiting Europe, they were still desirous to gain some more information about dollars, and requested me to teach them the art of making them of tin or lead; for many of them believe that the English are able, by a certain process, to change those metals into silver. As they considered me an adept in every art, except divinity, they were much disappointed when I told them that I neither understood the secret, nor believed that there was any mortal who did. This statement they discredited, and maintained that the English, as they were rich and had many great ships and splendid factories in Canton, and had no means of obtaining riches except by this art, must of necessity be able to change the inferior metals into gold. This same strange notion is believed in Siam; and I have been earnestly importuned by individuals to teach them this valuable art; silver ore has been sent to me also with the request, that I would extract the silver, and form it into dollars. The reason of their so frequently conspiring against me seems to have been, that I acted with liberality and honesty towards every one, and did not engage in trade; and hence they inferred that I made silver and coined money, and by these means had always a stock on hand sufficient to defray my expenses.

After staying several days at Leto, we again got under weigh; but the wind being still unfavourable, we proceeded slowly, and on the 2d September came to anchor in the deep and spacious harbour of Ke-shan-so. The town from which this harbour takes its name is pleasantly situated, and its environs are well cultivated. The people were polite and industrious; they manufacture a sort of cloth, which consists partly of cotton and partly of silk; it is very strong, and finds a ready sale in every part of China. They are wealthy, and trade to a considerable extent with the junks which touch here on their way to Teen-tsin. Many junks were in the harbour at the same time with ours, and trade was very brisk. On shore, refreshments of every description were cheap. The people seemed fond of horsemanship; and while we were there, ladies had horse-races, in which they greatly excelled.

The fame of the English men-of-war had spread consternation and awe among the people here; and I endeavoured, so far as was in my power, to correct the erroneous opinions which they had entertained.

Vice seemed as prevalent here as at Leto; the sailors borrowed money in advance, and before we left the harbour, every farthing of it was expended. I predicted to them that such would be the consequence of their vicious conduct:—that prediction was now fulfilled; the poor fellows became desperate, and, as they had no other object on which to vent their rage but myself, they exceedingly wearied and annoyed me. Did I ever offer an earnest prayer to God, it was at this time: I besought him to be gracious to them and to me, and to make a display of his almighty power, in order to convince them of their nothingness, and to console and strengthen my own heart. The following morning the weather was very sultry; I was roused from sleep by loud peals of thunder; and soon after I had awaked, the lightning struck our junk; the shock was awfully tremendous;—the masts had been split from top to bottom, but, most mercifully, the hull had received no injury. This event spread consternation among the sailors; and with dejected countenances, they scarcely dared to raise their heads, while they looked on me as the servant of Shang-te, and as one who enjoyed his protection. From this time they ceased to ridicule me, and on the other hand treated me with great respect. The elements seemed, at this time, to have conspired against us; winds and tide were contrary, and our progress was scarcely perceptible.

In the neighbourhood of Ke-shan-so is Kan-chow, one of the principal ports of Shantung. The trading vessels anchor near the shore, and their supercargoes go up to the town by a small river. There is here a market for Indian and European merchandise, almost all kinds of which bear a tolerable price. The duties are quite low, and the mandarins have very little control over the trade. It may be stated that, in general, the Shantung people are far more honest than the inhabitants of the southern provinces, though the latter treat them with disrespect, as greatly their inferiors.

On the 8th of September we passed Ting-ching, a fortress situated near the shore, on the frontiers of Chihle and Shantung provinces; it seemed to be a pretty large place, surrounded by a high wall. We saw some excellent plantations in its vicinity, and the country, generally, presented a very lively aspect, with many verdant scenes, which the wearied eye seeks for in vain on the naked rocks of Shantung.

On the 9th we were in great danger. Soon after we had anchored near the mouth of the Pei-ho (or Pih-ho, the White River,) a gale suddenly arose, and raged for about six hours. Several junks, which had left the harbour of Leto with us, were wrecked; but a merciful God preserved our vessel. As the wind blew from the north, the agreeable temperature of the air was soon changed to a piercing cold. Though we were full thirty miles distant from the shore, the water was so much blown back by the force of the wind, that a man could easily wade over the sand bar; and our sailors went out in different directions to catch crabs, which were very numerous. But in a few days afterwards, a favourable south wind blew, when the water increased, and rose to the point from which it had fallen. In a little time large numbers of boats were seen coming from the mouth of the river, to offer assistance in towing the junk in from the sea.

We had approached a considerable distance towards the shore before we saw the land, it being almost on a level with the sea. The first objects which we could discern were two small

forts; these are situated near the mouth of the
river, and within the last few years have been
considerably repaired. The natives, who came
on board, were rather rude in manners, and
poorly clothed. Scarcely had we anchored, when
some opium dealers from Teen-tsin came along
side; they stated, that in consequence of the heir
of the crown having died by opium-smoking,
very severe edicts had been published against
the use of the drug, and that because the difficulty of trading in the article at the city was
so great, they had come out to purchase such
quantities of it as might be for sale on board
our junk.

The entrance of the Pei-ho presents nothing
but scenes of wretchedness; and the whole
adjacent country seemed to be as dreary as a
desert. While the southern winds blow, the
coast is often overflowed to a considerable extent; and the country more inland affords very
little to attract attention, being diversified only
by stacks of salt, and by numerous tumuli which
mark the abodes of the dead. The forts are
nearly square, and are surrounded by single walls;
they evince very little advance in the art of
fortification. The people told me, that when
the vessels of the last English embassy were

anchored off the Pei-ho, a detachment of soldiers
—infantry and cavalry—was sent hither to ward
off any attack that might be made. The impression made on the minds of the people by the
appearance of those ships is still very perceptible.
I frequently heard unrestrained remarks concerning barbarian fierceness and thirst after conquest,
mixed with eulogiums on the equitable government of the English at Singapore. The people
wondered how a few barbarians, without the
transforming influence of the Celestial Empire,
could arrive at a state of civilization very little
inferior to that of " the middle kingdom." They
rejoiced that the water at the bar of the Pei-ho
was too shallow to afford a passage for men-of-
war (which, however, is not the case; when the
south wind prevails, there is water enough for
ships of the largest class); and that its course
was too rapid to allow the English vessels to
ascend the river. While these things were mentioned with exultation, it was remarked by one
who was present, that the barbarians had " fire-
ships," which could proceed up the river without
the aid of trackers; this remark greatly astonished
them, and excited their fears: which, however,
were quieted when I assured them that those
barbarians, as they called them, though valiant,

would never make an attack unless provoked, and that, if the Celestial Empire never provoked them, there would not be the least cause to fear.

Though our visitors here were numerous, they cared very little about me, and treated me in the same manner as they did the other passengers. Most of the inhabitants, who reside near the shore, are poor fishermen; their food consists, almost exclusively, of Barbadoes millet, boiled like rice, and mixed with water in various proportions, according to the circumstances of the individuals;—if they are rich, the quantity of water is small; if poor, as is usually the case, the quantity is large. They eat with astonishing rapidity, cramming their mouths full of millet and vegetables, if they are fortunate enough to obtain any of the latter. Most of the inhabitants live in this way; and only a few persons who are wealthy, and the settlers from Keangnan, Fuhkeen, and Canton provinces, enjoy the luxury of rice. In a district so sterile as this, the poor inhabitants labour hard and to little purpose, in trying to obtain from the productions of the soil the means of subsistence.

The village of Ta-koo, near which we anchored, is a fair specimen of the architecture along the banks of the Pei-ho; and it is only on the banks of the river, throughout these dreary regions, that the people fix their dwellings. The houses are generally low and square, with high walls towards the streets; they are well adapted to keep out the piercing cold of winter, but are constructed with little regard to convenience. The houses of all the inhabitants, however rich, are built of mud, excepting only those of the mandarins, which are of brick. The hovels of the poor have but one room, which is, at the same time, their dormitory, kitchen, and parlour. In these mean abodes, which, to keep them warm, are stopped up at all points, the people pass the dreary days of winter; and often with no other prospect than that of starving. Their chief enjoyment is the pipe. Rich individuals, to relieve the pressing wants of the populace, sometimes give them small quantities of warm millet; and the emperor, to protect them against the inclemency of the season, compassionately bestows on them a few jackets. I had much conversation with these people, who seemed to be rude but hardy, poor but cheerful, and lively but quarrelsome. The number of these wretched beings is very great, and many, it is said, perish annually by the cold of winter. On account of this overflowing population, wages are low, and provisions dear; most of the articles for domestic consumption are brought from other districts and provinces; hence many of the necessaries of life, even such as fuel, are sold at an enormous price. It is happy for this barren region that it is situated in the vicinity of the capital; and that large quantities of silver, the chief article of exportation, are constantly flowing thither from the other parts of the empire.

Some mandarins from Ta-koo came on board our junk; their rank and the extent of their authority were announced to us by a herald who preceded them. They came to give us permission to proceed up the river; this permission, however, had to be bought by presents, and more than half a day was occupied in making the bargain.

Before we left this place, I gave a public dinner to all on board, both passengers and sailors. This induced one of their company to intimate to me, that, in order to conciliate the favour of Ma-tsoo-po, some offerings should be made to her. I replied, " Never, since I came on board, have I seen her even taste of the offerings made to her; it is strange that she should be so in want, as to need any offerings from me." " But," answered the man, " the sailors will take care that nothing of what she refuses is lost." " It is better," said I, " to give directly to the sailors, whatever is intended for them ; and let Ma-tsoo-po, if she is really a goddess, feed on ambrosia, and not upon the base spirits and food which you usually place before her; if she has any being, let her provide for herself; if she is merely an image, better throw her idol with its satellites into the sea, than have them here to encumber the junk." " These are barbarian notions," rejoined my antagonist, " which are so deeply rooted in your fierce breast, as to lead you to trample on the laws of the Celestial Empire." " Barbarian reasoning is conclusive reasoning," I again replied; " if you are afraid to throw the idol into the waves, I will do it, and abide the consequences. You have heard the truth, that there is only one God, even as there is only one sun in the firmament. Without his mercy, in-evitable punishment will overtake you, for having defied *his* authority, and given yourself up to the service of dumb idols; reform, or you are lost!" The man was silenced and confounded, and only replied, " Let the sailors feast, and Ma-tsoo-po hunger."

As soon as we were again ready to proceed, about thirty men came on board to assist in towing the junk; they were very thinly clothed, and seemed to be in great want; some dry rice that was given to them they devoured with inexpressible delight. When there was not wind sufficient to move the junk, these men, joined by some of our sailors, towed her along against the rapid stream; for the Pei-ho has no regular tides, but *constantly* flows into the sea with more or less rapidity. During the ebb tide, when there was not water enough to enable us to proceed, we stopped, and went on shore.

The large and numerous stacks of salt along the river, especially at Teen-tsin, cannot fail to arrest the attention of strangers. The quantity is very great, and seems sufficient to supply the whole empire; it has been accumulating during the reign of five emperors; and it still continues to accumulate. This salt is formed in vats near the sea shore; from thence it is transported to the neighbourhood of Ta-koo, where it is compactly piled up on hillocks of mud, and covered with bamboo mattings; in this situation it remains for some time, when it is finally put into bags and carried to Teen-tsin, and kept for a great number of years, before it can be sold. More than eight hundred boats are constantly employed in transporting this article; and thousands of persons gain a livelihood by it, some of whom become very rich: the principal salt merchants, it is said, are the richest persons in the empire.

Along the banks of the Pei-ho are many villages and hamlets, and all are built of the same material and in the same style as at Ta-koo. Large fields of Barbadoes millet, pulse, and turnips, were seen in the neighbourhood; these were carefully cultivated and watered by women, who seem to enjoy more liberty here than in the southern provinces. Even the very poorest of them were well dressed; but their feet were much cramped, which gave them a hobbling gait, and compelled them to use sticks when they walked. The young and rising population seemed to be very great. The ass, here rather a small and meagre animal, is the principal beast employed in the cultivation of the soil. The implements of husbandry are very simple, and even rude. Though this country has been inhabited for a great many centuries, the roads for their miserable carriages are few, and in some places even a foot-path for a lonely traveller can scarcely be found.

My attention was frequently attracted by the inscription *Tsew-teen*, " wine-tavern," which was written over the doors of many houses. Upon inquiry I found that the use of spirituous liquors, especially that distilled from *suh-leang* grain, was very general, and intemperance, with its usual consequences, very prevalent. It is rather surprising that no wine is extracted from the excellent grapes which grow abundantly on the banks of the Pei-ho, and constitute the choicest fruit of the country. Other fruits, such as apples and pears, are found here, though in kind they are not so numerous, and in quality are by no means so good as those of Europe.

We proceeded up the river with great cheerfulness; the men who towed our junk took care to supply themselves well with rice, and were very active in their service. Several junks were in company with us, and a quarrel between our sailors and some Fuhkeen men broke out, the consequences of which might have been very serious. Some of our men had already armed themselves with pikes, and were placing themselves in battle array, when, happily, terms of peace were agreed on by a few of the senior members of the party. Several years ago a quarrel, which originated between two junks, brought all the Fuhkeen and Chaou-chow men in the neighbourhood into action; both parties fought fiercely, but confined themselves princi-

pally to loud and boisterous altercation; the
mandarins, who always know how to profit by
such contentions, soon took a lively interest in
the affair, and by endeavouring to gain something
from the purses of the combatants, immediately
restored peace and tranquillity among them.
Similar consequences were feared in the present
case, on which account the men were the more
willing to desist from the strife; they were farther
prompted to keep peace by the prospect of trading
with some merchants, who had come on board
for that object. Indeed, as the voyage was
undertaken for the purpose of trading, our men
constantly engaged in that business; and when
there were no opportunities of trading with
strangers, they would carry on a traffic among
themselves; but, unhappily, their treasure did
not always increase so fast as the cargo diminished.

My anxiety was greatly increased by our approach to Peking. A visit to the capital of the
Chinese empire—an object of no little solicitude,
after many perils, and much loss of time—was
now near in prospect. How this visit would be
viewed by the Chinese government, I knew not;
hitherto they had taken no notice of me; but a
crisis had now come; as a missionary, anxious

to promote the welfare of my fellow-creatures, and more willing to be sacrificed in a great cause, than to remain an idle spectator of the misery entailed on China by idolatry, I could not remain concealed at a place where there are so many mandarins—it was expected that the local authorities would interfere. Almost friendless, with small pecuniary resources, without any personal knowledge of the country and its inhabitants, I was forced to prepare for the worst. Considerations of this kind, accompanied by the most reasonable conjecture, that I could do nothing for the accomplishment of the great enterprise, would have intimidated and dispirited me, if a power from on High had not continually and graciously upheld and strengthened me. Naturally timid, and without talent and resources in myself, yet by Divine aid, and by *that* alone, I was foremost in times of danger, and to such a degree, that the Chinese sailors would often call me a bravado.

Fully persuaded that I was not prompted by self-interest and vain-glory, but by a sense of duty as a missionary, and deeply impressed by the greatness and all-sufficiency of the Saviour's power and gracious assistance enjoyed in former days, I grounded my hope of security on

protection under the shadow of *his* wings, and
my expectation of success on the promises of *his*
holy word. It has long been the firm conviction
of my heart, that in these latter days the glory of
the Lord will be revealed to China; and that,
the dragon being dethroned, Christ will be the
sole king and object of adoration throughout this
extensive empire. This lively hope of China's
speedy deliverance from the thraldom of Satan by
the hand of our great Lord, Jesus Christ—the
King of kings, to whom all nations, even China,
are given as an inheritance, constantly prompts
me to action, and makes me willing rather to
perish in the attempt of carrying the gospel to
China, than to wait quietly on the frontiers,
deterred by the numerous obstacles which seem
to forbid an entrance into the country.

I am fully aware that I shall be stigmatized as
a headstrong enthusiast, an unprincipled rambler,
who rashly sallies forth, without waiting for any
indications of divine providence, without first
seeing the door opened by the hand of the Lord;
as one fond of novelty, anxious to have a name,
fickle in his purposes, who leaves a promising
field, and restlessly hurries away to another;
all of whose endeavours will not only prove
useless, but will actually impede the progress of

the Saviour's cause. I shall not be very anxious to vindicate myself against such charges, though some of them are very well founded, until the result of my labours shall be made known to my accusers. I have weighed the arguments for and against the course I am endeavouring to pursue, and have formed the resolution to publish the gospel to the inhabitants of China Proper, in all the ways, and by all the means, which the Lord our God appoints in his word and by his providence; to persevere in the most indefatigable manner so long as there remains any hope of success; and rather to be blotted out from the list of mortals, than to behold with indifference the uncontrolled triumph of Satan over the Chinese. Yet still I am not ignorant of my own nothingness, nor of the formidable obstacles which, on every side, shut up the way and impede our progress; and I can only say, "Lord, here I am, use me according to thy holy pleasure."

Should any individuals be prompted to extol my conduct, I would meet and repel such commendation by my thorough consciousness of possessing not the least merit; let such persons rather than thus vainly spend their breath, come forth, and join in the holy cause with zeal and wisdom superior to any who have gone before

them; the field is wide, the harvest truly great,
and the labourers are few. Egotism, obtrusive
monster! lurks through these pages; it is my
sincere wish, therefore, to be completely swallowed up in the Lord's great work, and to labour
unknown and disregarded, cherishing the joyful
hope that my reward is in heaven, and my name,
though a very unworthy one, written in " the book
of life." I return to my detail.

In the afternoon, September 22d, we passed
a grove, on the left bank of the river Pei-ho,
which is said to have been visited by the Emperor
Keen-lung. It contains a few houses, but is at
present a mere jungle. On the opposite bank
we observed a shop, having a sign with this
inscription, written in large capitals, *Idols and
Budhas of all descriptions newly made and
repaired.* This sign told plainly the condition
of the people around me, and called forth earnest
intercession on their behalf.

CHAPTER III.

THE scene, as we approached Teen-tsin, became very lively. Great numbers of boats and junks, almost blocking up the passage, and crowds of people on shore, bespoke a place of considerable trade. After experiencing much difficulty from the vessels which thronged us on every side, we at length came to anchor in the suburbs of the city, in a line with several junks lately arrived from Soakah, and were saluted by the merry peals of the gong. I had been accustomed to consider myself quite a stranger among these people, and was therefore surprised to see the eyes of many of them immediately fixed on me. My skill as a physician was soon put in requisition. The next day, while passing the junk on my way to the shore, I was hailed by a number of voices, as the *seensang*—" teacher," or "doctor;" and, on looking around me, I saw many smiling faces, and numerous hands stretched out to invite me to sit down. These people proved to be some of my old friends, who, a long time before, had received medicines and books, for which they still seemed very grateful. They lauded my noble conduct in leaving off barbarian customs, and in escaping from the land of barbarians, to come under the shield of the "son of heaven." They approved of my design in not only benefiting some straggling rascals (according to their own expression) in the out-ports of China, but in coming also a great distance, to assist the faithful subjects of the Celestial Empire. They knew even that *seensang neang,* "the lady teacher," (my late wife,) had died; and condoled with me on account of my irreparable loss.

It very soon appeared that I was known here as a missionary, as well as in Siam; and hence I thought it my duty to act boldly, but at the same time with prudence. Some captains and pilots, afflicted either with diseased eyes or with rheumatism, were my first patients. They lived in a miserable hovel near the banks of the river, and were preparing to smoke the "delicious drug," when I entered, and upbraided them sharply for their licentiousness. From my severe remarks on their conduct, they concluded that I had some remedy for the use of the drug, and intimated their opinion to others. The success of my first practice gained me the esteem and friendship of a whole clan or tribe of the Chinese, who never ceased to importune me to cure their natural or imaginary physical defects. The diseases of the poorer classes, here, seemed as numerous as in any part of India. They generally complained of the unskilfulness of their doctors, whose blunders I had frequently to correct. Chinese doctors are, usually, unsuccessful literati, or persons fond of study. They claim the title of doctor as soon as they have read a number of books on the subject of medicine, without showing by practice that they are entitled to the appellation. Their minute examination of the pulse, which is frequently very correct, gives them some claim to the title of able practitioners. Anatomy, a correct knowledge of which must be gained from dissection, the Chinese regard as founded on metaphysical speculations, and not in truth. Their materia medica is confined chiefly to herbs, which are the principal ingredients of their prescriptions. They have some very excellent plants, but injure and weaken their effect, by mixing them up, as they do, often sixty or seventy in one dose. They generally foretell the precise time of the patient's restoration, but are often found mistaken. To stand against men of this description, who are so very wise in their own imagination, was not an easy task; but I always convinced them, by facts, that our theories, when reduced to practice, would have the most salutary effect.

Kam-sea, a merchant of considerable property from Fuhkeen, and a resident at Teen-tsin, invited me to his house; this was on the 15th of the 8th moon, and consequently during the *Chungtsew** festival. Mandarins in great numbers hastened to the temples; priests dressed in black,—friars and nuns clothed in rags; and an immense number of beggars paraded the streets; and when I passed, filled the air with their importunate cries. All the avenues were thronged; and in the shops,—generally filled with Chinese manufactures, but some also with European commodities,—trade seemed to be brisk. The

---

* That is, the festival of middle-autumn. This is a very great festival among the Chinese, and is observed partially throughout the whole month, by sending presents of cakes and fruit from one person to another; but it is chiefly celebrated on the 15th and 16th days: on the 15th, oblations are made to the moon, and on the 16th, the people and children amuse themselves with what they call "pursuing the moon." The legend respecting this popular festival is, that an emperor of the Tang dynasty being led, one night, to the palace of the moon, saw there an assembly of nymphs, playing on instruments of music; and, on his return, commanded persons to dress and sing, in imitation of what he had seen.

town, which stretches several miles along the
banks of the river, equals Canton in the bustle of
its busy population, and surpasses it in the importance of its native trade.   The streets are
unpaved ; and the houses aré built of mud : but
within they are well furnished, with accommodations in the best Chinese style.   A great many
of the shop-keepers, and scme of the most
wealthy people in the place, are from Fuhkeen ;
and the native merchants, though well trained to
their business, are outdone by the superior skill
of the traders from the south.

Kam-sea's house is situated in the middle of
the city, and is well furnished ; he received me
cordially, and offered me a commodious room.
The crowd of people at his house was great, and
many questions were asked by them concerning
me ; but as the Fuhkeen men acknowledged me
to be their fellow-citizen, these questions were
easily set at rest.   A mandarin of high rank,
who heard of my arrival, said—" This man,
though a stranger, is a true Chinese ; and, as
several persons seem anxious to prevent his
going up to the capital, I will give him a pass-
port, for it would be wrong, that, after having
come all the way from Siam, he should not see
the ' *dragon's face.*'"

The curiosity to see me was, during several days, very great; and the captain's anxiety much increased, when he saw that I attracted the attention of so many individuals. There were some, who even muttered that I had come to make a map of the country, in order to become the leader in a premeditated assault on the empire. Yet all these objections were soon silenced, when I opened my medicine chest, and with a liberal hand supplied every applicant. God, in his mercy, bestowed a blessing on these exertions, and gave me favour in the eyes of the people. Several persons of rank and influence paid me frequent visits, and held long conversations with me. They were polite and even servile in their manners. Their inquiries, most of them trivial, were principally directed to Siam; and their remarks concerning Europe were exceedingly childish. The concourse of people became so great, at length, that I was obliged to hide myself. A gentleman, who lived opposite to the house where I resided, wishing to purchase me from the captain, with a view to attract customers by my presence, offered to pay for me the sum of 2000 taels of silver (about 2700 dollars). My patients had now become so numerous as to engross all my attention; from very early in the morning till late at night, I was constantly beset by them, and often severely tried. Yet I had frequent opportunities of making known to them the doctrines of the gospel, and of pointing out the way of eternal life.

It had been my intention to proceed from Teen-tsin up to Peking, a journey which is made in two days. To effect this, it would have been necessary to learn the dialect spoken in this province, and to have obtained the acquaintance of some persons resident at the capital. For the accomplishment of the first, there was not sufficient time, unless I should resolve to abandon the junk in which I had arrived, and to stay over the winter; but for the attainment of the latter, some individuals very kindly offered their services. I thought it best, therefore, to stay and to observe the leadings of Providence. Some experiments which I made to cure the habit of opium-smoking proved so successful, that they attracted general notice, and drew the attention of some mandarins, who even stooped to pay me a visit, and to request my aid, stating that his imperial majesty was highly enraged, because so many of his subjects indulged in this practice. But, as soon as the Chaou-chow and

Fuhkeen men observed that the native patients were becoming too numerous, they got angry, saying, " This is our doctor, and not yours ;" and, as this argument was not quite intelligible, they drove many of the poor fellows away by force. In a few days, moreover, the whole stock of medicines I had with me was exhausted, and I had to send away, with regret, those poor wretches who really stood in want of assistance.

In the mean time our men went on with their trade. Under the superintendence of some officers who had farmed the duties, they began to unload, and to transport the goods to the storehouses. Many a trick was played in order to avoid the payment of duties, although they were very light. Indeed, the sailors' merchandise was almost entirely exempt from all charges. As soon as the goods were removed to the warehouses, the resident merchants made their purchases, and paid immediately for their goods in sycee silver. These transactions were managed in the most quiet and honest manner, and to the benefit of both parties. On the sugar and tin very little profit was gained, but more than one hundred per cent. was made on the sapan-wood and pepper, the principal articles of our cargo. European calicoes yielded a profit

of only fifty per cent.; other commodities, imported by Canton men, sold very high. On
account of the severe prohibitions, there was a
stagnation in the opium trade. One individual,
a Canton merchant, had been seized by government; and large quantities of the drug, imported
from Canton, could find no purchasers.

The trade of Teen-tsin is quite extensive.
More than five hundred junks arrive annually
from the southern ports of China, and from
Cochin-China and Siam. The river is so
thronged with junks, and the mercantile transactions give such life and motion to the scene,
as strongly to remind one of Liverpool. As
the land in this vicinity yields few productions,
and the capital swallows up immense stores,
the importations required to supply the wants
of the people must be very great. Though the
market was well furnished, the different articles
commanded a good price. In no other port of
China is trade so lucrative as in this; but no
where else are so many dangers to be encountered. A great many junks were wrecked
this year; and this is the case every season;
and hence the profits realized on the whole
amount of shipping are comparatively small.
Teen-tsin would open a fine field for foreign

enterprise; there is a great demand for European woollens, but the high prices which they bear prevent the inhabitants from making extensive purchases. I was quite surprised to see so much sycee silver in circulation. The quantity of it was so great, that there seemed to be no difficulty in collecting thousands of taels, at the shortest notice. A regular trade with silver is carried on by a great many individuals. The value of the tael, here, varies from thirteen to fourteen hundred cash. Some of the firms issue bills, which are as current as bank-notes in England. Teen-tsin, possessing so many advantages for commerce, may very safely be recommended to the attention of European merchants.

By inquiries, I found that the people cared very little about their imperial government. They were only anxious to gain a livelihood and accumulate riches. They seemed to know the emperor only by name, and were quite unacquainted with his character. Even the military operations in western Tartary were almost unknown to them. Nothing had spread such consternation amongst them as the late death of the heir of the crown, which was occasioned by opium-smoking. The emperor felt

this loss very keenly.   The belief that there
will be a change in the present dynasty is very
general.   But in case of such an event, the
people of Teen-tsin would hear of it with almost
as much indifference as they would the news
of a change in the French government.   The
local officers were generally much dreaded, but
also much imposed upon.   They are less tyran-
nical here, in the neighbourhood of the emperor,
judging from what the people told me, than
they are in the distant provinces.   When they
appear abroad it is with much pageantry, but
with little real dignity.   Indeed, I saw nothing
remarkable in their deportment.   No war junks
nor soldiers were to be met with,—though the
latter were said to exist.   To possess fire-arms
is a high crime, and the person found guilty of
so doing is severely punished.   Bows and arrows
are in common use.   There are no military
stores, but great stores of grain.   The grain
junks were, at this season, on their return home.

The features of the inhabitants of this district
more resemble the European than those of any
Asiatics I have hitherto seen.   The eye had less
of the depressed curve in the interior angle
than what is common, and so characteristic, in
a Chinese countenance.   And, as the counte-

nance is often the index of the heart, so the character of these people is more congenial to the European, than is that of the inhabitants of the southern provinces. They are not void of courage; though they are too grovelling to undertake any thing arduous or noble, and too narrow-minded to extend their views beyond their own province and the opposite kingdom of Corea. They are neat in their dress; the furs which they wear are costly; their food is simple; and they are polite in their manners. The females are fair, and tidy in their appearance,—enjoy perfect liberty, and walk abroad as they please.

The dialect spoken by the inhabitants of Teen-tsin abounds with gutturals; and for roughness is not unlike the language of the Swiss. The people speak with amazing rapidity, scarcely allowing time to trace their ideas. Though their dialect bears considerable resemblance to the mandarin, yet it contains so many local phrases, and corruptions of that dialect, as to be almost unintelligible to those who are acquainted only with the mandarin tongue.

The natives here seemed to be no bigots in religion. Their priests were poorly fed, and their temples in bad repair. The priests wear all kinds of clothing; and, except by their shaved heads, can scarcely be distinguished from the common people. Frequently I have seen them come on board the junk to beg a little rice, and recite their prayers, with a view to obtain money. But, notwithstanding the degradation of the priests, and the utter contempt in which their principles and precepts are held, every house has its *lares*, its sacrifices, and offerings; and devotions, if such they may be called, are performed with more strictness even than by the inhabitants of the southern provinces. Such conduct is a disgrace to human nature, and without excuse; " because that which may be known of God is manifest in them; for God hath showed it unto them." (Rom. i. 19.) Yet, prostituting the knowledge of a Supreme Ruler, they bow down before an image of wood or stone, and say,—" *This is my Creator.*"

I made many inquiries, in order to ascertain whether there were any Roman Catholics in this part of the country, but no trace, not even of their having once been here, could be found. There were Mohammedans, however, and with some of them I had opportunities of conversing. They seemed tenacious enough of their creed, so far as it regarded food,—they would not even dine with a heathen; but in their notions of deity they were not at all correct. In their dress, they differ very little from their heathen neighbours; and they are quite like them also in their morals. Though they are somewhat numerous, they never influence public opinion, or shew any anxiety to make proselytes.

The number of inhabitants which belong to the *middling classes*, properly so called, is not large. A few individuals are immensely rich; but the great mass of the population are sunk in abject poverty. I saw very little among the inhabitants of Teen-tsin, that could give them a just claim to be called a literary people. They are industrious, but not skilful workmen; and even their industry furnishes few articles for exportation. In a few manufactures, such as tapestry, coarse woollens, and glass, they succeed well. With such an overflowing population, it would be wise policy in the government to allow emigration, and to open a trade with foreign nations, in order to furnish sufficient employment and sustenance for the increasing multitudes of people; otherwise there is reason to fear, lest, ere long, pressed by want and hunger, they fall back upon and destroy those whom they have been taught to revere as their political fathers.

I am inclined to believe, from all that I have seen of this people, that they are susceptible of great improvement, and that reform might more reasonably be expected among them, because of the extreme simplicity of their manners. Teen-tsin, as has been already observed, presents an inviting field to the enterprising merchant; but to the christian philanthropist, whose attention may be directed to these regions, it not only affords an inviting field, but presents claims— *claims* which ought not to be disregarded.

Our sailors, having disposed of their part of the cargo, and obtained their full wages, gave themselves up to gambling—the general diversion of this place. Nor did they desist from this practice until most of them had lost every thing they possessed. They had now to borrow money in order to purchase clothes to protect them against the inclemency of the weather; new scenes of contention and quarrelling were daily exhibited; and the lives, as well as the persons of some individuals, put in great jeopardy. They also indulged freely in the use of spirituous liquors, which were very strong and intoxicating; and finally they betook themselves to wretched females. In these circumstances their misery was extreme; several of them were seized upon by their creditors, some hid themselves, and others absconded.

As we had arrived here so late in the season, just at the time when many of the junks were about leaving, it was necessary to shorten our stay, lest the Pei-ho, freezing up, should detain us over the winter. On the 17th of October we began to move slowly down the river. Before leaving Teen-tsin I received numerous presents, which were accompanied with many wishes for my welfare. A great many persons came to take an affectionate leave of me at our departure. At the earnest request of some individuals, I was constrained to promise that, if God should permit, I would return the next year; and, in the case of such a visit, some of them engaged to accompany me to the capital—while others wanted to make with me a journey overland from Teen-tsin to Hea-mun (Amoy). I can scarcely speak in too high terms of the kindness I enjoyed during the whole time I was at this place; and the reason for such unexpected treatment I must ascribe to the merciful interposition of the Almighty, under whose banner I entered on this undertaking. The favour and kindness experienced in Teen-tsin were a rich compensation for my former bereavements and trials. My health also was again restored, and I could cheerfully perform the duties devolving upon me.

We all had provided ourselves with furs; and we were now, at length, proceeding to Leaoutung, which is situated on the north of the gulf of Petchelee, on the frontiers of Mantchou Tartary. As Teen-tsin furnishes no articles for maritime exportation except the *tsaou*, or "date," the junks arriving there sell their cargo, and then proceed to some of the ports of Leaou-tung, where a part of their money is invested in peas and drugs. Though we had the current in our favour, we were a long time in reaching Ta-koo, and this because the sailors were fonder of gambling than of working the junk. At Ta-koo we were delayed several days, waiting for our captain and one of the passengers, who were left behind. While at this place I was invited by the port master to dine with him on shore, but was prevented by the inclemency of the weather; several physicians, also, came on board, to consult with me concerning difficult cases, and received my instructions with much docility. After further delay, occasioned by a strong north wind, we finally got under weigh, October 28th, with a native pilot on board. We soon passed the Shaloo-poo-teen islands; and, having a very strong

breeze in our favour, arrived at the harbour of
Kin-chow, in the district of Fung-teen-foo, about
fifteen leagues distant from Moukden, the celebrated capital of Mantchouria.   The persons
with whom I conversed about the place told me
that it differed very little from the other cities in
this district.   The Mantchou Tartars who live
hereabouts are numerous, and lead an idle life,
being principally in the employ of the emperor,
either directly or indirectly.   There seems to be
but little jealousy between them and the labouring class of Chinese.

There are two other harbours in this district,
viz., Nan-kin (or southern Kin-chow, so called
to distinguish it from the northern place of the
same name), and Kae-chow.   The latter is the
most spacious and deep, and is capable of containing a large fleet.   The harbour of Kin-chow
is shallow, surrounded by rocks, and exposed to
southern gales.   Junks cannot approach within
several miles of the shore, and all the cargo must
be brought off in lighters. This country abounds
with peas, drugs, and cattle of every kind.   It
is, on the whole, well cultivated, and inhabited
principally by Mantchou Tartars, who, in their
appearance, differ very little from the Chinese.
The Fuhkeen men, here, also, have the trade

at their command; and quite a large number of junks annually visit the harbours of Leaoutung.

It was a long time after we arrived at Kinchow before we could go on shore, on account of the high sea. It became generally known among the inhabitants, ere I had left the junk, that I was a physician, and anxious to do good; and I was, therefore, very politely invited to take up my residence in one of the principal mercantile houses. It was midnight when we arrived on shore, and found a rich entertainment and good lodgings provided. The next morning crowds thronged to see me; and patients were more numerous than I had any where else found them, and this because they have among themselves no doctors of any note. I went immediately to work, and gained their confidence in a very high degree. There was not in the whole place, nor even in the circuit of several English miles, one female to be seen. Being rather surprised at such a curious fact, I learned, on inquiry, that the whole female population had been removed by the civil authorities, with a view to prevent debauchery among the many sailors who annually visit this port. I could not but admire this arrangement, and the more especially, because it

H

had been adopted by heathen authorities, and
so effectually put a stop to every kind of licentiousness.

Kin-chow itself has very little to attract the
attention of visitors; it is not a large or handsome place. The houses are built of granite
(which abounds here); and are without any accommodations, except a peculiar kind of sleeping
places, which are formed of brick, and so constructed, that they can be heated by fires kindled
beneath them.

On the summit of a high mountain in the
neighbourhood there is a small temple, and also
several others on the low ground in the vicinity.
One of the latter I visited: it was constructed
in the Chinese style, and the idols in it were so
deformed, that they even provoked a smile from
my Chinese guide. In the library of one of
the priests I found a treatise on repentance,
consisting of several volumes. There are here
many horses and carriages; but the carriages
are very clumsy. The camel is likewise common
here, and may be purchased very cheap. The
Chinese inhabitants, of whom many are emigrants
from Shantung, speak a purer dialect than those
at Teen-tsin. They are reserved in their intercourse, and in the habit of doing menial service;

while the Fuhkeen men carry on the trade, and
man the native fishing craft. After having supplied the manifold wants of my patients in this
place, I distributed to them the word of life, and
gained their esteem and affection.

The 9th of November was a very pleasant
day; but during the night the wind changed,
and a strong northerly breeze began to blow. In
a few hours the rivers and creeks were frozen up.
The cold was so piercing, that I was obliged to
take the most active exercise, in order to keep
myself warm ; while the Chinese around me,
covered with rags and furs, laid down and kept
themselves quiet. The wind, at length, blew a
gale, and we were in imminent danger of being
wrecked ; but the almighty hand of God preserved us, whilst a large junk, better manned
than ours, was dashed in pieces, near to us.
Business was for some days quite at a stand,
and I had reason to fear the junk would be
ice-bound. The sailors on shore whiled away
the time, smoking opium day and night. Some
of them bought quails, and set them fighting
for amusement. Indeed, there was not the least
anxiety manifested in regard to the vessel ; and
it was owing to the unremitting severity of the
cold, that we were, at last, driven away from

Kin-chow. The sailors delayed so long on shore,
that the favourable winds were now passed away;
and, dissatisfied with the dispensations of Divine
Providence, they murmured, and gave themselves
up again to gambling and opium smoking.

On the 17th of November we finally got
under way, passed along the rugged coast of
Leaoutung, and, on the next day, reached the
province of Shantung. Uuluckily for us, snow
now began to fall, and our sailors thought it
expedient to come to anchor, though we had a
fair breeze, which would have enabled us to
make the Shantung promontory. My strongest
arguments and representations were all to no
purpose:—" Down with the anchor, enter the
cabins, smoke opium, and take rest," was the
general cry among the men. The next day
they showed no disposition to proceed, and went
on shore to buy fuel. When we were again
under way, and the wind was forcing us round
the promontory, the sailors thought it best to
come to anchor at Toa-sik-tow (or Ta-shih-taou),
near the promontory, where there is a large
harbour. This place is too rocky to yield any
provisions; but some of the adjacent country is
well cultivated, and furnishes good supplies.
The inhabitants carry on some trade in drugs,

but are generally very poor. The sailors crammed our junk, already well filled, till every corner was overflowing with cabbages and other vegetables; even the narrow place where we dined was stuffed full. "We *must* trade," was their answer, when I objected to these proceedings.

A favourable breeze now began to blow, and I tried to persuade the men to quit the shore, and get the junk under way. They, however, told the pilot plainly, that they did not wish to sail; but after many intreaties, he finally prevailed on them to weigh anchor. A fair wind had almost borne us out of sight of the promontory, when the breeze veered round to west, and the sailors immediately resolved to return and anchor: all sails, therefore, were hoisted in order to hasten the return; but the wind changing back again to a fair point, they were unable to effect their purpose, and so cast anchor. They continued in this situation, exposed to a heavy sea, till the wind abated; then they entered the harbour, and went on shore, the same as previously,—wholly regardless of the wind, which had now again become fair. I strongly expostulated with them, and urged them to go out to sea, but—"It is not a lucky day," was their reply. Nor was it till after a wearisome delay, and when

other junks, leaving the harbour, had set them
an example, that they were, at length, prevailed
on to get under way. We had not proceeded
more than fifty leagues, when the fellows resolved once more to return, but were prevented
by strong northerly gales, which now drove us,
nolens volens, down the coast.

Though the sea was amazingly high, when we
came to the channel of Formosa we saw many
fishing boats, in all directions. I have never
met with more daring seamen than those from
Fuhkeen. With the most perfect carelessness,
they go, four in number, in a small boat, over
the foaming billows; while their larger vessels
are driven about, and in danger of being swallowed up by the sea. Formerly, these same
men, who gain a livelihood by fishing, were
desperate pirates, and attacked every vessel they
could find. The vigilance of the government
has produced this change; and, at present, piratical depredations are very unfrequent in the
channel of Formosa.

On the 10th of December, after having suffered severely from various hardships, and having
had our sails torn in pieces by the violent gales,
we at length saw a promontory in the province
of Canton, — much to the joy of us all. At

Soah-boe, (or Shan-wei,) a place three days' sail
from Canton, our captain went on shore, in order
to obtain a permit to enter.

We proceeded slowly in the mean time, and I
engaged one of my friends to go with me to
Macao, where, I was told, many barbarians lived.
All the sailors, my companions in many dangers,
took an affectionate leave of me; and in a few
hours after I arrived at Macao, on the evening
of the 13th December, and was kindly received
by Dr. and Mrs. Morrison.

The reader of these details should remember,
that what has been done is only a feeble beginning of what must ensue. We will hope and
pray, that God in his mercy may, very soon,
open a wider door of access; and we will work
so long as the Lord grants health, strength, and
opportunity. I sincerely wish that something
more efficient might be done for opening *a free
intercourse with China*, and would feel myself
highly favoured, if I could be subservient, in a
small degree, in hastening forward such an event.
In the merciful providence of our God and Saviour, it may be confidently hoped, that the doors
to China will be thrown open. By whom this
will be done, or in what way, is of very little
importance; every well wisher and co-operator

will anxiously desire, that all glory may be rendered to God, the giver of every good gift.

The kindness wherewith I was received by the foreign residents at Macao and Canton, formed quite a contrast with the account the Chinese had given me of " barbarian character," and demands my liveliest gratitude. Praise to God, the Most High, for his gracious protection and help, for his mercy and his grace !

JOURNAL

OF A

SECOND VOYAGE ALONG THE COAST OF CHINA, &c.

CHAPTER I.

THE expedition of which I am to give an outline originated in the desire of the factory of the Hon. East India Company in China, to facilitate mercantile enterprise, and to acquire information respecting those ports where commerce might be established. We were instructed to use no force except for self-defence; but by every means so to conciliate the natives, as to establish trade on a basis which would be permanent. We were to visit the coasts of China, Corea, Japan, and the Loo-Choo islands. Mr. Lindsay, our chief and supercargo, a man of the most humane disposition, refined manners, and enthusiastic in such an enterprise, was conversant with the

Chinese language. Capt. Rees, the commander, an able seaman and surveyor, was anxious to make accurate charts of the different harbours.

We had also a draughtsman among the officers. There was also a learned Chinese on board. I was charged with the office of interpreter and surgeon. Our ship, "The Lord Amherst," was in very good condition, and commanded by able officers.

On the 25th of February, 1832, we went on board our ship, lying in Macao roads, but from adverse winds and fogs were unable to sail till the 27th. Next day we passed the Lae-moon passage, where was good anchorage, but, from our eagerness to proceed, we did not anchor. That night we were exposed to a heavy gale, during which my cabin was filled with water. Before we reached the open sea, some servants of the Budha temple in the Lae-moon passage accosted us, and begged for rice. To grant such a request seemed very harmless; but with the interpretation they are known to give to such an act, a Christian can scarcely feel satisfied to do it. For it is customary with the Chinese, previous to every voyage, to implore the protection of Ma-tsoo-po, goddess of the sea, and queen of heaven. They bestow their gifts upon the

priests, who, after presenting them before the
idol, convert them to their own use. While
offering them to the idol, a priest also recites
prayers, and burns incense before her, to conciliate her favours. Our gift, therefore, was
considered an offering to an idol, and was highly
unworthy of professed Christians.

The wind blowing strong from the north-east,
our progress against it was very slow. March
5th, we came to anchor at Ma-kung, in the district of Hae-fung. Here we were hailed by the
natives, who seemed unused to see foreigners,
and exceedingly delighted at our arrival. They
ushered us into their houses, and gave us sweet-
meats and tea. This village or town seemed
very extensive and populous. Their houses
were spacious, but very dirty; and most of the
inhabitants go out to fish.

It was soon known that we had medicines
to give them, when repeated applications were
made by those afflicted with various diseases, and
they shewed themselves grateful. Here we began to distribute christian books. They had
never been seen before, and their contents excited wonder. To see this poor friendly people,
anxious for the word of eternal life, but unable
to obtain it, is truly distressing.

The next day many people came on board; they were very inoffensive, and behaved with great propriety. The appearance, however, of a military officer of the lowest rank, gave them much alarm. This man was extremely proud and ignorant, and took no notice whatever of any objects in the ship. One of his servants was very boisterous in asking a present for his master, for his condescension in coming on board. As we did not gratify his wish, he stole a pipe, and marched off with the stateliness of a bigoted " Celestial." I had here the pleasure of hearing the inquiries of the people about the word of eternal life. One of them was very desirous to know whether the books which were distributed were good books, and when convinced of this, his expressions of delight were extreme.

Towards evening, having left the ship, we ascended a mountain in the neighbourhood. At the foot of this were a few hovels of fishermen, as wretched as human dwellings can be; yet there was a small temple, with an image in it, and a few incense sticks. Even the smallest villages have these buildings, reminding the Christian to strive to become individually the temple of the living God. The small patches of land which were cultivated with great care by the

natives, presented a pleasing sight among the
barren rocks. We had a long conversation with
the poor people, who, though clad in rags, and
scarcely provided with the necessaries of life,
were yet cheerful and communicative. They
were natives of the Kea district, whose inhabitants speak a dialect more resembling the mandarin than the natives of any other part of Canton
province. They are industrious cultivators of
the ground, barbers, smiths, and carpenters. As
their population is too dense, they leave their
country for foreign lands, especially for the
Indian Archipelago. At Banca and Borneo they
are the principal miners, and at Singapore and
Batavia, the artisans. They occupy much of
the interior of Formosa, and are spread throughout the Canton province as barbers and servants.

When we had descended the hill, the scene
presented to our view was sublime—a boundless
prospect of the tranquil ocean, and the adjacent
country spread out at our feet. The whole ridge
of the mountain was planted with fir-trees. This
economy is necessary, as the wood of natural
growth is very scarce; and from the supplies required by the immense population, fuel is rapidly
decreasing.

The dense fogs which we had experienced at

Macao still continued frequently to envelope us. We arrived, March 9, in the bay of Kea-tsze. The inhabitants soon hailed us with joy; amongst them was a very intelligent youth who shortly became so familiar with us, that he offered his services as a sailor. We were thwarted in our desire to ascend the little stream where the town was built, by the stern commands of the officers of two war junks anchored in a small bay. Our young friend was with us in the boat, and would have suffered severe punishment from these tyrants, for being in the contaminating atmosphere of barbarians, had we not rowed away and put him into a native boat. The commanders of these junks were Fuh-keen men; they would scarcely admit more than two of us on board, and when in their presence, insisted that we should *stand*, which, however, we refused to do. In the course of the conversation, they upbraided us for our wanton attempt to ascend the river, which would expose them to very severe punishment. They and many of their sailors were devoted opium-smokers, and of the most depraved character.

In the afternoon we visited some villages at the entrance of the bay. Viewed from a distance, their appearance is most romantic; the houses,

built of brick, rise up among the high trees, of
which there are a multitude overshadowing them.
But on a nearer approach the charm vanishes.
Large quantities of manure, near the houses, in-
fect the air; the houses themselves have scarcely
any furniture, and are exceedingly filthy; the
lanes are narrow, and the whole built without
plan or convenience. Great crowds of people
followed us in every direction. Of the young,
also, whom we every where observed to be numerous, the boys (for the girls were confined in
the houses with their feet bound up) in multitudes
accompanied us, with shouts and gambols, to
show their delight. I distributed several books
to the people, which excited much interest, as
well as wonder, that we should possess books
in their language, and should distribute them
" without money and without price." The shore
here, consisting of numerous projecting rocks,
presents an imposing aspect; along this we
walked till we arrived at an old fort. The
wall of this, in part, was massive rock, and able
to resist a heavy bombardment. A ravine in the
neighbourhood contains a mineral acid.

The next day, which was very fair, we made
an excursion to the right of Kea-tsze. Here are
extensive saline works, consisting of an elevated

bed of mud, where the sea water is partially evaporated. After this it is boiled till the pure salt appears. The monopoly of salt is one of the most important revenues of the Celestial Empire. The merchants who deal in it are generally the richest individuals in the country. Yet the monopoly, though under the conduct of certain officers, is generally so conducted as to become very oppressive to the poor, and a heavy national burden.

On the dry ground the natives cultivated the sugar cane, and prepared it for use. The soil is here very sandy, and productive of only a few vegetables. Yet such is Chinese industry, that they sow here and reap on the most barren soil; and though they cannot boast of abundance, they receive a sufficiency. After proceeding in various directions, we finally came to a bridge, the first we had hitherto seen. There was no railing for the sides. At the end was a temple, where some elderly men waited for us, and very gravely questioned us about our country. The filth and stench were here intolerable. Though the crowd of people around us was very numerous, we had no reason to complain of their rudeness or want of respect. It gave me great pleasure to leave with them the words of eternal life. Eternity will show how many a soul may be benefited by the perusal of one little tract.

Notwithstanding the severe prohibitions of the mandarins, we went up the river. In the midst of it stands a rock, and upon it a huge image of the goddess of the sea. Every where the monuments of superstition, and of the most lamentable degradation, meet our eyes. We were pursued by several mandarin boats, which, however, could not overtake us. The people on shore pressingly invited us to visit Kea-tsze. We judged it best not to go on shore, to avoid implicating the people in guilt and danger from our intercourse. It is distressing to see that men are forbidden free intercourse with men, to please the whim of a few tyrants.

March 17th, we were again obliged to come to anchor at Shin-tseuen. The adjacent country is fertile and sown with wheat. The inhabitants were very poor, and were consumed with cutaneous diseases. We proceeded up an inlet, on the left bank of which stands Shin-tseuen. One branch of the inlet turns westward, and a short distance up is a village named Shih-Chow. The old mandarin stationed at the fort at the entrance was very anxious that we should return. Several of inferior rank shewed us the greatest kindness. I asked them why we were not allowed to walk upon our common earth. "The laws of the empire forbid it," was the answer. "You boast of equity and reason in your government: where is the equity or reason of laws against the common laws of nature?" "There is none," they replied. "Why then are you so very anxious to shut us out from intercourse with a people who would gladly receive us?" To this they gave no reply, but inquired our names, and the name of our ship. We always made it our great endeavour to conciliate the people. As the Chinese are not of that misanthropic cast of mind which foreigners generally believe, we succeeded in our endeavour so far, that though our stay was but short, they invariably became attached to us.

On the 22d, we arrived at———and found unsafe anchorage amidst surrounding rocks. The shore is here a large sandy plain, destitute of vegetation, except the wild pine apple. In crossing this plain I was strongly reminded of the Arabian desert. There is a fort at the hill, where the half-starved soldiers were much frightened at our appearance, and closed the gates behind them. The walls were very weak, and crumbled down at the least motion.

The inhabitants living at a distance beyond
the desert, very soon heard the arrival of our
ship, and came off in great numbers to provide
us refreshments. Having received very pressing
invitations to visit them on shore, we crossed
over the barren tract, and came at last to Kang-
lae. This is a very large village, situated near
an inlet, which reaches far inland, and resembles
the water of a deep river. Nothing could exceed the joy of the inhabitants, whom curiosity
and the hope of gain from the sale of a few
articles had called together. But the stench
arising from the sloughs of manure was so
offensive, that we were speedily compelled to
retreat from this bustling scene. Here were
people engaged in the manufacture of sugar, the
staple article of export in most of the districts
already visited by us. Of this, the larger part
goes to the northern ports. Every where the
population is abundant to overflowing; and it
would be a humane act of the emperor, should
he send the surplus of them to the Indian Archipelago, where large and fertile tracts of land
might be allotted to them for cultivation and
subsistence. Though he connives at the emigration of male subjects from Canton and Fuhkeen province, yet he never permits females to

leave their country. The consequence is, that Chinese emigrants intermarry with the natives where they reside : and hence, in the offspring are combined the natural vices of both parents, while there is little proficiency in the virtues of either. The greater part of the emigrants, however, live in celibacy and wantonness : those who are fortunate enough to gain a little money, speedily return to their native land to enjoy it, thus draining the colonies of wealth and population. Hence, it is hardly possible that Chinese colonies should extend and flourish to that degree which the industry of the people might lead us to expect. Other nations are desirous to aid colonization in all ways, but the Chinese government assiduously opposes and obstructs it. In the public papers, frequent mention is made of the transforming and salutary influence of the Celestial Empire upon the conduct of its subjects. This could actually be exemplified amid the jungles of Borneo, Lingan, Biletou, &c., were practical virtue, rather than ostentation, the real object of the Chinese government.

After many days of dark weather, we finally enjoyed a fair day, and a favourable breeze for a few hours carried us to How-ta, where we anchored ;

a considerable village in the neighbourhood of
Nan-aou, (or Namoh.) We saw the numerous
junks lying at anchor at Ting-hae, (or Ching-
hae-heen.) The trade here has always been
brisk and advantageous, for the government
choose to be unusually liberal to the overflowing population, which here threatened rebellion,
if not permitted to engage in mercantile speculations, and to embark as colonists for foreign
countries. All the districts belonging to Fuh-
chow-Foo, to which Ting-hae likewise appertains,
send forth a great number of colonists, who spare
neither danger or toil to gain a scanty livelihood
in their foreign homes. A part of their hard
earnings is annually remitted to their kindred
who are left in their native land ; and it is astonishing to see what hardships they will suffer, to
procure and send home this pittance. A man of
tried honesty is appointed to collect the individual subscriptions of the emigrants, who also
engages to go home with them, and there make
an equitable distribution to the donees. The
subscriptions are regularly noted down, and a
certain per centage paid to this commissioner.
Before he goes on board, a banquet is given by
the subscribers, and then he embarks with all
the wishes which human voices can utter, for his

prosperous passage. On arriving at his native
shores, he is welcomed by all those who are
anxiously waiting for this supply. The amount
of these remittances is often large, and there are
instances where junks have taken on board more
than sixty thousand dollars for this purpose.
Notwithstanding the great precaution taken to
find a proper man for so important a trust, it
often happens that he runs away with the money
entrusted to him, and the poor families, whose
sole dependence it was, are reduced to starvation.
Good faith is surely not a virtue of which the
Chinese can generally boast, though there are
honourable individual exceptions; at the same
time, it must be admitted, that their affection
towards their kindred is very strong; neither
time nor distance can withdraw their attention
from the beloved objects they left behind in their
native land. If an emigrant can send but a dollar
he will send it; he will himself fast in order to
save it; indeed, he will never send home a letter
unless accompanied with some present; he will
rather entirely cease writing than send nothing
more substantial than paper. There are also
swindlers among the colonists, who, on their
arrival from China, engage in extensive mercantile speculations, and having acquired credit, and

got much property in their hands, either run away, or abide the consequences in a jail.

The condition of the emigrants in general, on their arrival in a foreign country, is most miserable, without clothing, or money for one day's subsistence. Sometimes they have not money enough to pay their passage from home (six or twelve dollars,) and they become bondmen to any body who pays this sum for them, or fall a prey to extortioners, who claim their services for more than a year. The junks which transport them in great numbers, remind one of an African slaver. The deck is filled with them, and there the poor wretches are exposed to the inclemency of the weather and without any shelter, for the cargo fills the junk below. Their food consists of dry rice and an allowance of water; but when the passages are very long, there is often a want of both, and many of them actually starve to death. As soon as they arrive, they fall with a ravenous appetite upon the fruits of India, and many die by dysentery and fever. The climate also has often an enervating effect upon them; but they very soon recover from it, and resume their industrious habits. But disappointed hopes render them languid in their pursuits; they came to amass dollars, and can scarcely get cents; they expected to live in plenty, but can earn a bare subsistence. Many therefore become thieves and gamblers to gratify their covetous desires. This is not strange, for it is generally the degraded and vicious of the people who leave their country for foreign parts, and there they rather advance than recede in vice. The propagation of the gospel among such a class of men, is therefore attended with numerous difficulties, from the prevailing corruptions.

March 27th we anchored in sight of the city of Nan-aou, and the next day resolved to visit the war junks stationed here. They signified by their hands and by words, that we must be off immediately, pointing to the shore where his excellency, the commander-in-chief, resided. We succeeded, however, in getting on board a very large rice-trader from Formosa, driven hither by one of the N. E. gales, which are very common in the channel of Formosa. The captain of this junk seemed to understand true politeness well; and when censured by the commanders of the war junks for receiving us, he mildly replied, " How could I transgress so against the laws of hospitality?" He very soon silenced a boisterous mandarin, and Mr. Lindsay's winning manners contributed not a little to remove their objections.

We afterwards approached the city in a boat, but as his excellency had strictly forbidden all intercourse with us, we did not wait upon him as we first designed. Conscious of their own weakness, they are always fearful that the fierce barbarians will assume too much liberty if permitted to enter at all.

There are two forts on an island eastward of the city, and another smaller one nearer to it. The city itself has a romantic appearance when viewed from a distance. It is one of the principal naval stations of the empire, as the island, Nan-aou, was formerly the haunt of pirates, who infested all the Chinese seas. Hence so many forts were erected; but they are at present almost fallen to ruins, like all the military defences of the Celestial Empire. In ascending a hill, Pih-shan-gan, we reached a most romantic spot, covered with cottages and wheat fields. A streamlet issuing from the hill falls into the sea near a little hamlet. The people were rather disposed to shun us, on account of the neighbourhood of the mandarins.

We now left the coast of Canton, and began to sail along the shores of Fuhkeen. The same barren rocks, the same sterile soil, present themselves to the eye of the passenger. The fishermen

I

whom we saw in all directions, were not very anxious to approach us, though we encouraged them by great rewards. We anchored westward of four islands, bearing the names of Tiger, Lion, Dragon, and Elephant, and east of an offing of perforated rock. We landed at the village of Gaou-keo, which is built on a peninsula, and inhabited by fishermen. The hill we ascended exhibited a great variety of stones and strata of earth. Though the inhabitants were very civil, yet they were very cautious in their intercourse. They asked of what ship and country we were, and from their conversation we understood that they were partially acquainted with Europeans before.

The islands here are universally as barren as can be conceived, yet the larger of them are the abodes of fishermen. Formerly the pirates had possession of most of these islands. They were Fuhkeen men, from the Fung-gan district. The owners of their ships generally resided at Amoy or Formosa. Very many of the sailors were men driven to desperation by the mandarins; the rest were worthless vagabonds. Though the Chinese character is generally exempt from cruelty, these men were so degenerate and hardened that they committed the most unheard of

crimes from mere wantonness. In their engagements with the imperial fleet they were often
victorious, for many of their sailors were taken
from the flower of the nation; whilst the imperial
fleet has chiefly on board half-starved beings,
taken from the dregs of the people, and regardless of military honour. A regular system of
piratical extortion once threatened to put a stop
to the coasting trade, and to interrupt the supplies which came to the capital by way of Teen-
tsin. The chiefs of the pirates gave passports to
the trading vessels, and thereby strictly enforced
their claim to the command of the sea-ports.
Such a ruinous system could not long continue,
and hence the mandarins bribed the chiefs by
the offer of military rank and service under the
imperial banner. They accepted the offer; and
many of them to this period are renowned naval
commanders, whilst a few have been executed.

The sea seems here to be receding; for the
lands belonging to this people ten years ago
were sea, and are yearly increasing in extent.
Not far from this fishing village is Chang-poo-
heen. We could merely discern that it was an
extensive place; for it was already the dusk of
the evening, and we could not reach it. The
natives were very inquisitive respecting our

cargo, and complained bitterly of the system of exclusion enforced by the mandarins. " How gladly," said they, " would we, if permitted, cultivate amicable intercourse with you! but we are always forbidden to obey the impulse of our hearts!"

CHAPTER II.

AFTER many delays we finally arrived at Amoy. This place is situated on a very large island, on the left side of a bay, which deeply indents the country, and forms numerous islands. The city is very extensive, and contains at least two hundred thousand inhabitants. All its streets are narrow, the temples numerous, and a few large houses owned by wealthy merchants. Its excellent harbour has made it, from time immemorial, one of the greatest emporiums of the empire, and one of the most important markets of Asia. Vessels can sail up close to the houses, load and unload with the greatest facility, have shelter from all winds, and in entering or leaving the port, experience no danger of getting ashore. The whole adjacent country being sterile, forced the inhabitants to seek some means of subsistence. Endowed with an enterprising spirit and unwearied in the pursuit of gain, they visited all parts of the Chinese empire, gradually became bold sailors, and settled as merchants all along the coast. Thus they colonized Formosa, which from that period to this has been their granary; visited and settled in the Indian Archipelago, Cochin-China, and Siam. A population constantly overflowing demanded constant resources for their subsistence, and this they found in colonization. This they have promoted all along the coast of China up to Mantchou Tartary. As soon as the colonists amass sufficient money they return home, which they leave again when all is spent.

This constant emigration of the male part of the people contributes very much to the destruction of domestic happiness. It is a general custom among them to drown a large proportion of the new-born female children. This unnatural crime is so common among them, that it is perpetrated without any feeling, and even in a laughing mood; and to ask a man of any distinction whether he has daughters, is a mark of great rudeness. Neither the government nor the moral sayings of their sages have put a stop to this nefarious custom. The father has authority over the lives of his children, and disposes of them according to his pleasure. The boys enjoy

the greater share of parental affection. Their
birth is considered one of the greatest and most
fortunate events in a family. They are cherished
and indulged to a high degree ; and if the father
dies, the son assumes a certain authority over
his mother. There is also carried on a regular
traffic in females. These facts are as revolting
to humanity as disgusting to detail. They may
serve, however, to stimulate the zeal of christian
females to promote the welfare of one of the
largest portions of their sex, by giving them the
glorious gospel of our Saviour — that gospel,
which alone restores females to their proper
rank in society. It is pleasing to observe, that
there is now a benevolent association in England
for the express purpose of instructing Chinese
females at Malacca. If this institution can ever
exert any influence upon China in this way, for
which we sincerely pray, we are persuaded that
the degradation and oppression under which the
nation now groans will be much alleviated.

Amoy was formerly a resort for ships of different foreign nations. The English were forced
to relinquish the trade by the severe extortions
to which they were subject. The Dutch continued it for a longer time, but neglected it when
their influence at Formosa ceased. The Spanish

have nominal permission to trade there to this day, but they have preferred to send their ships to Macao. They retaliated upon the Chinese junks which annually arrive at Manilla from Amoy and Shang-hae, by imposing upon them higher duties than they themselves paid at Amoy. This has embittered the Chinese against them, given rise to smuggling, and greatly impeded the trade.

We arrived at Amoy harbour about three o'clock. Scarcely had we come to anchor when a mandarin boat approached, and one of the boatmen joyfully exclaimed, " Oh! she is a trader!" A young man now came forward, and delivered us a paper sent by a principal mandarin, desiring us to report " whence we came, and for what purpose we had entered the harbour." At the same time he invited us to an entertainment the next day at his master's house, where we should see the Te-tuh, or admiral. Two mandarins with gold buttons came very shortly after, and also desired our report. They were followed by two others, one with a blue and the other with a white button, who were exceedingly reserved. An elderly man, belonging to the custom-house office, was of quite a different character. He told us very candidly that this

was the best place to which we could come,
because the wealthiest merchants resided here,
who would gladly engage with us in mercantile
business.

Scarcely had we dined when the two mandarins
first mentioned brought us notice, " that the admiral desired us to leave the harbour as speedily
as possible, and they would supply us with
water." We thanked them for this show of
hospitality, and merely replied, that we could by
no means be guilty of so great a breach of
politeness as to neglect paying our respects to
his excellency before our departure; that as the
wind was against us, we had time enough to
spare. We begged them to treat us as we
treated their countrymen when they arrived at
our colonies. This tended to soften their harsh
language, and confound their reasoning about
the inviolable laws of the Celestial Empire.
But nothing inspired them with so much respect
as our well-mounted long guns, which silently
spoke more in our behalf than the best harangue
of Demosthenes could have done. Several respectable merchants were anxious to come on
board; but as no permission had been given,
while they deeply regretted it, they did not venture to come on deck.

April 3.—Several boats anchored around us, to keep off the natives; some watermen, by feeing the mandarin on duty, got permission to come on board.

When several mandarins, our friends of yesterday, came on board, we were again importuned to leave the harbour immediately. They pretended to be very hospitable towards us, and professed themselves our sincere friends,—hence they had stationed boats around us, that we might not suffer from the treacherous people. We simply replied, that " according to our foreign customs, *friends* are not watched like thieves, and *guests* are not driven away like scoundrels." This answer seemed so conclusive that they began now to talk about the probability of an audience with his excellency, the admiral. He had pledged himself to provide us provisions. But as the trade with foreigners was restricted to Canton, he could give us no permission to trade.

In going up to the city we passed a large rock with an inscription on it, the purport of which we were too distant to ascertain. Before landing, a mandarin with a white button, who had been aboard the ship, and had shown us every attention, came up to us in a boat. He apologized for his sudden appearance, and offered himself as our guide through this unknown place. He had evidently been despatched by his superiors to prevent our landing, but feeling the uselessness of the order, he did not once mention it. In our walk around, we saw many shops well furnished with the necessaries and the luxuries of life, such as could scarcely be supposed in a district almost destitute of any natural productions. The insufferable stench, and the great crowd of people, prevented our penetrating far. We visited several respectable merchants, who treated us with every mark of civility, and would have entered into commercial speculations with us, had not the presence of the mandarins overawed them. Many large houses which we passed bespoke the wealth of the inmates. A military escort attended us, which rendered our visit very awkward, though the commander repeatedly assured us, that it was merely for our protection. When we objected to this, that the people were friendly to strangers, and gave every sign of being delighted with our visit, the mandarin replied, "These are the orders from our superiors; I cannot justify them myself; but come to-morrow again, and you will enjoy greater liberty."

We sailed afterwards up the inlet. At the
entrance we found from six to ten fathoms of
water, so that the largest ships could anchor opposite the city. There were, in all, about one
hundred and fifty junks in the harbour, many of
them undergoing repairs in the docks, which are
very commodious. Daily arrivals from Formosa,
with cargoes of rice, increased the number.
Notwithstanding the abundant supply, rice was
very dear, and soon after our departure rose to
an enormous price. Farther up the inlet are
shoals and numerous rocks above water. On
our return to the ship we found that our learned
China-man had fallen overboard, but was provi-
dentially rescued by our second mate, Mr. Jemi-
son, a gentleman of great intrepidity.

April 4.—I was roused by the arrival of all
the mandarins who had formerly been aboard.
They told us that we had nothing to expect, but
must immediately leave the port. At the same
time we received a document from the Te-tuh,
containing an imperial edict, issued the twenty-
first year of Kea King, (1817, a year after the
British embassy,) to the officers in the Fuhkeen
and Che-keang provinces. They were not to
permit a barbarian ship to come near the coast
of those two provinces, not to allow her to anchor

for a moment, but to drive her instantly away, and not to connive at the people's going on board.

All these orders had been neglected by the admiral, in our case, yet did he plead this document as the sole rule of his conduct. The last clause, however, he had overstepped by his severity, in cruelly beating the people who came " along-side" of us, merely to look at our ships ; with the design not only to intimidate them, but also to disgrace us in the eyes of the natives as unworthy of notice. In this design he failed, for though the people seemed astonished at his harsh treatment to us, they could not forbear to be kind to strangers whom they considered as their friends.

We often conversed with them upon the things which concerned their eternal happiness ; we gave them books, exhorted them to read them with diligence, and we left this kind-hearted people, with a deep impression of their unhappiness in being formed for improvement from foreign intercourse, yet always debarred from it. How deplorable it is to behold such numbers of rational beings in a state of deep ignorance! Whatever other attainments they may have made, their idolatry is degrading to humanity; their superstitions, a stain upon the human understanding. How do they stand when viewed in their relations to their Creator and Protector? How can we regard them in reference to their God and Saviour? Though they are ignorant of these relations, they have immortal souls capable of being enlightened, and responsible for the neglect of their highest duties. A government discountenancing any mental advancement cannot deserve applause, whatever the temporal advantages may be from laws in favour of stupidity. Every candid reader will agree with me, that no government has a right to seclude its subjects from all foreign intercourse. There are innate rights which no human prohibition can destroy, and the right of reciprocal intercourse between the nations of the world is one of these.

What authority on earth, even of the Chinese emperor, as "vicegerent of heaven over all the globe," can enact laws forbidding to acknowledge the Creator of the universe, and the Saviour of the world? This, in effect, has been done in China. Though we cannot alter their laws to exclude foreigners and the true religion, yet we do not consider them so binding upon us, as inhabitants of the same planet, and Christians in faith and practice, that we may not enter the empire. We have strenuously debated these two points with them : and the mandarins have conceded that this system of exclusion is unreasonable, but throw the whole work of reform upon the emperor. This convenient way of ridding themselves of conscientious scruples, may be styled *political popery;* nothing is more common throughout the empire.

Whilst we were in a temple near a fort at the entrance of the inlet, whither we had been invited to come to an audience at noon, those poor people who happened to come into the neighbourhood of the ship were treated most barbarously. After being severely beaten on board the war-junks, so that we might hear the lamentations of the sufferers, they were then exposed in the pillory with a canque* about the neck, and a label inscribed with their crime; not of leaguing with barbarians, or going aboard,

* This is an instrument of corporeal punishment often used in China. It is made of two oblong pieces of wood, which, when joined, form a square. Each of the pieces is hollowed out a little at the place where they are to join; and this hollow encircles the neck of the criminal, round which the "canque" is placed. It is sometimes very heavy, and the criminal, while wearing it, can neither raise his hand to his mouth, nor see where to set his feet. He is sometimes obliged to carry it for weeks, or even months.

but of *looking at* the barbarian ship.   Thus the
mere sight of us was contaminating!   We could
not have been worse treated, even if we had had
the plague aboard.   Only a few people before
this had come on board, and they were immediately driven away.   The clerk, who had previously invited us to his master's house, came in
a great hurry, earnestly beseeching us not to
mention this invitation, for, if known, it would
cost him his life.

Towards noon we put off in a boat, to present
our petition to the Te-tuh.   In our way up to
the temple we passed ranks of soldiers, dressed
in tiger uniform; some without a nose, others
with one eye, and the greater number old and
emaciated beings.   Their officers, who were in
full uniform, armed with bows, and very elegantly dressed, presented a striking contrast to
the soldiers.   In a hall adjoining the temple, we
found the admiral and the Tsung-ping-kwan of
Kin-mun, a military station in the neighbourhood, besides several others.   We yielded the
point of *standing* in their presence.   This circumstance, trivial in itself, encouraged the mandarins to treat us insolently.   After having
handed the petition, we were requested to retire
to the temple, till we should receive an answer.

Wang, the clerk, became the bearer of our messages. Our request to buy provisions from the merchants, was refused. The admiral, who was no personal enemy, but rather our friend, agreed to depute a person to act as comprador. In the course of our conversation, we stated our friendly intention in coming to this port. Mr. Lindsay expostulated with all the firmness and politeness of an Englishman. The *unalterable* laws of the Celestial Empire were held forth to justify the treatment we had experienced. " If the laws are indeed unalterable," we replied, " then we ought to come hither freely, for the ancient edict issued under Kang-he, permitted foreigners to enter all Chinese ports. The unchangeable laws, which, as you assert, allow not the least deviation from ancient custom, are in our favour, and we plead them in our behalf. We allow your junks to enter all our Indian ports; they come and trade freely, without being surrounded by our men of war, or inspected in their intercourse with our fellow-subjects. Moreover, we allow your nation, and especially the natives of this province, to settle in our colonies and to enjoy the same liberties as our own people, without being oppressed by any authorities. If we, therefore, asked in return, not all of the same privileges, but only the permission to trade to every port, our demand is just by the common law of nations. Besides, we have been repeatedly told, that the emperor compassionates foreigners; this compassion has never reached us yet, and we humbly hope that we may participate in it, by being permitted to trade to these ports according to ancient custom."

This whole conversation was not very palatable to the mandarins. We were frequently interrupted, and I myself was charged with impoliteness in adducing the honesty we had exhibited, as a pledge that we would leave the port after obtaining provisions. " Don't fear," continued I, " that we shall not perform what we promised." " *Fear* you ! " the Tsung-ping-kwan replied, " fear *you !* " exclaimed he, with a contemptuous sneer. After inviting them to come aboard the ship, and receiving a scornful refusal, we returned.

We had now tried what could be effected by petition, and by unresisting submission, and were forced to give ourselves up to the mercy of these Celestials. After dinner we took an excursion round an island opposite to Amoy. All the surrounding country is barren rock, except some valleys capable of cultivation, where a few potatoes grow. These vales are tilled with the greatest care, and richly repay the labours of the peasant. The country has a romantic appearance. There is something grand in the sight of those undulating, barren ridges of hills along the Chinese coast. We have frequently gazed from the top of those hills upon the tracts of land spread beneath us, and oft did I sing,—

> " O'er the gloomy hills of darkness
> Look, my soul, be still and gaze.
> All the promises do travail
> With a glorious day of grace:
> Blessed jubilee !
> Let the glorious morning dawn."

While musing thus, I turned and saw a poor man carrying a burden, but willing to converse upon the things of eternal life. I felt consoled by this, and rejoiced that I was permitted to tread upon these barren hills. To-day we entered a village at the foot of a very high hill, and were gladly received by the inhabitants. They did not hesitate to converse freely upon any topic which we introduced. I had the pleasure to add a few books to the well-worn library of an old man; he examined them carefully. The houses were built very substantially, and kept tolerably clean; but the occupants were very poor people, of whom the

male part were either at work at Amoy, or were
gone to foreign parts. At the beach we were
shocked at the spectacle of a pretty new-born
babe, which shortly before had been killed.
We asked some of the bystanders what this
meant. They answered with indifference, " It is
only a girl." It is a general custom in this
district to drown female infants immediately
after their birth. Respectable families seldom
take the trouble, as they express themselves, to
rear these useless girls. They consider themselves the arbiters of their children's lives, and
entitled to take them away when they can fore-
see that their prolongation would only entail
misery. As the numerous emigrations of the
male population render it probable that their
daughters, if permitted to live, would not be
married, they choose this . shorter way to rid
themselves of the encumbrance of supporting
them.

Thus are the pledges of conjugal love, the
most precious gift of the Most High, the most
important trust confided to men by the Supreme
Being, deliberately murdered. Brutes love their
young, and cherish and defend them; but man
can divest himself of natural affection, and
degrade himself far below the brute creation.

I had sent my servant, Eu, on shore during the night, to visit his family, which resides here. He came off during the night with provisions. The people who came with him were astonished at the barbarous treatment which we had hitherto experienced. They blamed us for having yielded too much to the mandarins. Since matters had come to this state, however, they saw no possibility of opening a private intercourse with the natives. They deeply regretted this result. When they saw our ship enter their port, they had flattered themselves with the hope of renewing the foreign trade which was formerly carried on here.

April 5.—We waited till this time to receive a comprador from the admiral; but instead of this we perceived that our "friends" were making warlike preparations. They went so far as to point the guns of the war-junks at us. Though this could but cause us smile—for the most martial preparations in China, directed by those possessing neither skill nor courage, can never intimidate any European sloop of war—yet we could hence perceive their ill-will emboldened by our tacit submission.

In the afternoon we enjoyed a magnificent view from one of the highest peaks in the environs of Amoy. The islands at the mouth of the harbour, Hin-mun in the back-ground, and all the many hills, valleys, with the villages interposed, and the city, all before us, afforded us one of the highest enjoyments we had had. Oh! when will this populous district become the Lord's?

The Amoy people, though otherwise very reasonable men, have always shown themselves bigoted heathen. Whether at home or abroad, they have everywhere built splendid temples, chiefly in honour of Ma-tsoo-po, " the queen of heaven," to whose intercession they attribute the increase of their wealth. They rival Rome in the adoration of images, and are most devout after a profitable voyage, or an escape from storm. From their intercourse with foreign ports they have often enjoyed the high privilege of becoming acquainted with the gospel, and they have often rejected the great salvation. Proud, selfish, and stubborn, they find it entirely agreeable to reject a religion, at the portal of which is inscribed *humility*. But we look for better times.

The mandarin boats, which followed us wherever we went, kept at a respectful distance, and scarcely attempted landing where we did; so that we enjoyed the undisturbed privilege of conversing with the natives. To-day we distributed more books than usual. They were at first cautious in taking them; but seeing that we asked nothing in return, they made no scruple to accept them, and with gratitude.

We were to-day unexpectedly visited by a sailor, who " claimed friendship" with me. He had formerly seen me in Mantchou Tartary, and received some medicines for his brother which had restored him to health. Anxious to show his gratitude, he had asked permission to come on board. The mandarins had granted it under condition that he became our comprador. He described, in the most lively colours, the alarm which our unexpected appearance had excited in the breasts of the mandarins. We sent him with a list of the articles needed, and he was very prompt in procuring them. We cannot account for the fact, that the inferior mandarins have not been permitted to hold any farther intercourse with us, unless their superiors feared that they would be seduced by our arguments to favour us.

April 6.—To-day I received applications for medicines from mandarins of the highest rank, who were afflicted with the " itch." In our excursion of to-day we received, on our return, a military escort. These soldiers were much astonished at the singular structure of our muskets. When we asked them the reason of this escort, we were told again that it was merely for our protection against the people; though they have always shown themselves our warmest friends, and sympathized with us whenever we were treated insolently.

Our poor sailor came on board this evening very much agitated. He had been made responsible for our leaving the port. The junk to which he belonged was now ready to sail for Formosa, but could not proceed till we had left the port. He was also threatened with corporeal punishment if he failed to persuade us to depart. He besought us, therefore, with tears, to leave the harbour early the next day; or if we could not do this to move farther out. We could not doubt the sincerity of this man, but regretted that the mandarins must have recourse to such expedients, to make up for the want of personal bravery, and to enable them to report to the emperor that they had driven away the barbarians.

April 7. — To-day we got under way. I cannot omit to notice a few more particulars respecting this most celebrated emporium of

Fuhkeen, and one of the greatest in Asia. Its harbour is excellent, and accessible to the largest men of war. The natives of this district seem to be born traders and sailors. Their barren country, which furnishes employment for only a few hands, but far more their inclination, prompts them to leave their home, either for Formosa or the principal emporium of the Chinese empire, or the Indian Archipelago, or for the fisheries along their native shores. Wherever they go, they are rarely found in a state of abject poverty; on the contrary, they are often wealthy, and command the trade of whole islands and provinces, as well by their capital as by their superior enterprise and industry. Strongly attached to their early home, they either return as soon as they have acquired a small property, or they make large remittances. Many of the merchants, settled in the north part of China, return annually with their profits. It is not surprising, therefore, that a large amount of Chinese shipping belongs to Amoy merchants, and that the greater part of capital employed in the coasting trade is their property. Hence this barren tract is one of the richest in China, from the enterprise of the inhabitants. Here is doubtless one of the best harbours for European mercantile enterprise, both for its situation, its wealth, and the stores of all Chinese exports. At an early period the Portuguese traded here; the Dutch followed them; the English for a long time had a factory here; and the Spanish have to this day a nominal right to come hither. The cause of the cessation of trade has not been so much the prohibition of the emperor, as the great extortion to which it was subject. The renewal of commerce will have the most beneficial influence both upon the nation engaging in it, and upon the Chinese.

It is highly desirable that a Christian mission should be established here. The facilities for disseminating the divine word are greater in this place that in any other part of China. The Spanish have a mission in the environs; but it seems to be almost unknown. Though I have had intercourse with thousands of Amoy men, I have never met with one Christian among them.

Boldness, pride, and generosity are characteristics of the natives. They have always been obstinate against governmental encroachments. They were the last who kept up resistance to the Tartar usurpation; and many of them preferred a voluntary exile in Formosa or India, to compliance with the customs of their conquerors and submission to barbarians. They defended themselves bravely at Formosa, and became notorious for piracy. Successful in resisting the attacks of the imperial fleet, they established a maritime government; and were never entirely subdued by force, but finally yielded to persuasion and bribery.

Literary fame is no object of their ambition; but they generally learn to count and to make up bills. Their language differs widely from the mandarin dialect, and they are obliged to learn this with the same labour as we acquire Latin. In their dealings, they have a name for honesty above all other Chinese. Though incessantly hunting for gain, they are not mean, and they are anxious to establish a fair character. Solicitous to cultivate friendship with strangers, they have always associated with them freely, whenever beyond the reach of government. They have been frequently entrusted with high offices, by those foreign states where they have resided as colonists. One of their descendants, as late as the middle of the last century, ascended the throne of Siam. I am acquainted with his son, who became a physician instead of a king, but who, notwithstanding this degradation, possesses royal virtues, and too much sagacity to be a usurper. He is wise enough to prefer a quiet humble life, to the pageantry of royalty, with the disaffection of a nation, indignant at seeing a foreigner on the throne.

When we had left our anchorage, and got beyond the reach of the fort, their large guns were fired, and most of the men of war joined them in this act of heroism. Several of them escorted us out, to protect us, no doubt, from the treacherous natives. However, we had no reason to complain, for we had received all the necessaries we had requested, though in a very awkward manner. His excellency even sent us several boat-loads of stores, as a present, for which, however, we paid the people, who were compelled to furnish them.

On the whole, we may say the Amoy mandarins heaped all possible insult upon us, to render us despicable in the view of the people, and to maintain the dignity of the Celestial Empire. Other ships which may come hereafter will avoid all this by entering the harbour without delay, and anchoring among the junks. They ought not to move before their reasonable demands are complied with, as they will thereby gain their end, expedite the business, and less trouble both mandarins and people. The natives suggested this course to us, of which we made experiment in other ports, and to our great advantage. The most trivial things, if not firmly demanded, will meet a refusal from the Chinese. Justice and forbearance should be on our side; we should do our utmost to conciliate, by unequivocal acts of kindness; we should prove ourselves Christians by honest dealings, and philanthropists by our religion; yet we should never allow any native to be unjustly punished on our account. They regard us as their friends, and we claim friendship with them. We have surely no right to interfere with the internal laws of a country, where we are merely tolerated as merchants; but we may restrain the unlawful acts committed on our account by the guardians of the laws.

April 9.—After an unsuccessful attempt to proceed, we got under way, and reached the Pang-hoo, or Piscadores, anchoring at Se-seu, a very barren island. These numerous islands, various in extent, are all extremely sterile; but having good harbours, they serve as a refuge for the junks, which continually pass between Formosa and China. As the north-east wind generally blows strong a greater part of the year in the Formosa channel, many junks must be lost, if they could not find shelter among them.

On the largest of the islands there are the ruins
of a fort, built by the Dutch, called Hung-maon-
ching—" Red-bristle fort." The Chinese garrison
is very numerous here, because the security of
Formosa depends upon the possession of these
islands. Several war-junks are also stationed in
the harbour. Though the colonists have tried
their utmost to draw something for subsistence
from so unfruitful soil, yet they would be reduced to starvation but for the supplies of rice
from Formosa. Government also favours them
greatly. There was lately a scarcity of grain,
and the government sent the Tsung-ping Kwan
to distribute large quantities among them. The
majority of the inhabitants are emigrants from
the Kin-mun district, of Fuhkeen province, and
in general very poor.

We went ashore, where a great number of the
populace were present at a play, given at the
expense of a captain of a junk. Scarcely had
the people beheld our books, when they grasped
them with eagerness, and read them with great
attention. The village has a very wretched
appearance, but the houses are built substantially of granite. We walked up an eminence,
followed by several people, who put to us very
curious questions, and gave themselves the air

of merchants. We were surprised to find a light-house on the highest part of the island, for this is a thing no where seen on all the Chinese coast; perhaps it was built by the Dutch. Scarcely had we gone down to the beach, when an old mandarin, with a blue button, ordered us very peremptorily to stop. He then seated himself, and, with a firm voice, commanded us to leave the port immediately, since his excellency, Woo, who resided on the opposite islands, would by no means allow us to stay.

April 10.—The old mandarin made us another visit. When he delivered his message yesterday, the people around us showed him so little respect, that he found his authoritative orders would be lost upon us if not duly repeated. He came, therefore, with his whole retinue, and put again the usual questions—from what country, where we embarked, &c. They were all in good humour, and rather childish at the sight of so many novelties. The present of a few lion buttons so pleased the old mandarin as to change his commands to requests. He informed us, that in his native place several Christians are living, who are under the charge of an European missionary — very probably

Spanish. He repeated the name of Maria, mother of heaven, and showed that he was a convert, or, at least, acquainted with papacy. When leaving us, he advised us to go to Formosa, where we might trade. There were several junks in the harbour, waiting a favourable wind to return to Formosa for cargoes of rice.

CHAPTER III.

APRIL 11.—On awaking this morning we were near the level coast of Formosa. The island, which has become celebrated since the establishment of the Dutch on some parts of it, at present forms the granary of Fuhkeen. It produces immense quantities of rice, and furnishes many cargoes of sugar. The Formosan camphor is generally known, and exported to all parts of Europe. Though the greater part of the island has been subjected to China, the eastern portion, lying beyond the range of hills which passes through the island, is still in possession of the aborigines. They are described as a harmless race, when not provoked, but relentless when once enraged. As we saw no individual of them, we are enabled to speak only from report. Frequent rebellion has tended to retard greatly the growing prosperity of the island. The colonists, as I have said, are chiefly

K 3

Fuhkeen men, who, after their arrival, laboured hard to acquire a little property. The mandarins here, who were free from the immediate control of their superiors, concluded that they might safely oppress these emigrants, who were but the dregs of the Chinese population. The colonists, on their part, considered themselves entitled to higher privileges than in their mother country, and opposed obstinacy to oppression. The spirit of discontent was also encouraged by the success of the rebels in repelling their enemies. When all resources fail, they retire to the mountains, and defend their liberty against all the attacks of the numerous troops, which the emperor constantly sends against them, to regain and maintain his authority. There is a very brisk trade with this fruitful island, but chiefly in the hands of Fuhkeen merchants, who have advanced the capital for clearing the rice-fields, and for the cultivation of sugar. There are no junks strictly belonging to this island; all the shipping is the property of the Amoy merchants.

It was at the early period of the Dutch conquest that Christianity was preached to the Formosans. Several ministers of the Dutch church, which was at that time imbued with the spirit of the reformers, here spread the saving knowledge of the gospel. There are still extant a few books upon Christianity, which they published in the Formosan language. They seem, from the number of their converts, to have been very successful; and great emulation was created at Batavia, in deciding who should first be sent to Formosa. While reading their simple and short relation of their missionary efforts, we must regret that the conquest of the island by the Chinese has probably left little traces of the true gospel. We spared no trouble to ascertain this point, but found every one ignorant of the facts.

After anchoring, we were immediately visited by great numbers of fishermen. They did not show the least suspicion; on the contrary, they treated us as old acquaintance, and promised to bring off some merchants to effect purchases. They were very eager to possess books, and came along-side in great numbers, earnestly craving them. As I can remember no effort here to spread the gospel since the Chinese conquest, I rejoiced to embrace this opportunity of giving them, at least, the means to know it. They were very thankful, and promised to read what had been freely given them.

We afterwards went on shore, and had a view

of the whole coast; the soil of which appears to
be entirely alluvial. The sea recedes from the
land so rapidly, that many harbours, once good,
are now inaccessible, even for small junks.
Formosa has always been deficient in good
harbours, and ships were obliged, even at the
capital, to lie at a great distance from the shore,
near the Fort Zelandia. But latterly the land is
increased to such a degree, that large shoals
have become visible all along the coast, and the
approach to it is consequently dangerous. The
place which we visited bears the name of Woo-
teaou-keang, where several junks were lying in
shore, with scarce two feet water at ebb tide.
The soil is a black sand, and, as far as the eye
can reach, there is neither shrub or grass.
Carts, with wheels, but without spokes, and
drawn by buffaloes, are used to carry the cargo
through the water to the vessels. The village
is very mean, but inhabited by some mercantile
agents, whose houses are two days' journey in
the interior. They have also hemp-for exportation. We saw a few agents, or clerks of the
mandarins, residing here, as overseers of the exports. The people, though secluded from intercourse with Europeans, exhibited great interest
to know every thing respecting our ship and

our country. Their inquiries were very appropriate, and were continued till properly answered.
At the same time we had to lament the profligacy
which reigns throughout the island, and especially in the sea-ports. When will the glorious gospel banish from the earth all the pests of mankind?

We found here many readers, very anxious to
possess our books. Several natives set off to
call hither some merchants residing in the
district of Kea-e. The capital of this district is a
very large town, upon a river which empties itself
into the sea at Woo-teaou-keang, in lat. 23° 38′,
long. 120° 21′. We waited about two days for
the merchants, but they did not arrive. At
length we saw the mandarin clerks stepping on
board, with presents of tea and fruits. By ascertaining the prices of our goods, they endeavoured
to give us hope that they would probably trade.
But unable to wait longer in so bad an anchorage, we got under way.

April 15.—We narrowly escaped running
ashore near the island of Nan-jih, which belongs
to Footeen district. Several junks had anchored
in this harbour, some of which we visited, and
were advised to go to Shang-hae in Keang-nan,
where we might find a ready market for our
cargo. The people were communicative, and

expressed their fears that we should be unable
to do much in trade, because the natives were
suffering starvation; " How could they afford
money to buy cloth ? "

April 16.—We entered the Hae-tan passage,
a very labyrinth of islands and rocks, between the
Fuhkeen coast and the large island of Hae-tan.
We were near striking a rock, and escaped with
much difficulty and peril. Few ships have sailed
through this passage, and it would be well that
none but small craft should attempt it again.
When we had anchored at Wan-gan, a fish-boat
came along-side, but the boatmen did not, at
first, venture to come on board. However, we
prevailed on them to sell their fish ; and they
were at length emboldened to come up to us.
As soon as they had looked around a little, their
fears vanished, and their tongues were loosed.
They had never seen a ship, and their astonishment was very great in viewing its superior
structure. " What a people are they ! " was
their general exclamation. In the cabin, they
were struck with its order, and admired its
carpets. Scarcely could the savages of the
Pacific islands show more curiosity and amaze-
ment than these natives did. They engaged
immediately to bring off customers for our cargo,

and hastened home to give an account of all the strange things they had seen.

April 17.—During the night we heard the report of guns, the sure sign of the approach of war junks. Early in the morning we received a visit from the rear-admiral, an old stupid opium-smoker, who behaved in the most disrespectful and even insulting manner. It was remarked, by his companion, a mandarin with a crystal button, that he had lost his understanding by the immoderate use of this drug. We should otherwise have been at a loss to account for his silly behaviour and insolent language. However, Mr. Lindsay made to both of them a present of pictures, with which they were very highly delighted. The inferior mandarin pledged himself to bring off some purchasers.

Near our anchorage, is the city of Chin-tan, now chiefly in ruins. We ascended a hill which commanded a view of all the adjacent region. On the top was a platform, and some stones, engraved with unknown characters, which seemed to have been placed there many centuries ago. The inhabitants had cultivated, with the most assiduous care, every inch of arable land, and we could not but admire their ingenuity in watering their terraced plats. The city itself is extensive, but thinly peopled at present, for the pirates had destroyed it. We saw a few shops, and distributed some books. Close upon the shore, at the entrance of the city, stands a pyramid, about seventy feet high, very neatly built of massy granite, erected during the Ming dynasty. We entered it, and the more we examined it, the more we were led to admire its workmanship and durability. In front is an ancient temple, far gone to decay. We saw also many dilapidated images of Budha, with negro head and hair, very similar to those in Siam. This temple seemed to have been entirely abandoned. How earnestly should we pray that this may be the fate of all the fanes of idolatry, and that in their place may rise the temples of the living God! Whilst our company was examining the pyramid, I read and explained some passages from the tracts to the surrounding people, who were very much astonished at this new doctrine. They received gratefully some of our tracts, and took the utmost care to carry them away without being observed.

In the afternoon we visited the young mandarin who had been aboard. He had just risen from smoking opium, which had stupified him to such a degree, that he had forgotten his promise to bring purchasers. His whole war junk seemed a den of opium-smokers, for all the crew, in imitation of their noble captain, indulged freely in this narcotic. He told us that our ships had, a century ago, traded to this place. There was nothing but the utmost politeness in his conversation, at the same time that all his remarks showed a total want of moral principle. He seemed to be a little ashamed of the miserable appearance of his junk compared with our ship. He had a few cannon, made of cast iron, which seemed to be in the worst state imaginable.

There were several merchants desirous of coming on board, who were pursued by the mandarin boats, but escaped by a speedy flight. We returned to our ship and found her already under way, after being obliged to cut the cable of our friend, the rear-admiral. On our return, we met a fishing boat in tow of the mandarin boats, which, we afterwards heard, to our great mortification, had arrested the poor people because they had approached too near us. Doubtless their punishment will be as severe as that of the populace at Amoy; we regret that we did not rescue them from the hands of such cruel men. During the night, the war junks fired their

guns continually, and threw up rockets also, both
of which we imitated with very good effect.

April 18.—Owing to a continued calm, we are
still amidst the groups of islands. The want
of charts of this intricate passage, rendered our
situation very perilous. We shoaled aft to three
fathoms; and were actually at a loss how to get
off again. Having anchored opposite to a fishing
village, we visited the natives, who were at first
very shy, but when they perceived our peaceable
intentions, they became very familiar. They were
much struck with the construction of our fowling-
pieces, so different from their matchlocks, and
mistook them for opium pipes. Their hospitality formed a striking contrast to their extreme
poverty, for they invited us into their dirty hovels,
and shared with us their scanty supper. I gave
them the Holy Scriptures, by which they may
become rich in God, and find their present
miseries alleviated by the joyful and firm hope
of eternal riches.

We exchanged with them rice for fish. This
excited all the inhabitants to come and enjoy the
luxury, which they had not known for a long
time, of eating a sufficiency of rice. The smoke,
which was soon rising in every direction, showed

that we had provided them a banquet at so very trifling expense.

April 19.—To-day was a perfect calm, and we had therefore no alternative but to wait patiently or impatiently for a breeze. In the meanwhile, several fish-boats came to barter fish for rice, and were highly delighted with their profitable bargain. On their return home they fell into' the hands of the mandarin boatmen, who towed them to the admiral's junk. We much fear that they will suffer severely for having had intercourse with the barbarians.

A very polite note was put on board, making inquiries after us, and inviting us on shore. We expected to see a very great man, who had taken the trouble to invite the strangers, but found only a pawnbroker. He gave himself an air of much importance, and seemed anxious to inform government of our arrival; yet he behaved with much politeness, and showed also much sound understanding. We were so happy to-day as to get out of this dangerous passage, and to find ourselves once more in the open sea.

April 21.—We went on shore at Pih-keun-shan island, which is not far from the entrance of Fuh-chow harbour. The fertility of the island astonished us, for we had hitherto seen only sterility. The inhabitants had not cultivated it to the extent of which it was capable, but availed themselves principally of its pasturage for their goats. The natives lived in the most wretched hovels imaginable, and were filthy and rude in appearance. We could not have obtained a correct idea of pirates better than by seeing these natives, whose very physiognomy betokened great ferocity. Their language differed widely from all the dialects which we had yet heard. However, they could write, and thus assisted, our intercourse was mutually intelligible. There were no females among them, nor any comforts to distinguish them from mere savages. I left here some books, the perusal of which may arouse their untutored minds to reflection.

While advancing towards Fuh-chow, the capital of Fuh-keen province, we met several war-junks, despatched, doubtless, in quest of us. We happened to direct our spy-glass towards one of them, which so intimidated the crew that they ran below decks, and did not re-appear till they were sure of having escaped the danger. We could only ascribe their panic to mistaking the glass for a gun, which they supposed pointed at them.

April 22.—It is the commemoration of the Lord's resurrection. How far from all Christian society! How long have I been separated from the communion of the saints!

We arrived to-day in the harbour of Fuh-chow, after having, the day before, slightly touched the ground. The whole atmosphere was shrouded in darkness, which obscured the landmarks at the entrance of the harbour; yet we had excellent pilots on board, who brought us in safely. We are now come to that district whence the greatest quantity of tea is furnished for consumption in Europe.

The hills where the tea is cultivated, stretch abroad in every direction. The soil does not yield a sufficient quantity of rice for home consumption; however, the exports of timber, bamboo, and teas, more than balance the imports of rice and cotton. The whole region is very romantic: ridges of undulating hills, naked in part, and partly cultivated, in form of terraces, up to the top, give the whole a most picturesque aspect. The river, which leads up to the capital, is broad and navigable as far as the city. Here are no fragments of ancient edifices, or other classic ruins, but a display of Chinese industry and skill in all its variety. The villages and hamlets are very numerous all along the river; often in beautiful situations. The Dutch anciently traded at this port; but even the remembrance of it is now lost. Our appearance, therefore, struck the inhabitants with astonishment. The entrance of the river is in lat. 26° 6′, lon. 119° 55′. As soon as we had anchored, we were visited by the inhabitants of the adjacent village. They made no inquiries after trifles, but were anxious to ascertain the prices of our cargo, and invited us to their village. Fertile fields, sown with wheat, naked rocks, and plains of sand, gave a diversified aspect to the whole environs. We visited our friends in their houses, and held very long conversations with them, principally upon trade. They received the books with hearty pleasure, and read them most diligently. After going through the village, and scrambling over several cliffs, we were intending to return, but were pressingly invited by a merchant to partake of a supper, which he had prepared for us in a public hall. We supped, therefore, upon very good fare, among an immense crowd, who were extravagantly delighted to see us their guests, and urgent that we should partake freely of their refreshments. We felt very happy in the midst of these cheerful people, who did not act on the principle of the mandarins, that barbarians must be treated as enemies.

April 24.—Ignorant of the situation of Fuh-chow, we started in search of it. Steering north by west, the first object which drew our attention was a war-junk, anchored in a little bay. Hitherto we had not been annoyed by them, and we began to cherish the hope that we might escape their vexatious visits. The beautiful scenery on the banks of the river, which reminded me of the Rhine, in Germany, was enlivened by the numerous hamlets in all directions. We came to the entrance of a second river, which is more shallow than the first by which we came in. Near the junction, a village is built, with a granite jetty: on both sides are dismantled forts, apparently without garrisons. As soon as the mandarin on the opposite side espied us, he immediately ordered us to return. But finding us obstinate, he tried to terrify us by the tremendous peal of the gong. When every measure failed, he gave us over to the mercy of the other boats in pursuit of us. But as none of them could come up with us, they gave up the pursuit, and returned to their stations. When we had passed the narrow point of the river at Min-gan, the boats molested us no more, and we had the pleasure of admiring the cascades, which fell down the rocky declivities. Farther up is

an island, in the midst of the river: the water
shoals from seven to five and a half fathoms.
On the southern bank is a large pagoda, with
high, towering hills, in the back ground, cultivated up to the very summit. Many junks were
passing to and fro, to which we distributed books.

The river, which is here two miles broad,
divides into two branches; the northern, and
largest of which, leads to Fuh-chow. There is
a lofty mountain, bearing north-west one half
west from this: near the north bank of the river
is a large shoal, with two fathoms water; on the
south, varying from one to three fathoms. Perceiving, at a distance, a forest of junks, which we
supposed near the city, we steered for them, and
the city gradually opened to view. On a nearer
approach, the numerous small craft were found
to be coasters from the Che-keang province, and
vessels constructed purposely for the carriage of
timber and bamboo. The next object which
arrested our attention, was a great stone bridge;
a rude, but substantial structure, built quite across
this broad river. The natives, from all quarters,
crowded around us, to behold the novel sight of
foreigners. We speedily stepped ashore, and
found an easy passage through all the crowds,
whose politeness was by no means inferior to

their curiosity. As we had drawn up a petition, we proceeded in quest of the governor, passing through a very long street, both sides of which were lined with shops, richly supplied with every variety of merchandise. Many dwellings were spacious and commodious; and, though of wood, were built in an elegant Chinese style. The eyes of all were fixed upon us, and their reiterated inquiries were satisfied, by simply distributing a small pamphlet, which had been written " *upon the English nation.*" Scarcely any means adopted to promote a friendly intercourse, proved so effectual as the circulation of this paper. My patience was exhausted by the time of our arrival at the city gates, from whence we proceeded slowly to the Heën's office. Here we were encompassed by a crowd of curious police runners, who were incessant with their common'-place questions, till the arrival of a demure mandarin, who asked no more than was indispensably necessary, keeping his eyes at the same time fixed upon the ground. We were then shown into a small temple, and assured that supper was preparing. Meanwhile, we were invited to take a little warm water. Scarcely had we finished this water repast, when a servant came with a torch, and screaming, commanded his fellow-

L

servants to conduct us to another house of plenty. Our swift guides had all provided themselves with torches, and re-conducted us back to the city gate, and hurried us through the long street, which we had just passed. In the way, we met a strange and gaudy procession, or rather masquerade, apparently in honour of some god, whose huge image was borne by people dressed in yellow. Our sudden appearance amidst such a train, threw them into confusion. We hurried away, however, though weary and hungry, in the hopes of being conducted to good fare and lodgings. How great, then, was our surprise, to find ourselves suddenly surrounded by a number of mandarins, who insolently directed us to step immediately into our boat and depart. Hwang, a " civil" mandarin, with a white crystal button, continued to enact his authoritative injunctions to ears now deafened by his insolence. They, however, enforced their orders, by pressing us towards the water's edge, and leaving us no alternative, but to enter the boat or the water. Their greatest wonder was, that we should find our way to the city without a guide; and regarding this as impossible, they fixed on a young gentleman and myself, as the leaders of the party. They affirmed that they had seen us some time

since; confounding us with some sailors who
had been cast away near Hae-tan, and brought
to Fuh-chow.

As we, however, expostulated with them on
their inhospitable treatment, and insisted on our
right to quarters, they promised to bring us to a
boat for lodging. This we found overcrowded
with people, who had no previous intimation of
our coming; so we were under the necessity of
taking our abode in the custom-house, a very
airy mansion. But it did not end here. Hwang
contrived to entice us to a temple, where he had
assembled his fellow-mandarins to sit in judgment over us. Thus far he succeeded in drawing
us from our lodgings, but failed in his design,
which he urged very hard, of sending us into
the street for the night. After a long and useless
debate, we quietly made quarters for ourselves
in the room where our disappointed judges were
sitting. In order to secure tranquillity, we posted
a sentinel at the door, who had, however, to
perform the duty but a quarter of an hour, when
the mandarins all dispersed, greatly ashamed of
their unsuccessful stratagem.

April 25.—I was first aroused by them this
morning. Hwang, in very insinuating terms,
inquired after our books. When satisfied on this

point, he again tried to persuade me that I was
a Chinaman, very kindly entreating me to write
down the contents of the petition, that he might
report it to the governor. We had come, however, to have an audience with his excellency,
and therefore could only thank him for his kind
officiousness. Last night we had been regaled
upon warm water and sweet-meats, and this
morning we were expected to breakfast on board
a boat; but being vile barbarians, were by no
means allowed to take food on the shore of the
Celestial Empire. Instead of attending to these
proposals, we examined the stone bridge before
mentioned. It is about four hundred and twenty
paces long, built upon thirty-five huge pillars of
granite, and bears the name of Wan-show,
" Myriads of ages!" Though built with extreme rudeness, and having all the defects of
unskilful architecture, it is one of the most famous
bridges in the empire. Durability is a praise
which it well deserves, considering its great
length, the rapidity of the current, and the total
absence of arches.

Finding that we were only embarrassed continually by the mandarins, we went out of their
way, and visited other parts of the city; and
were making preparations to re-embark, when

our friend Hwang made his appearance in a
large boat, inviting us to come aboard. We had
had too many proofs of his studied insolence to
make another trial. There was a large Soo-
chow junk in the harbour, the crew of which
were very anxious to see us, and show their
friendliness.

In our return we walked along the shore.
Nothing could surpass the enjoyment we had in
passing through so beautiful a country; and
though we had to scramble over many preci-
pices, our trouble was richly compensated by the
sublime prospects we enjoyed. We distributed
several books to eager and grateful readers.
Botany might here have had a large field for
its researches; but unfortunately none of us understood any thing of it. Many people came
near us, and inquired the prices of various
articles.

The natives spoke with admiration of Mingan,
a fortress built on the declivity of a hill. We
stopped at the place, and ascended the hill by
granite steps till we saw one of the finest places
imaginable. The fortifications were built in the
form of terraces; several large trees overshadowed
the precipitous sides; gardens adorned both the
valley and the fort; and the town was situated

at the foot of this romantic hill. Nothing can describe our agreeable surprise, when, after having ascended one terrace, another enchanting view opened; thus continuing, one after another, till we arrived at the summit, when we could overlook multitudes of the gardens and plantations beneath us. When we descended to the town, we were soon surrounded by the inquisitive natives and sportive children. When we left, some mandarin boats escorted us, to protect us, as we were told. When we had gone some distance, one of the boats came nearer, and wished to make some arrangements in regard to trade, but was interrupted by the sudden arrival of a second one.

April 26.—Mr. L. and the captain took proper care that the unjust punishments of the natives, who might approach us, should not be repeated here, as at Amoy. We were visited by the mandarin of this district, a civil and sagacious old man. He had received orders from the deputy-governor of Fuhkeen province to procure a certain number of our Christian books for the inspection of the emperor. I gave him, accordingly, one copy of " Scripture Lessons," a tract on Gambling, " Heaven's Mirror," a full delineation of Christianity, besides a few other books

of which he had copies before. I was highly
delighted that God, in his wisdom, was sending
his glorious gospel to Peking, that it might be
fully examined and known in the palace. Taou-
Kwang has never shewn himself an enemy to
popery. In all his edicts against the sects and
heresies in his dominions, he does not even
mention the name of Christian. Though I
know nothing of his character, except that he
delights more in pleasure than in business, I
humbly hope that the perusal of the word of
God will impress his mind favourably towards
the gospel. It is the first time that the Chinese
government has taken the trouble to examine the
oracles of God. The depravity of the human
heart, which is as great in the rulers of China as
anywhere, I fear will not permit them to perceive
the glory of God in a crucified Saviour. Yet it
is the cause of God. The mighty God and the
Saviour will advocate his own cause, and defend
it by his omnipotent arm. His mercy embraces
China as well as enlightened Europe. The
Chinese are his creatures as well as ourselves,
and the gospel is given for their salvation likewise. His wisdom will find ways to convey it to
their minds. Though we are unable to fathom
his purposes, we wait for the glorious day when

the door will be thrown open, and the gospel ride triumphantly through the land.

I began, to-day, my medicinal operations with a great number of sick people. To this even the mandarins could not object.

April 27.—A reinforcement of war ، junks arrived, and the behaviour of the mandarins was immediately changed. Though they had promised us to give the people full permission to come aboard, they now not only threatened them, but ourselves also. We therefore went and complained to the admiral, who promised redress. Towards evening the junks were moored close around us. We requested the admiral to remove so far as to permit our ship to swing round with the tide, which he refused. The captain sent some people on board his junk, who cut his cable. This spread general consternation, and the following day the whole fleet withdrew into the river.

April 29.—As soon as the fleet had withdrawn, we were visited by great numbers of traders and patients. Yang, the local literary mandarin, came to expostulate with us on account of the damage done. He was a Mohammedan, from Sze-chuen province, and appeared to know a little of the doctrines of the Koran, for he was very careful not

to eat pork. Some Arabic sentences were familiar
to him, but the Chinese organs of speech can
scarcely pronounce the Arabic well. His joy
was very great to find some among the sailors
who had the same creed. He denied that he
worshipped idols, but was by no means superior
to his Pagan countrymen in his moral character.
Whilst affirming that the Mohammedans never
tell lies, and with every important assertion repeating the imprecation, " May heaven's thunder
strike me," he told the most palpable falsehoods,
unmindful of his dreadful oath. I made several
inquiries respecting the Mohammedans of China.
Many of them appear to be the descendants of
Turkish tribes west of China. They were never
numerous, nor ever had influence in the councils
of government. They pretend to serve no idols ;
but, if they are officers under government, this is
almost unavoidable ; for at the stated festivals
every mandarin must appear in the temple, and
make his prostrations. On such occasions, however, they solve their scruples by the excuse that
their heart does not participate in this abominable
worship, but they externally comply with it as a
mere governmental usage.

We were to-day invited to the ceremony of
hearing a reply to our petition, which had been

addressed to the viceroy of Fuhkeen. We found
a number of mandarins in a boat moored opposite
to a military station, Tang-ko, and among them
the adjutant of his excellency. Instead of receiving a reply to our own petition, we were
presented with an answer to a statement drawn
up from our petition by a military mandarin, and
presented to the viceroy. This answer contained
a refusal of our request. No barbarian ships
were allowed to come to this place, and no tea
could be exported by way of sea. We drew up
another petition, therefore, and humbly expressed
our wish for a direct answer, not to the representations of others, but to our own.

In the mean time I was fully employed in
healing the sick, who came in crowds from all
quarters. They were afflicted with cutaneous
diseases and ophthalmic complaints. A great
many complained of the " heart-ache," others of
the asthma, and not a few of coughs. I was
highly rejoiced that they came and afforded
so good opportunities of proving our friendly
intentions. Some among them were suffering
intensely, and after being relieved, shewed themselves very grateful. Their presents were numerous, and their letters of thanks very hearty;
I had often more than a hundred a day, and

might have had triple the number, if I had had time to attend to all the applicants.

I praise God for the grace bestowed upon me, to be a distributor of his holy word. Here was ample opportunity to communicate these holy treasures; for the people were anxious to see and study the books which the emperor was to examine. Often when I came upon deck all hands were stretched out to receive them; a scuffle would ensue, and loud complaints were vented by them whose wishes were not satisfied. I frequently visited the adjacent villages; the houses were comfortable, except from their want of cleanliness. The people themselves seemed to bestow little care to wash their persons and preserve neatness; and hence the frequency of cutaneous diseases. They were invariably friendly, when we entered their dwellings, and communicative upon all our questions. After passing through the villages, we generally found a temple built with great care. But a small part of this was destined to religious purposes, the larger part was a stage. This seems to be true of all the temples we saw, and is truly characteristic of the regard in which the Chinese hold their idols, and of the manner of worship which they offer to them.

May 2.—After waiting long for an answer to our petition, we found that all the promises given us were intended merely to encourage our hopes, till they could find some means of sending us empty away. Even Yang, our steady visitor, took no longer the trouble to come and confer with us. Instead of this, two very *fierce* edicts had been issued against us, prohibiting every body from coming on board. We had expressly stipulated, *free intercourse*, and this had been granted and affirmed repeatedly, so that this breach of promise was the more irritating. We therefore decided formally to enter the harbour, or rather the river.

May 3. This decision produced immediate effect. The mandarins are now mild and yielding, and have become sureties for our permission to trade.

The patients become daily more numerous and clamorous, and the number of books distributed increases. Our trade also wears a very favourable aspect, so that we begin to be reconciled to our situation; withal we rejoice, that none of the natives are punished for holding intercourse with us.

At the close of our daily business, which generally lasted eight or ten hours, we often traversed the extensive rice fields. The people have shown much ingenuity in laying out these fields. To satisfy immediate want, seems to be the object of the Chinese peasant. Instead of cultivating grain, and a variety of vegetables equally nutritious, he is satisfied to plant the rice, and seldom cultivates vegetables to any extent. Every corner is planted with rice, and, in the cold season, with wheat, for they have here two crops a-year.

Their daily food, with scarcely any variation, is rice, with a few vegetables as a relish. Meats seldom fall to the lot of the common people, except on holidays, and even the higher ranks consume meat more sparingly than the common people in Europe or America. No Chinese in the southern provinces, will admit that he has made a meal, unless he has eaten a sufficient quantity of rice. Even at their grand festivals, where a great variety of dishes is prepared, they end with rice. It is not surprising, therefore, that they undervalue all other vegetable diets, and bestow so much pains to supply each member of their families with a sufficiency of rice.

Gardening rarely engages their attention, for, though fond of flowers, they prefer the artificial to the natural. They are very skilful in the fabrication of them, and females, of all ages and ranks, constantly purchase them as ornaments of the hair.

We received, to-day, a paper written with red ink, from a person pretending to be very anxious for our welfare, because some of his ancestors had been saved from a watery grave by people of our nation. He had heard that we were in imminent danger of death, if we were so daring as to advance farther, and so pertinacious as not to retire out of the river; that our destruction had been agreed on, but the Tartar general, who was to have executed this bloody work, not agreeing to it, we were still permitted to breathe. Whoever originated this plot, (and we strongly suspect the mandarins,) ought to have been surprised at the consternation which our entrance into the harbour immediately threw among all our adversaries; not even the most feeble resistance was offered. The mandarins were humble and kind; the soldiers withdrew every where from our path, and the most perfect tranquillity prevailed. The people rejoiced at this happy change, and improved the opportunity to secure our friendship. Their letters of civility and advice were numerous, and their demonstrations of kind feeling still more frequent. To receive such treatment from the people, and then to read, what has so often been repeated, that the Chinese nation detest foreigners, and are averse from all intercourse with them, led us to doubt this assertion. My little experience rather leads me to think them a most social people, whenever free from the immediate influence of the mandarins. But to say that the Chinese government discountenances and severely prohibits intercourse with strangers, is strictly true. In general, the officers were never more annoyed than when the people showed themselves our friends, and we returned their kind feelings. They frequently endeavoured to give us the worst ideas of the stupid and treacherous natives, while trying to prepossess them against us also by the most abusive edicts; but on each side unsuccessfully, for the veil was too thin to hide their palpable falsehoods.

May 6.—It is the Lord's day, and an excessive crowd of customers are on board. We received to-day a chart of the river, executed by our friend who had given us the previous warning. He pointed out the station of the ambush, and described the batteries destined to blow us up. But his exhortations were lost upon the fierce

barbarians, who could not believe any danger
was to be apprehended, while the mandarins
were so dispirited.

This was to me one of the most happy days
spent in China. There was a real desire for books;
and the applications for them were made in so
earnest a manner as to preclude a refusal. I am
ignorant of the effect produced by their perusal,
but some of the blessed effects of divine truth
upon the hearts of the readers will remain.
Considering it as the work of God, and as the
salvation of souls from eternal condemnation,
I am prepared to hope and believe that our
Almighty God will give growth to the good seed
sown. There are great obstacles to the efficacy
of the divine word, but it is quick and powerful,
sharper than any two-edged sword, and is a
discerner of the thoughts of the heart. Occasionally I sat down with the people, and spoke
about their eternal peace. Though these words
sounded strange to their ears, since every thing
beyond the reach of sense is strange and unintelligible to a Chinese mind, yet the words will
not be entirely lost. I have often by comparisons
made the doctrines palpable to their comprehen-
sion. They will listen for a time, but after this

it is quite useless to recommence; for they generally withdraw their attention and turn their conversation to other topics.

The number of patients is rather increasing;
and many of them come from a great distance.
They are very urgent in their requests, and so
sure of the good effects of the medicines, that
they apply them with the greatest confidence.
I received several papers expressive of their
gratitude, and a great number of presents.

Hitherto we had never seen any native Christian, but to-day we perceived a man with a paper
rolled up in his hand, which he was anxious to
hide from the other people. He asked me
whether I knew the objects there represented.
Upon examination I found it a representation of
the Trinity, executed in Spain. From his conversation I perceived him to be very ignorant of
Christianity, but he adduced decisive proof of
being a real believer. He showed me the cross
which his wife wore around her neck, with a
rosary. Yang, the mandarin, had previously
informed us that the number of native Christians
in his district was very great, especially among
the boat people. This man confirmed Yang's
information, said they were all very poor, and
had no European among them. He could give

me no account of the rise and progress of Christianity here, neither did he seem to be aware of the extent to which it was known in other countries.

May 12.—The native Christians came in greater numbers. One of them handed a paper, to prove that popery was the same as our religion. He claimed fraternity with us, and used every means of persuasion to convince us, that as our religion was the same, we ought to show benevolence towards our poor brethren. Another handed us a paper, expressing his great surprise that we should be in possession of the *holy book*, which contains the relation of the Saviour's life; the more so, because they themselves had begun only last year to print this holy book; and how it could so soon have reached us, he was unable to explain. At the same time, he warned us against giving this holy book to any people afflicted with the blindness of heathenism, because they would not understand its contents. He also requested some prayer-books, which he might study privately. I was anxious to see those parts of the holy book which his friends had already printed, but he refused to produce them. After receiving a manual for prayer he departed highly gratified. I do not know how far he was interested in the spread of the Bible; but his objections to the distribution of it among the heathen are light, and unworthy of a Christian. Yet I should rejoice if they would print the Bible, or the New Testament only, and circulate it among themselves at least, if they are too narrow-minded to impart it to the heathen.

I have been very desirous to converse with some of the native priests, and to-day was rejoiced to see a well-dressed young man introduce himself as a Christian teacher. Whilst all the other Christians were rude and illiterate, he exhibited much polish in his manners, and was well versed in Chinese literature. Yet his knowledge of Christianity was very superficial and unsatisfactory; but he promised to study diligently to become acquainted with the heavenly doctrines. I supplied him amply with Christian books.

When will the time come that the converts to Christianity will be genuine converts; Christians by grace, cleansed from all sins by the efficacious application of Christ's blood!

During this period we had been very successful in trade, and we might have traded to a greater amount if we had not demanded too high a price, and been desirous to retain our cargo

for the northern ports. Mr. L. therefore, resolved to leave this port for Ning-po. Thither
the mandarins had directed us, and earnestly
requested us to go for the disposal of the remainder of our cargo.

May 16.—Two naval officers, one of whom
had addressed a letter to Mr. L. came to make
us a visit. In this elaborate and quaint communication he justified their conduct in inter-
fering with our stipulated arrangements, by the
orders received from the viceroy, and excused
themselves for the degradation of our coming
into their very harbour by the dispensation of
fate. Instead of cherishing hostile feelings, they
crave our friendship, and beseech us as friends
to leave the port. The writer of the letter, who
seems to have expressed the sentiments of his
brother officers, was a man of very polished
manners and cultivated mind. He frankly acknowledged his mistake in supposing us warriors
rather than merchants. " Whenever," added he,
" your ship may arrive here again we will immediately arrange the articles for trading, so that
myself will not be implicated in the danger, and
you will lose no time." We asked him whether
he desired us to interest ourselves that he might
regain the rank which he had lost on our account.

" Only quit the harbour," he replied, " and I shall regain lost favour."

May 17.—We got under way after receiving a final visit from our warm friend who had so often warned us against the " imminent danger." To-day he acquainted us that he was a *Keu-jin*, a literary graduate of the third degree, anxious to go to the capital and pass the examination, in order to obtain a higher rank. As he was short of money, however, he applied to Mr. L. for a present adequate to defray his travelling expenses to Peking. Dissatisfied with receiving so little he left us.

CHAPTER IV.

MAY 21.—Highly pleased with our reception at Fuh-chow, we now steered towards Che-keang. Many fishermen, natives of this province, came aboard, and showed much vivacity and decorum. They examined every corner of the vessel; inquired the use of the various parts; and retired, delighted with what they had seen. In general, they were not tall, but stout, and apparently inured to hardship. The Fuhkeen fishermen, who spend several months of the year along the coasts of Keang-nan and Che-keang, in fishery and occasional piracies, are very daring and rough seamen. No weather can detain them in the harbours. In the highest seas they will venture out of their smacks into a small boat, scarcely sufficient to contain four persons. A great many of them, every year, therefore, are drowned. All this peril is endured to obtain a scanty pittance to sustain their lives, for they are generally very poor, and often even wanting rice.

May 25.—Yesterday, we entered the Chu-san passage, which leads to Ning-po. We did not here observe the same crowded population which we had elsewhere seen. All around us was silent as the grave. Only a few villages, and some temples, were visible in the distant and still recesses of the mountains enclosing us. We soon saw several junks entering and leaving, one of which, from Fuhkeen, we boarded, and found the captain inquisitive, but an inveterate opium-smoker. He showed us a Chinese map; and, being aware of its geographical errors, he was desirous of correcting and extending his information. The Chinese, in general, are very tenacious of their errors, more especially in geography and in nautical science. We, therefore, admired the more this man's candour. He was from Formosa, and was slightly acquainted with our nation, from the perusal of the pamphlet before mentioned. His cargo consisted of sugar, destined for the Shang-hae market, whither at least a hundred junks from Formosa annually repair. Whilst we were conversing with these boatmen, a mandarin boat passed, and fired a few crackers, to intimidate us. This called forth a laugh even from the sailors of the junk. When we returned to the ship, several mandarin boats had already come along-side. In their exterior there was nothing superior, nor any thing interesting in their questions. They retired very soon, requesting us to wait further orders before we proceeded to Ning-po, and left us.

We pursued our course through a most extraordinary passage, having the appearance of a broad river. The tide was running very strong, producing in some places an eddy, which makes the passage very dangerous. In vain we sought anchorage, for the depth of the water exceeded the length of our cable, till, after long search, we found twenty-five fathoms, close to some junks, and anchored for the night.

We saw verdant hills, but very few dwellings. It is surprising to us to observe so much fertile ground uncultivated. We could never find the reason for a thing so extraordinary in China.

May 26.—We set out to-day in our long-boat for Ning-po. Ignorant of its situation, we followed the junks, which entered the river by a passage between the land and an island. By not keeping at a proper distance from the shore we got upon a rock, from which, however, we

succeeded in getting off again. Scarcely any
body impeded our progress, till we came to a
war-junk, where we were hailed. On the top
of a hill, at the entrance, is a fort, the best we
have hitherto seen in China. The buildings in
it have something Gothic in appearance; and
though the garrison is not numerous, yet the
fort is so excellently situated as entirely to command the river. The course at the entrance of
the river is south-west: not far up is an island,
or rather a rock, which we first thought was the
" Triangle" of the charts. The harbour presented a very lively scene. Junks were anchored
in all directions; and, judging from the great
number of vessels constantly entering and leaving
the port, trade must be in a very flourishing
condition. Chin-hae, the place at the entrance,
is a walled town, with a great number of ships
outside.

As soon as the mandarins got sight of us,
they despatched a boat in pursuit, which being
unable to overtake us, ran ashore, when the
soldiers in her jumped out, and ordered us to
stop. It may appear strange that we did not
obey this summons; but it must be remembered that our object was to deliver a petition to
the principal magistrate of Ning-po, and that the

local mandarins, as at this place, dislike nothing more than our gaining access to the higher mandarins. They failed, however, here, as well as every where, though they prevailed on a few naked boys to throw stones at us.

The banks of this river are so low that dykes are very necessary : the whole region, with the exception of long ridges of sterile hills, is highly cultivated. It was the time of wheat harvest, and all the people were in the fields, cutting their corn, which this year amply repaid their labour. Even in the houses of the peasants we remarked more comfort and neatness than in the parts we had hitherto visited. To a mandarin boat which had come up with us we gave a report of our ship, and passed on undisturbed towards Ning-po, situated about eleven miles up the river. The noise of junk-building, and the large quantities of timber which were piled up on both sides of the stream, announced the neighbourhood of Ning-po. The people looked very disdainfully at us, and repeatedly called out hih-kwei, " black devils." In the middle of the city the river divides into two branches, neither of which has fresh water. The junks here were larger and more numerous than at Fuh-chow. While in search of the principal office we passed a broad street, well lined with the most elegant shops, which even exceed those at Canton. European manufactures, as well as Chinese, were here displayed to much advantage. Mirrors and pictures also, with the most splendid silks, embellished and decorated the scene.

We were first shown to the office of the Che-heen, a magistrate of a small district, several of which make a Foo. Our names were noted down, the particulars of our voyage inquired into, and this, as well as all the other accounts, delivered in writing. As soon as we had duly reported, the Che-heen, who was an elderly man, and wore a white button, came out, and offered to introduce us to the Che-Foo. We followed him at some distance amidst a numerous crowd, and finally came to a large hall with many books, destined for the examination of the lowest graduates, the Sew-tsae. The police runners belonging to this office are very numerous, but by no means kept the people in order who thronged the passage, and could not be prevailed on to leave their stations.

The Che-Foo, a stout man, of a very pleasing countenance, with a blue button, soon made his appearance. Mr. Lindsay formally delivered his petition. He began immediately to read it; and after having finished it, he turned towards us and said, " This matter deserves our attention ; we ought to deliberate upon the subject. In the mean while I shall provide you with a lodging and board. Don't you think this is right? " Upon receiving answer in the affirmative, he immediately ordered his servants to conduct us to our lodgings. We crossed a floating bridge, and arrived at the leang-kung, Fuhkeen hall. This was an extensive building, with spacious rooms, adorned with Chinese pictures and idols. A very sumptuous supper was served up in the evening, and every attention shown us to make us comfortable. We were fully sensible of this uncommon degree of kindness, and made no remarks upon the dirty room where we were to pass the night. In front of it were different idols, all gilt; one of them was inscribed with the name of the emperor, and received his regular supply of incense with much more attention than his neighbours.

May 27.—During the whole night the vociferating crowds had never wholly left us. To-day they re-assembled, and were not less anxious to satisfy their curiosity than yesterday. Yet they observed decorum towards us, and one hint from us would silence the most clamorous crowd. Several merchants made inquiries after the prices of our merchandise. Some of the inferior officers asked us what were the countries bordering on our territories in Asia, and how far our power extended. We were upon the point of going out to view the city when we received a visit from several mandarins, both military and civil. Two of these were Turkomans by descent, and Mohammedans by profession. Ma, one of them, was a tall man, with a blue button, and had passed some time at Macao and Canton. He was a very intelligent man, well acquainted with the customs of foreigners, and versed in all the diplomatic arts of mandarins. The mandarins in general are exceedingly ignorant of all the concerns of foreign countries which are either not immediately under the sway of the Celestial Empire, or bordering upon it. They were astonished to hear that our India possessions were separated only by forests and mountains from the Chinese province of Yunnan, and could scarcely believe that we were so near them. Ma, however, waived these topics of petty alarms, and entered into a full discussion upon the European powers which traded to China. He referred to Arabia and Persia as the cradle of

Mohammedanism, and tried to repeat some Arabic phrases to show his adherence to the system of religion which was delivered in that language. He was ample in his praise of European character, highly extolled the advantages of a trade with them, and frequently addressed the other mandarins upon the subject with true Persian flattery, and empty Chinese compliments. Yet his conversation was most interesting, and would have been valuable but for being intermixed with too palpable adulation. We received apparently the most cordial farewell of the mandarins, who, whilst we were going to the long boat, came down towards the river, and bowed as long as we were in sight. The people, who by this time had read our "Pamphlet" on the English nation, were highly gratified with such an exhibition, and showed us the utmost attention. We bought several articles from the shops, inquired after others for exportation, and answered all the numerous questions of the natives.

Returning by a circuitous route to our boat, we came to the city wall, a very massive structure, but overgrown with weeds, and in a state of decay. We had here a view of the whole city. In extent it may vie with Fuh-chow, and in population is not inferior to many of the large

trading towns of Europe. It surpasses any
thing Chinese which we have yet seen, in the
regularity and magnificence of the buildings, and
is behind none in mercantile fame. The Portuguese traded to this place as early as the sixteenth century. They found here a ready market
for European products, and they exported hence
to Japan a great amount of silk. After being
once expelled they renewed it again, and other
European nations participated with them in the
trade, till the extortions became so great as to
limit the foreign merchants to Canton. The
English East India Company maintained a factory here till the last century. Whilst we were
at Ning-po, we received a list of the ships which
had formerly been at this port. They seemed
to be very numerous; but at the present time no
traces of the foreign trade are to be seen, though
the old people retain still a faint remembrance
of the foreigners. Here the celebrated Jesuits
from France, near the end of the seventeenth
century, landed, and obtained permission to settle
at Peking. Two of them became the constant
attendants of the emperor, Kang-he, in all his
travels, and were the partners of his dangers in
the Tartarian war. What great results might
one have expected from such an opportunity,

both to benefit the highest personages in the empire, and to impart to the people the blessings of Christianity! In these hopes we have been greatly disappointed. Instead of introducing the reign of truth, they created intrigue; in lieu of pure religion they spread popery. Though possessing the greatest talents, they never devoted them simply to the glory of their Saviour; they never employed them in giving to the benighted heathen, in their own language, the blessed gospel of our Lord Jesus Christ. This is truly lamentable; that they should bestow such labours, encounter such sacrifices, and defend their tenets with such heroism, to found an *earthly religion*, which confers few blessings in this life, and leads to a doubtful eternity. In offering these sentiments, there is no design to depreciate their talents, or to vilify their religious zeal; but it is the language of deep regret to see the salvation of the soul neglected amidst the best opportunities of securing it; and the most trifling ceremonies predominate over the eternal welfare of men, which should have been the *prime* object in all their operations. But to return.

Highly delighted with the hospitable reception we experienced, we attributed it to the influence which the perusal of our little tract had had

upon the natives. Crowds of people were collected at the beach to give us a kind farewell,
whilst mandarins of all ranks vied with each
other in their expressions of friendship.

May 28.—In our return we remarked the
dangers of this passage ; the water shoaled from
sixteen to one and a half fathoms. We were
to-day visited by great numbers of mandarins.
Among them were two naval officers, an aid of
the admiral, and a messenger from the Che-Foo.
The former stated his excellency was coming the
next day to pay us a visit. It was therefore
necessary to stay and obey in silence, till he
should decide according to our wishes. They
again inquired respecting our cargo, and one of
them remarked, "You have nowhere sold any
thing; how can you expect to effect any sales
here?" As we, however, gave him proof of the
contrary, he departed quietly. Several war-junks,
in the mean time, had anchored near us. After
having surveyed the passage, we got under way
for the entrance of Ning-po river. This sudden
resolution threw all the mandarins into consternation. They immediately left our ship, hoisted
sail, and followed us.

Having arrived at our anchorage, we fired
three salutes, which roused the soldiers from

their stupor. We now went to visit the Che-
heën, of Chin-hae, who had pressingly invited
us to call when we came down two days before.
The concourse of people was very great, and
neither threats nor blows could deter them
from looking at us. Though prohibited to land,
we ascended a stone pier, and went up to a
temple, which served also for a public hall and a
stage. Here we met our friends the mandarins,
and both the Mohammedans, Ma and Le, whom
we had seen at Ning-po, joined them. They
earnestly expostulated with us for approaching
so near the city. We replied, that our laws
permitted their vessels to come immediately into
our ports, without petitioning government, and
therefore we in return expected the same liberal
treatment. To this they could not object, as
they had declared themselves our warm friends;
but they remarked, that our premature entrance
would involve the local mandarins in trouble.
We promised to interpose with the admiral in
their behalf; and, as his excellency also had
made large professions of friendship, we hoped
he would yield to our representation. Meanwhile, the people were all gazing upon us,
highly enjoying the novel sight. In our return,
we distributed many tracts, to grateful readers;

afterwards, we went aboard a large war-junk. The commander asked some impertinent questions, for his spirit was wounded, or rather, his national pride had been severely hurt; therefore, he painted in the most lively colours the displeasure of his excellency, which they must experience. After promising our aid to soften his excellency's wrath, he replied, " Before your face he will be friendly, and grant your request; but behind your backs, he will reprimand us severely, and punish us besides." We visited afterwards his fellow-officers, who took it less to heart. They granted that our way of despatching business was the best; " but what could they do who must act according to the laws of their country?" After having given them a store of consolation from the Chinese classics, we returned to our ship, little moved by the charge of rash encroachment.

It will seem strange, that whatever step we take, we are accused of wantonly transgressing the laws of the Celestial Empire. To persons unacquainted with the laws and regulations of exclusion, this must be inexplicable. " Do not approach our country!" is the general prohibition, which would be violently enforced, if it could be with safety. Conscious of their physical weakness, and persuaded of the impracticability of their unreasonable law, the naval officers, who guard the coast against intruders, always endeavour to prevail by threats, which they never carry into execution, or by repeating the prohibitions of the " inviolable laws." Both measures are vain, when once a vessel enters the harbours. They are there ready to furnish provisions, if required, and to allow a certain trade to be carried on, which they cannot prevent. The only condition they make is, to leave the harbour within a stipulated time, after which they report to their superior mandarins, that they have driven away the barbarian ship. Future traders visiting the coast ought to remember this. The more they understand the spirit of the system, the better they will be able, without injury to the mandarins, to obtain their object.

May 29.—This morning the admiral arrived, and was saluted by many a shot from the guns, whilst we only fired three salutes, which re-echoed through hill and dale. To make the event more solemn, the soldiers blew upon a horn, like that of a herdsman, and accompanied this dismal sound with the gong. As soon as his excellency arrived, measures were taken to

seize the people, who had become numerous, and were anxious to trade. We saved
the soldiers the trouble of beating them, and
sent a very polite note aboard the war-junk,
entreating of the mandarins free permission for
the people to come and go.

In the afternoon, we visited several villages
farther up the river, where we had before lodged
a night. So dense is the population here, that
the greatest industry, exerted upon a soil so
fertile, can barely procure their subsistence, from
the small extent of ground. In our excursion,
we went to the salt-boilers, and visited many
neat shops. Even this, our innocent walk,
created suspicion in the mandarins, who disliked
the friendly reception which the inhabitants gave
us. We explained to them, that it was not our
wish to oppose the laws of the empire, but we
could not believe that there were any laws *com-
pelling* to such misanthropy. Why not give the
people opportunity to see our faces; and, as
fellow-men, why not be allowed to visit their
abodes? To all this they replied, " Your reasoning is very good, but our laws forbid you
this intercourse."

May 30. — We were to-day invited to an
audience to hear an answer to our petition. The

Che-heën of Chin-hae, talked very reasonably; but some of the mandarins used most outrageous language, and uttered palpable falsehoods. After a preamble about the difficulties of carrying on trade without the special permission of the emperor, they showed us a circular, issued by the deputy-governor of Fuhkeen, strictly prohibiting all trade with us. They were pleased to call us deceitful and crafty barbarians, who, like rats, sneaked into every corner. Though this order was only addressed to the officers, and by no means a reply to our petition, yet we were indignant that such words had been used against us; and showed that our conduct had always been just the opposite. This answer alarmed them; and they finally regretted having shown us a document, which only provoked us, and did them not the least good. It was evident, that the mandarins intended to excuse their future oppressions, by a recital of laws, which had been prescribed as their general rule of conduct towards foreigners.

May 31.— To-day we removed to another anchorage, because the strength of the tide continually endangered our cable. As we had received no reply to our petition, and the communication from the mandarins had rather ended in dissatisfaction on our part, and vexation on theirs, a new audience was to take place to-day, when all things should be settled. To render this new conference the more formal and satisfactory, the highest personages were to attend; for we had drawn up a remonstrance for the higher authorities. We found the two military commanders, both of the general officers, and a civil mandarin, with a blue button, seated under a canopy, in the open air. On each side they had stationed soldiers, with fire-arms, regularly drawn up in line; and to heighten the solemnity, a great many military officers, of all ranks, surrounded them; whilst flags, in the back ground, gave to the whole a martial aspect. The spectators were exceedingly numerous, but were quiet and orderly. After being previously instructed in the ceremonies, we proceeded slowly into the assembly, and after some explanation, were seated. The admiral seemed an elderly man, of very dark complexion, good humoured, and of winning aspect. He wore two peacock feathers, as proof of the merits of his government over some barbarian tribes in the empire. The other military mandarin had nothing extraordinary in his appearance, but seemed to be present merely to echo the words of his superior. Nothing could be more striking than their contrast with the literary mandarin, whose looks and language both immediately showed the bitterest enmity against barbarians. The admiral began with stating, that many years ago an English factory had been established at Ning-po; but having long been discontinued, it was very inconvenient now to recommence it. The civil mandarin commented upon this in the most virulent language, till he was interrupted by Mr. Lindsay. He briefly stated the reasons of our coming hither, not as enemies, but friends, desirous to revive those old regulations which unhappily had fallen into disuse. We founded our hope of trading on their justice and generosity. We allowed that opposing laws existed; but more ancient regulations, (which, according to the Chinese sentiment, are preferable,) gave us full liberty to trade to this harbour. Under such circumstances, we were highly grieved that such abusive language had been used against us in a public paper. As soon as this sentence was uttered, they exclaimed against our rudeness; and to silence our reproaches, handed us a copy of the letter with which the deputy-governor had accompanied our books to the emperor. Though we had received the repeated promise of the

governor that he would properly represent our
cause, and would co-operate with us in having
the harbours of the north opened, yet we perceived from this document, that he only asked
imperial sanction to what he had done in driving
the barbarians off, without a moment's delay.
He also requested that the degradation of several
officers, who had been remiss, should be confirmed, and concluded with expressing his anxiety
to learn the imperial pleasure. We then presented our petition, which they at first refused to
receive. None of the general officers could read:
the literary mandarin, therefore, glanced it over,
and explained to them its contents, The petition
was then returned to us, but we did not receive
it. When we expressed our gratitude for the
attention received, the admiral replied, that even
if our sovereigns had been at war, we should
have been treated in the same manner, for we
were strangers.

After the audience, Le and Ma, our two
friends, visited us, in order to come to some
understanding about the trade. I deeply regretted that the people were not allowed to
come aboard, since I was thereby cut off from
the performance of my duties. All our remonstrances upon this subject proved fruitless; and

I had even to give up the patients with whom I had commenced some days before. This was distressing to me, for amongst so friendly a people, I had expected a rich harvest. I felt persuaded that the distribution of books here, would be more useful than even at Fuh-chow, and so far as it was tried, the experiment had confirmed my opinion.

June 1.—Some Fuhkeen merchants visited us to-day, and expressed a desire to trade, but also the impossibility of doing so on account of the mandarins. When they went away, they assured us that we should get no customers, unless we boldly entered the river, and left the mandarins no alternative but compliance with our wishes. This afternoon we went ashore. As soon as we had entered the river, a mandarin boat came up, desiring us to return. On shore we were surrounded by soldiers, armed with swords and sticks. We spoke of the delay in fulfilling their promise to trade, but received no satisfactory reply. Ma told us that he had been absent to-day, because he was obliged to accompany the admiral to a temple, where he publicly and solemnly worshipped the idols. As this was so directly opposed to the injunctions of Mohammed, I asked him whether he did not consider himself polluted by being present at idolatrous worship. He disclaimed all actual participation, and considered it as a mere ceremony.

June 2.— New visits from our merchants. They seemed to be in earnest to purchase, but shewed a great deal of roguery. Yun, a naval commander of a war-junk, of Fuhkeen parents, and my friend, came aboard with a mandarin wearing a gold button. They told us that all the mandarins stationed at Ting-hae, at the entrance of the passage to this harbour, were to be degraded for permitting us to pass, but he himself had endeavoured to avoid this hard sentence by bribes. As for himself he heartily wished that his superiors were on better terms with us, and that they would give permission to trade, to the mutual advantage of both parties. His admiral cherished the same sentiments towards us, and contested the point very warmly with the other mandarins. " He argued strongly to facilitate intercourse with you; he even made the Che-Foo his enemy, who returned indignant to Ning-po. He is also anxious to visit you, but the fear of E, the Taou-tae, prevents him from doing so. Our viceroy, who will refuse you the trade, has represented the matter to the emperor. The only course to be adopted in

such circumstances, is to send an intrepid, royal
envoy, to his imperial majesty, to arrange these
mercantile concerns. If he is a man who can
overawe vile intrigue, and maintain his point
against all objections, and if he has full authority
to demand, he will surely succeed."

This was his private opinion, which, in some
degree, coincided with the advice received from
Ma and other mandarins.

The guns of the fort were again fired whilst
his excellency, the admiral, went to worship the
idols. We begin to suspect that he is imploring
their assistance to drive us away. We were
anxious to know what all the martial preparations on shore and at the mouth of the river
meant; and were told that the navy had been
collected to repress the annoyance of the fishermen, who are come hither with their boats, in
order to have the names of the districts to which
they belong inscribed, to prevent piracy. " His
excellency has been previously engaged to settle
their quarrels, but is by no means come hither
to meddle with you, nor are the batteries and
camps for any other purpose than for display on
account of the fishermen."

We had long admired from afar a sloping
embankment, made of square granite blocks,

united together by iron hooks, as a specimen of
Chinese industry and ingenuity. It was made
in the reign of Kang-he, and had withstood the
rage of the waves more than a century. This is
the best proof of its superior structure, and shows
that sloping dikes resist the fury of the waves far
better than massive perpendicular embankments.
To-day we visited this monument of Kang-he's
glorious reign, and perceived that the present
generation had suffered so magnificent a work
to fall into decay. It has shared the fate of all
the forts which we have yet seen. Whilst we
were going round the city wall of Chin-hae,
crowds of people had assembled upon the wall
anxious to catch a glimpse of us. Wherever
they moved the stones tumbled down in great
quantities, bearing ample witness to the ruinous
state in which the successors of the most enlightened Chinese monarch have left the fortifications of the empire. Some of the soldiers
were stationed on the wall with matchlocks and
bows. I asked them the reason of so strange
accoutrements, and they replied, " We are come
to look at you in full dress." The embankment now appeared to be several miles in length.
When we had walked to the fort on the hill we
scaled the wall, but were requested to withdraw

and make a circuitous route back of more than
three miles, to which we readily agreed, to avoid
implicating the commanding officer of the fort.
All the way we were accompanied by a number
of sharp boys, our constant companions in all
our excursions. I admired the sound understanding which these children so fully exhibited.
What they might become with a different education I am unable to say; but I must regret that
no better institutions for the cultivation of their
minds are established than mere schools for reading and writing. When they are able to write a
legible hand and to compose a letter, they are
dismissed from the school. If they intend to
become literary graduates they tarry longer and
read the literature and laws of their country;
but, after all, their acquirements are very limited,
and general knowledge lies quite beyond their
attainments. How great a field therefore is
there in China to benefit the people by giving
their children a better education! But the sphere
for religious instruction is far greater, for this is
entirely neglected, and the juvenile mind here
never receives any direction to the knowledge of
its Creator and God.

In our return we met the first military commander of the fort. He was seated with two other

officers, and asked us very roughly, " Where have you been, sirs?" We replied, we have taken a walk and admired the industry and skill of your countrymen in forming so excellent an embankment. " But were you aware," he replied, " that I ordered the soldiers to stop you? These men do not know the rules of decorum, and therefore I was afraid something serious might befall you, and came hither." We thanked him for his care, and moved with all haste towards Chin-hae, for it had become late, and they would not allow us to pass through the city in order to shorten our return. The constant crowds of people, as we passed along, behaved with the greatest politeness and friendship.

June 3.—Ma, and his friend Le, came again on board. He explained the reason that we were treated with such suspicion. " You are," he said, " very clever; understand making charts, are well versed in the management of business, and always ready to act. We know all this, and are therefore on our guard. Some Coreans were last year shipwrecked near us; we permitted them to travel through different provinces, allowed them to see every thing, and to return by way of Leaou-tung to their native country; for this nation is stupid and take no notice of the things which fall under their immediate observation. Nevertheless, if, by a proper statement to the emperor, you can prove that your sole object is trade, and not the acquisition of power, we will unite our entreaties with yours that trade to this place may be established." He himself had brought off some money to show us that he was in earnest to purchase, and expressed his hearty wishes that others might do the same. They would wink at the trade with several merchants whom they had sent on board.

June 4.—Several mandarins, amongst them Sun, and a clerk from the admiral, came on board; the latter to convey the injunctions and advice of the admiral. He wrote down upon paper, that if we stayed one or two years no trade would be allowed. We understood that a messenger from the governor was expected to-morrow to examine into the conduct of the local mandarins towards us. This will involve the character, as well as the fortune of the admiral, and several petty officers, and therefore they are so desirous to get us away. At the same time it was stated to us that the admiral exceedingly regretted that he did not previously permit us to trade, as this would have shortened the business and saved him a great deal of trouble. We expressed our hope that in future the matters would be better managed.

When going up the river this evening we were forcibly stopped, but recourse to compulsory means (which, however, would have been better omitted) procured for us a free passage. We went near the admiral's junk to complain of this unprecedented behaviour. After all his repeated assurances of friendship, we were treated like enemies. The crew on board the junk were so numerous as completely to crowd her, and render all naval tactics useless. They betrayed great fear lest we should board them, notwithstanding our assurances that no hostile feelings had prompted us to come hither. All the mandarins present promised that our trade should immediately be settled, and pledged themselves that we might reckon on their co-operation.

June 5.—We had yesterday concluded our bargain with a merchant sent off by the mandarins. He promised to buy the whole cargo immediately, and to pay partly in raw silk, and partly in silver. This man seemed a respectable merchant in Ning-po, and in full earnest to effect purchases. He advised us to be firm in our conduct towards the mandarins.

We visited to-day the hall of audience, where

we also met with some inferior mandarins, who had come with the messenger from the governor of Fuhkeen. We were assured by them that to trade was a thing impossible; the matter, however, should be taken into consideration. Besides, they intended to send a statement in our behalf to their sovereign, that the matters might be properly arranged. After this confirmed refusal, Ma talked with Mr. L. in private about carrying on the smuggling trade, and asked with much interest whether the merchants had been on board to-day. So much for Chinese duplicity.

In order to prevent our walking abroad, they had drawn up two lines of military before the temple. We asked whether they considered us as prisoners, and to their great astonishment broke through the ranks. The people, by their extraordinary kindness, compensated for all the hostile treatment of the rulers, given under the name of friendship. We, on our part, endeavoured to screen them from the blows of the police runners, who were very liberal in dealing them out, and thereby occasioned much disturbance. One word of admonition from us to a dense crowd was sufficient to repress their noise and rudeness, and we were far more successful in managing them than were the creatures of the mandarins.

June 7.—To-day we received a document from the Taou-tae, enjoining upon us to obey implicitly the laws of the Celestial Empire, whose dominion extended over all the ocean, and whose power kept all the world in subjection and awe. We were strictly admonished to conform to established rules, and enjoined to quit the harbour immediately. We nevertheless urged the matter further, explained the practicability of the design, and returned a paper, insisting upon the fulfilment of the promises made us.

I have here given at full length an account of our intercourse with the mandarins, as a specimen of the unvaried diplomatic policy of the Celestial Empire. There is a short way of making an end of these wearisome negotiations, by presuming upon their professed friendship, and demanding the fulfilment of their promises. Had our ship been a private trader we should very soon have disposed of all our cargo without encroaching upon the laws of the country, by simply leaving them no alternative to performing their promises of trade. This was the course our merchants advised us to pursue; but we had definite instructions which did not allow us to follow our own judgment.

June 9.—Bad weather and an exposed anchorage forced us yesterday into the harbour. While our flag was waiving, we were asked whether this was not the bloody flag. They are always suspicious that we design to attack them, and betray their petty alarms on every occasion. The Taou-tae sent his clerk to-day with several despatches, in mild language, ordering us away. He quoted at the end the proverb, "Whoever obeys heaven, will prosper; whoever disobeys heaven, will perish." He here blends the institutions of the Chinese empire with the laws of heaven. One ought to possess an implicit faith in political popery, to be guided by such maxims. How absurd soever these theories may appear to foreigners, they are nevertheless the principal basis on which the Chinese found their treatment of foreign nations; and the same arrogance and misapplication of the name of justice pervades all their diplomatic documents. It may be called mere bombast; but whenever a serious application of these theories is made, the party concerned feels their injurious consequences.

June 10.—I had to-day the pleasure of distributing some books, and of administering to the bodily wants of some sick people. Some well-dressed persons seem to have been sent as

spies upon us. We treated them in a friendly
manner, and showed them every thing worth
seeing, and they speedily left us to report to the
admiral.

In order to prevent our going up the river,
they had locked the junks together by means of
bamboo. This line was broken to-day by our
long-boat, to the great amusement of some mandarins, who could not but laugh at such ineffectual measures of defence. His excellency, the
admiral, has long been very sick. I offered him
my assistance, but he refused it, and intimated
to us by Sun that he should recover without
medicine as soon as we had left the harbour.
Sun complained very much of the sufferings he
had to undergo from the duplicity of his col-
leagues. He warned us to be on our guard
against them, for they had two mouths; and
while they used to us the most friendly language,
they would asperse our characters and thwart
our plans whenever they were in the presence of
their superiors.

June 12.—We had finally resolved to leave
the harbour. Ma offered us six hundred dollars
demurrage, and a large stock of provisions,
which we refused; for we should otherwise have
been put on their records as beggars. Several

mandarins expressed their wish that when we came back next year matters might be so well arranged as to permit our trading without any further opposition. We received several presents, accompanied with the warmest wishes for our welfare. The highest officers did not scruple to acknowledge openly their regret that we had not been allowed to prosecute a trade which would have been so mutually advantageous. All articles of European imports are much dearer here than at Canton; and had we been permitted to trade, or even enforced the fulfilment of promises made us, we might have realized a considerable profit.

The curiosity of the people had always been very great. They had constantly flocked to the beach to look at the ship; and great crowds now assembled to see her quitting the harbour. The mandarins, during our short stay near Chin-hae, had used every means to frighten us; but finding that neither the firing of their cannon, nor the increase of their fleet, could intimidate us, they rallied at one point, waiting patiently the effect of persuasion. They promised themselves much from so subtle a negotiator as Ma, and were highly disappointed to see him so little successful.

June 15.—We left on the 13th, steering near

the triangle in four or five fathoms water, a depth sufficient for the entrance of any ship, and arrived the same day at a romantic island, Kin-tang, in the neighbourhood of Ning-po. Our anchorage was lat. 29° 55', long. 121° 54'. The mandarins had hinted to us that they would very gladly allow the people to come aboard if we chose to move out of the harbour. Though we placed little reliance on this assertion, we thought it well to reconnoitre the sea in this place, and to take in a new supply of water. The harbour is very commodious and safe, but the distance which we had entered was short.

In our excursions over this beautiful island we crossed hills and valleys, and halted at several temples and houses. The fertile valleys all run in the same direction, are intersected by rivulets, and yield a rich harvest to the cultivators. The hills are clothed with verdure, and furnish both fuel and timber. Most of the fruits which grow in the southern parts of Europe grow here luxuriantly; and perhaps every vegetable could be raised if the inhabitants would give themselves the trouble.

We ascended some of the highest peaks, from whence we could look over a great part of the island. The beauties of nature are here exhibited in every variety to a numerous and thriving people, who lack only the blessings of Christianity to enjoy true earthly bliss. They enjoy the fruits of their labours, because no extortioner or mandarin lives among them; and though they pay the customary taxes, yet they can easily afford it from the produce of their fertile soil. The temples were very numerous, and built on the most picturesque situations. We conversed with several priests, and acquainted them with the way of salvation. My books were rapidly distributed, and eagerly read by a great concourse of people. We admired the neatness which reigned in the houses, as well as in the dress of the natives. They expressed unrestrained joy to see us. In the midst of a beholding multitude, who had collected from all quarters of the island, we sat down to dine, to the great amusement of the spectators. The mandarins often characterise the common people as stupid; but this could apply very little to the company which we saw to-day, for their remarks were just, and their inquiries showed more intelligence than many of the mandarins. In our return we visited a school. I conversed with the school-master on the inexpediency of teaching young children, like his scholars, the refined principles of good government contained in their classical books. He could defend such a practice by no argument but custom. I urged him to cultivate the intellectual powers of his pupils, instead of merely teaching them a certain number of characters, of which they did not begin to learn the signification till the lapse of two years. He was polite enough to promise what he doubtless never intended to perform. Several idols are placed along the road in little shrines, to remind the people of their religion, and to excite their devotion by burning a little incense. To see so fine an island under the absolute sway of paganism, is a very mournful sight. This feeling is enhanced by reflecting upon the willingness to hear which the inhabitants constantly evinced. Many other islands have been visited by the blessed gospel, though the inhabitants were cannibals and hostile to missionary exertions; but this peaceful abode, where missionaries would by no means encounter all those obstacles which they meet in New Zealand and elsewhere has never known the blessed effects of the glad tidings of salvation. While we ought to bewail our lukewarmness, let us, prostrate, adore the mysterious ways of Providence, when savages are called to the enjoyment of heavenly light, and more civilized nations are left in darkness.

June 16.—We had a large number of visitors on board. Applications for medical aid were very numerous; they were eager to possess books as soon as they knew I distributed them; and it was a very cheerful day. The word of God will doubtless find some serious readers among the intelligent natives of Kin-tang, and when I revisit the island, there will be some individuals who know that Jesus Christ is come into the world to save sinners. This joyful hope animates me under all discouragements. I slight the obstacles, though apparently insurmountable, firmly looking up to the Saviour who has all power in heaven and earth.

In the absence of the gentlemen belonging to the expedition, I had a long conversation with our old comprador of Ning-po. He took the liberty of portraying the mandarins in true colours. He detested the duplicity of Ma, as the source of all our ill-fortune. The naval squadron, in the meanwhile, had been withdrawn and anchored at a great distance from our ship, while some boats were despatched to watch our movements. However, these boats did not stop the people who came on board to trade, nor did they interfere with us in any way. We now bade farewell to the Che-keang province and moved on our way towards Shang-hae in Keang-Soo province.

CHAPTER V.

June 19.—We reached the banks of the Yang-tsze-keang, which stretch out very far, and we had only four feet of water, but very regular soundings. The regions adjoining this river are so low that the shore was at first invisible. We went through a passage, which, so far as we know, had never been passed by a European vessel. Our endeavours to procure a pilot from the numerous fishing craft, proved vain; we had therefore no alternative but following the junks which steered towards the Shang-hae river. About mid-day we saw the low coast, rendered conspicuous by a grove of trees near the shore. In steering towards this harbour, there is no other landmark than a peak of a small island, the most northerly of the Archipelago, and called by the Chinese, if I remember right, Seu-kung-shan. There is a safe anchorage, and many of the junks destined to Shang-hae wait in this harbour for a favourable wind. From hence they steer in a north-western direction, and generally arrive in a day or two at the mouth of the Woo-sung river, which leads to Shang-hae. On all the banks, during several months of the year, there is fresh water. So long as no regular pilotage is established, and no survey of the banks taken, the entrance will continue to be dangerous for large ships. But so extensive an emporium well deserves the attention of hydrographers; so that we may soon be in the possession of charts, if the spirit of mercantile enterprise can give a stimulus to the art of the navigator.

June 20.—Early in the morning we set out in our long boat in search of Shang-hae. Several war-junks hove in sight yesterday, and displayed their bravery by firing guns. We were very long uncertain where to seek the mouth of the river, because it was about dawn, and the coast was every where so low and uniform as to render any opening almost imperceptible. Two forts, built on either shore of the river, whose entrance is broad, marked our course, bearing south by west. It was about 4 o'clock when we arrived, and were saluted by a discharge of fifteen guns from each fort, designed, by alarming, to prevent our entering forbidden ground. We cared very little for this ungracious reception, and proceeded to sound the entrance, where we found six fathoms; but, towards the right shore, the water shoals so as to leave only a channel for the passage of vessels. On the left is a town; a canal leading to Nanking branches off in a western direction. We were met here by several mandarin boats, which insisted on our immediate return.

The aspect of the country here differs widely from Che-keang; all is one fertile flat, not much above the level of the sea, well cultivated, without the least hill. The ravages occasioned by inundations are here very great, since no banks, made of this loamy soil, can resist the swollen river. In such low ground one would expect many meadows, but even the name of them is unknown. The Chinese have taken proper care to drain these marshy grounds of water, and to render them well adapted to the culture of rice, which requires a low and moist soil. They do not prize milk and butter, nor do they like to rear cattle for slaughter; hence they would derive no advantage from meadows. But to procure the immediate necessary of life, rice, as well as to furnish their tribute of grain to the capital, which in this province is very considerable, all their energy is directed to raise annually two crops of grain from this fertile soil, one of rice and another of wheat.

We visited some houses which are very spacious, serving at the same time for granaries and dwellings. The natives are diminutive in size, and very dirty in their persons, as well as in their houses. They shewed very little curiosity or alarm at seeing us come suddenly upon them. While walking through the luxuriant fields, then covered with a ripe crop of wheat, we saw every where the people busy gathering in their rich harvest. As far as the eye could reach over this extensive plain, there was no spot bare of cultivation, or of exuberant vegetation. The dwellings were built in small clusters; the inhabitants possessed just so much land as would maintain their families; these hamlets were very numerous. We saw several females engaged in weaving nankeen cloth, and afterwards examined the cotton of which it is made, and which is of the same colour as the cloth. While we were in the boat at anchor, we received numerous visits from the people, whose curiosity seemed to be raised by degrees, and who staid along-side, silently gazing upon us. They possessed neither the intelligence nor politeness of the Che-keang people. Some of the peasants could read, and we were glad to present them with our books; some hesitated in accepting them, fearing we should ask a great sum in return; others received them gratefully. We greatly astonished them by firing a fowling-piece, for though accustomed to the use of their unwieldy matchlocks, they could form no conception how the powder is ignited without the application of a match. In one of the houses, we saw stuck up a yellow paper given by the emperor, in token of his great respect towards an aged pair, who had lived a hundred years. This paper, with a large present, had been granted upon the representation of the local magistrate, who highly extolled this faithful pair. In reading the excellent sentiments contained in the paper, one could not avoid thinking that paternal government does really exist in theory, and that an occasional show is made in practice. I have often made these remarks to the natives, and exhorted them to value a national government founded on such amiable principles. They always laughed heartily at these remarks, and ascribed them either to my ignorance or egregious stupidity. " Our rulers," say they, " want money, and care little about the means by which it is obtained. If you know this, you know the principles and practice of our government."

We had now advanced half way up to the city, whither many junks were proceeding. Those belonging to this place are of an oblong form, and have generally four masts, and canvass sails. They seldom exceed two hundred tons burden, are all of them numbered, and have the place where they belong written in very large letters along the side. They are bad sailors, and are very frequently wrecked. They visit, principally, the harbours of Leaou-tung, or Mantchou Tartary, from whence they import oil-cakes and peas; whilst they export silks, and other manufactures of Keang-nan.

We very soon had the mortification of seeing several boats from the city, and from Woo-sung, arrive at the entrance, to stop our progress. They were very numerous, and had several military commanders on board, who insisted upon our immediate return; but our boat being a very good sailer, we got a-head of them, and at half-past four, arrived at Shang-hae. A crowd had already collected on the shore to catch a sight of us. We went up a stone pier, in front of a temple, dedicated to the queen of heaven, who seems to have many temples and worshippers in all the trading towns. Our first steps were directed towards the Taou-tae's, the office of the principal magistrate, to whom we had addressed a petition.

The city is built on the left side of the river, with houses generally very low, streets narrow, shops numerous, some magnificent temples, and excessive bustle. Our visit was very unwelcome. At the Taou-tae's office we were told that his excellency had left this, and repaired to Woo-sung, a town at the entrance, to have a conference with us. We expressed our regret at this news; but having once got to the city, we intended to take the opportunity of fully examining this great emporium of central Asia. The Che-heen of this district, a mandarin with a gold button, came out very soon to insult us, and upbraid us severely for coming hither. After calmly answering his objections, we reminded him that civility becomes the rulers of the Celestial Empire, and then returned to take up our quarters in the spacious temple where we had landed. Very soon we became acquainted with a man who held the office of interpreter, because he spoke both the Fuhkeen and mandarin dialects. I have known very few characters so stained with falsehood as this man's. His tongue was volatile; he was a regular opium smoker, and an abject slave of the mandarins. Surrounded by numerous police-runners, we had scarcely waited a quarter of an hour, when the Taou-tae's arrival was announced. He had come with the swiftness of lightning, and was ready to hear our petition. Before the ceremonial question of standing or sitting was adjusted, we passed more than half an hour in debate. He finally rose when we entered, and we also remained standing. He did not wait till Mr. L. addressed him, but said, in a very stern voice, " Why don't you go to Canton, and trade there? It is an unheard-of thing for any ship to come to Shang-hae. Conform to the established laws of the Celestial Empire, and don't trouble us with your presence." To this Mr. L. replied: " The trade with Canton is in a state of confusion; but that does not concern Keang-nan province. As we allow junks from Shang-hae to enter our ports, we think it right to have the same privilege of coming hither with our vessels." When he heard this, he grew very fierce, and said, " Do not permit them to come to your harbours, but drive them away." " This is impossible," said Mr. Lindsay. " Why?" " Because our government understands reason, and does not treat any nation unreasonably." After a great deal of altercation, we withdrew. We had not long sat down, when our petition was returned, and a copy shewn to us, to let us see that the original paper was superfluous. As we, however, had written it for the information of the higher mandarins, we refused to receive it back.

Some priests of the Taou sect had taken charge of our bodily wants. They provided us a plentiful supper, and shewed us every attention. Indeed, we could complain of none but the mandarins, who wanted to shut us up, in order to prevent our going about the city. We used a forcible argument to dissuade them from placing such restraints upon us, and they very soon desisted.

June 21.—Early in the morning, Mr. L. was ordered to depart. We regarded these commands very little, but visited a great part of the city before breakfast. I copied a fierce edict, which had been issued against us before our arrival, in consequence of some notice they had received from Che-keang, warning them to be on their guard against our intrusion. We bought several articles, though the most explicit injunctions had been issued against selling. As soon

as the mandarins perceived that we were firm
and reasonable in our demands, they became
polite, and yielded. All of them were opium
smokers; and among all the number, there was
not one respectable man who came under our
observation. They all expected to repel us by
haughtiness and force; but in this they so completely failed, that they now tried every means to
conciliate us.

While walking through the streets, I was
observed by great numbers of my former " pa-
rishioners." They called me by name, and were
anxious to express their joy at seeing me again;
but I beckoned to them with my hand, not to
endanger themselves by any show of affection
to me. They understood me, and reluctantly
complied. How often have I talked to this
people, and explained to them the gospel of our
glorious Redeemer! They are not ignorant of
his holy name, nor unacquainted with his sufferings for all mankind. Alas! it does not enter
their minds, that they must show a living faith
in order to become partakers of that grace which
is in Christ Jesus our Lord. Though I have
seen here very little fruit of preaching Christ
crucified, I am fully persuaded, that if circumstances had allowed a longer stay among them,

I might have gained a few for the gospel, for they were not entirely unfeeling.

We had boisterous weather in returning, but reached the ship just as she was entering the port, having been yesterday ashore. The naval officers had already been aboard, and ordered her immediately to leave the port. While entering, the guns from both batteries fired, the war-junks also gave us a few broadsides, which did as little harm as crackers. As soon as we anchored, the Tsung-ping-kwan, or river-admiral, came along-side, and told us, in plain language, that we were not allowed to anchor here for a moment. However, while we were debating this point, our captain fired a salute, in return for the many shots; which threw him into such consternation, for the report of our guns was very loud, that he immediately ordered his boat to return on shore.

June 22.—A very fresh breeze, which would have endangered our safety, had we been on the bank outside. But our gracious God protects us from all dangers, seen and unseen; his name be praised to all eternity!

In our petition, we had pointed out the advantages which would accrue to this province, if trade were permitted. We used the most cogent reasons, such as the emperor's great compassion towards foreigners, the trade of the Shang-hae merchants to our ports, &c., and humbly hoped these things might become a subject of deliberation. Instead of this, our petition was returned, accompanied with a very angry answer. The letter we retained, as a fair specimen of Chinese diplomacy, but refused to receive the petition, which had been once formally accepted.

While the captain was going up the river, we took a ramble in the Paou-shan district. This is on the left side of the river, a very large alluvial tract, increasing every year, as the sea recedes. As soon as we landed, the soldiers were regularly drawn up, armed with pikes, sabres, and matchlocks. We went to Woosung, a filthy, but populous town, accompanied by large numbers of people, to whom we gave books; and escorted also by several mandarins. We crossed many fertile fields, entered into numerous villages, and entertained ourselves with the people, who collected from all quarters. In this walk we had to jump over many ditches, which so wearied the mandarins, that they were disgusted with such obstinate intruders. Our return was rendered formal by a second display of the soldiery, who were drawn up along the

embankments. Their officers behaved like gentlemen, and spoke very friendly. We saw several
large iron guns mounted, of various calibres, with
heaps of stones near them, which serve instead
of balls. These warlike preparations were not
intended for us, according to the repeated
assurances of the officers, but for the customary
review of the troops.

June 23.—A dark day and fresh breeze, but
several boats came along-side. The people were
inquisitive, cringing, and even knelt when they
were about to enter the cabin. On the whole
they seem far inferior to the inhabitants of Ning-
po. The Taou-tae began to repent of his rash
measures, and begged us to give back his saucy
letter, that he might frame another according
to the model of those which we had received
at Ning-po; both of which requests were flatly
refused.

June 24.—We reasoned our friends out of the
use of the epithet E, " barbarians," which they
apply to all strangers indiscriminately. The idea
of cunning and treachery is always attached to
this name when uttered by the Chinese. As
foreigners trading to China have hitherto patiently
borne such an appellation, they have been treated
as barbarians. It was highly necessary to object

to this epithet, and to shew from its use in Chinese writings that the term conveyed reproach. From this time they abstained from the use of it, and called us foreigners, or Englishmen. They had the strongest objections to our purchasing any thing; but, regardless of this odious prohibition, we involved some people in danger to-day by buying of them a few trifles.

June 25.—A rainy and stormy day. During all this unpleasant weather, the soldiers, whom we really pity, are lodged under tents, and subject to the greatest hardships, all to no purpose. The greater part of them seem to be common ploughmen, forming a certain sort of land militia, calculated for the protection of the coast against the inroads of the fierce barbarians.

We received to-day a most insolent message, on which account we moved farther up the river, that we might come to a better understanding. As soon as they saw us so earnest, they were kind and yielding. The commander-in-chief, a general of very high rank, sent a message to tell us expressly that he was our warmest friend, and well acquainted with our heroic character, having formerly been an officer at Canton.

June 27.—Early in the morning we received a visit from the two naval officers, who had been frequently aboard. They had received orders to send us out of the harbour to-day; and if they failed in the attempt, they were to be degraded. To shew that they were in earnest, they unscrewed the button on their caps, which is the badge of their rank, and offered them to us as henceforth useless to themselves. The interpreter, who had no button to lose, told us that he should be imprisoned if we did not leave the harbour. " They were not the only persons implicated in the affair; but even his excellency, the commander-in-chief, would incur the imperial displeasure if we staid longer. The Taoutae, also, was very much afraid." One of the mandarins tried to weep, but the tears fell very sparingly; and on the whole this intended tragedy more resembled a farce than any thing else. If we had not been fully acquainted with the lying spirit which animated these men, if we had not known their baseness, it would have been unjust to disregard their entreaties. But they were the most worthless characters which we met with on all the coast, and so shameless as to deny an assertion uttered by them a quarter of an hour before. We simply told them that we wanted to trade; that after having traded we should depart immediately; that, as strangers, we never interfered with the maxims of their government, as to degrading or promoting officers; and that we were sorry to be the occasion of degradation to them. They afterwards came to tell us that they had been authorized to ask how much of all the produce of the country we wanted before we could leave. We gave them, therefore, a list of all things needed, when they gained more courage, and entered into a friendly conversation, interrupted only by their occasional groanings.

June 30.—All the restrictions to free intercourse are now taken off, though the papers posted up at every corner of Woo-sung, and most severely prohibiting the " treacherous people from all dealings with the barbarians," are not yet taken down. The mandarins themselves are anxious to oblige us, and persuade the people to sell their choice articles. This sudden change greatly astonishes the people. One shopkeeper gave a mandarin a ludicrous welcome, by contrasting the gravity with which they one day prohibit a thing, with the lightness with which they next day trample on their own injunction.

We visited a temple opposite the ship, which had been built by a mandarin of rank, and served as a place of public resort. There were several

huge idols, guardians of the river, and rulers of
the sea. The queen of heaven had also a shrine,
which was guarded by some demons, armed with
tridents. It was very natural that they should
ask me whether we also adored these idols.
They could not have given me a better text for
preaching. Accordingly, after dwelling upon the
great truth of an Almighty Creator of heaven and
earth, I reverted to the helplessness of their
idols, which they all admitted. The mandarins
laughed at these remarks. In general they
succeed in waiving an argument which they do
not intend to follow up, but I kept them to the
point, by referring to the mediatorial sacrifice of
our Lord Jesus Christ. O that this precious
doctrine might not be lost upon them! for all
whom we have met here are stained with guilt, and
irrevocably lost to all eternity, if divine power,
revealed and communicated through Jesus Christ,
do not rescue them.

Our conversation was to-day very familiar.
They did their utmost to convince us of their
friendly intention, and even hinted that they
had received the most explicit orders to this effect.
They claimed brotherhood with us, and declared
themselves our most devoted friends. We only
requested them to give us more substantial proofs

of their veracity than mere words, to which they agreed. A long time we sat in a loft of the temple, while hundreds of people crowded around, highly pleased to catch a glimpse of us when we were looking out of the windows. Though the crowd was excessive, not the least disturbance or alteration arose; for the mandarins did not beat them, and they had no occasion to retort the wrong.

We visited the fort on the left side, and saw the internal economy of the defences of the country. It was a very massive structure, and they had done their best to arrange the batteries; yet the most despicable force could take it, for they have no skill in fortification, but place their whole reliance on the thickness of the ramparts and walls. With the slightest inspection we perceived that both the forts were constructed after the European model, which they had probably received from the Jesuits. Though the river is here more than two miles broad, these forts might command it if the cannon carried to any considerable distance. But the powder is very bad, the guns are ill served and worse directed, their touch-holes are often very wide, they are made without proportion, and I am fully persuaded that some of them would more endanger the gunner's life than his at whom they were aimed. From the long peace which China has enjoyed, all their military works have fallen into decay. They even seem anxious that all should crumble to dust, and that wars should be blotted from remembrance. As far back as Chinese history informs, this empire was never so large as at this moment. The reigning Tartar family has grasped dominion in every direction, and been successful in all their ambitious enterprises. That so happy a termination of their warlike exploits should suggest to them that the nation is invincible, and can defend itself without fortifications, is not surprising. Their contempt of European tactics, without the aid of which they rendered whole nations, north and west of China, tributary, is as natural as the Turkish military bigotry, while they vanquished Europe.

Notwithstanding, it is really difficult to ascertain the means by which so extensive an empire is kept together. Persons in the least acquainted with Chinese institutions, can by no means ascribe it to the wisdom of the theoretical laws of the Celestial Empire. Many of them read excellently, but cannot be reduced to practice, because they are not adapted to existing circumstances. Others are trampled on both by mandarins and people, and few are strictly observed. Nor can we ascribe this political phenomenon to the internal vigour of the dynasty. So far as I have known the Tartars, they are great cowards, and they have received their political lessons from the Chinese. Apparently, the principal means which confirm their administration are bribes, which are profusely distributed to those who have the disposition to question their authority, and the power to enforce this questioning.

But in all this we ought to look higher, to an overruling Providence, which upholds nations by imperceptible means, and subverts kingdoms which can bid defiance to every earthly power.

That pacific disposition which generally marks the Chinese rulers is truly praiseworthy; for though often cruel, they detest bloodshed, and have generally made the greatest sacrifices to prevent it. We attach no blame, therefore, to their cowardice; but hope that, while they continue to be pacific, they will cease to be overbearing towards other nations, who have power to humble their arrogance.

We visited also the barracks, those abodes of misery for the ill clad and worse fed soldiers.

They are chiefly taken from the dregs of the people, such as have no other resource for a livelihood; the most emaciated in appearance, and the most immoral of the whole community. Though our arrival had subjected them to great hardships, many of them had contrived to get a new jacket, to appear at least decently. During the time of our visit, they endeavoured to be as friendly as possible: having no tea, they presented us with warm water. Their officers repeatedly exclaimed, " What a miserable state our men are in!" for the utmost wretchedness was depicted in their countenances. We saw the arrows hanging round upon the wall, but could espy no bows, which, they said, were on the opposite shore. There is little uniformity in their armour; some having swords, others matchlocks, a few pikes, &c. The division to which they belong is written in large characters upon the front of their jackets. Their dress is the same as that of the people; but they have a cap which marks the distinction. Some parts of the Chinese army have the character Yung— " valour," written upon their jackets *behind:* and it is rather characteristic of their bravery. Even the soldiers are forced to become agriculturists. In certain parts of the empire, fields

are laid out, which they cultivate for their subsistence; in other parts, where they have no
farms of their own, they hire themselves out as
servants to the peasants, and plough the fields,
till they are called for the military reviews. The
greater part of the officers are very illiterate, and
have risen from the ranks. There are, however,
military examinations, as well as literary, and
degrees of bachelor, master, and doctor, in military tactics, regularly conferred. They have the
same degrees as literary mandarins, and wear
the same badges of rank, buttons or knobs, on
their caps; yet they are regarded both by the
literary mandarins and the people with the
greatest contempt. Their salary is very small,
their resources slender, and their situation not
at all enviable. Many of the general officers are
Tartars, who enjoy great salaries, besides often
some lucrative civil offices. As long as the
peaceful state of China continues, their office is
but a sinecure. The army is no ways distinct
from the navy; an officer or private quitting the
one and entering the other without any difficulty,
for they both rank alike.

A great part of the navy is manned by
Fuhkeen men, and the natives of the eastern
part of Canton province. The common soldiers,

as well as their officers, belong generally to the place which they garrison. It is only in case of extreme danger that they are drawn off to the frontiers, and then by decimation. The actual military force differs greatly from the numbers on the books. It is the practice of the officers to draw the full allowances, without having the receivers in pay. It may suffice to leave them on paper, so long as the Celestial Empire wages a paper war with European powers, and she is too cautious to try the experiment of the sword.

By the various accounts which we had read in the " Lettres Edifantes," we were prompted to visit the island of Tsung-ming. Though we passed very near it in entering the Woo-sung river, yet we could scarcely perceive it, because it was so low. We set out at half-past nine, A. M., steered north-east by north, crossing banks, and passing near and between several other islands, all of which were formerly shoals, which have gradually increased in height and extent, till they are now habitable. On reaching Tsung-ming, we entered a creek, where we found a junk at anchor. The island is entirely alluvial, formed by the Yang-tsze-keang, and the whole country is low, and almost level with the sea. To facilitate agriculture, the people have intersected it by creeks, and thrown up some dykes, which prove an ineffectual barrier against the high tides. The country was very densely populated, in separate clusters of two or three bamboo cottages. The ground was sown with rice, Barbadoes millet, and some culinary herbs: we found also apricot and peach trees, and apples of very inferior quality.

We bent our walk towards Ho-chin, about two miles distant from the sea, and found it interesting and pleasant to pass through such richly cultivated fields. At first, the natives were much astonished at our sudden appearance, having never seen an European; but they soon became familiar and friendly, because we distributed books among them freely. It afforded me great satisfaction, as the first protestant missionary, to tread this spot, where once a regular mission of the Jesuits had been established. We had taken with us a great number of books, chiefly of the Scriptures. At first, they hesitated to receive them; but, on glancing at the contents, the people became clamorous for more. I satisfied their requests, as long as it was in my power, but had then the mortification to send away numerous applicants empty.

We scarcely any where experienced such

friendship as among these islanders, all of them
seeming very anxious to oblige us, and prove
that the Chinese character is exempt from misanthropy. Chin-ko itself is a very flourishing
place, with numerous shops, and many pawn-
brokers among them, who seemed to be the
richest men in the community. The concourse
of people was so great, that we could scarcely
pass through the streets; but there was no rudeness, and they rather seemed interested to show
us every thing worthy our attention. Finding
several persons in a temple engaged in gambling,
I presented them with a tract on gambling, when
they started up astonished at our unexpected
and unwelcome gift. At our departure, one man
offered Mr. L. the conveyance of a wheel-barrow,
which, being pushed on by one man, not only
accommodates with a seat, but with room for a
little baggage. We had a numerous train of
well-dressed persons, who continued their intelligent inquiries all the way. Striking also was
the appearance of so many healthy boys, playing
around us with their characteristic glee. They
were not entirely frivolous, however, but would
occasionally turn towards us and put some intelligent question, which, when satisfied, they
communicated to each other. Great numbers

stood on the shore to give us a hearty farewell, and lamenting that we could give them no more books. When we were approaching the forts at the entrance we were met by a mandarin boat, sent in pursuit of us. The officer stationed to guard against barbarians, drew upon himself a very severe punishment for his alleged failure in duty. He was led around blindfold, with a bamboo stuck through his ear, and a label, on which was written, " As a warning to the multitude, this culprit has his ear pierced for having neglected and disobeyed the martial laws, by the military commander-in-chief of Soo-sung."

It was in vain to lament such severity, for the great mandarins were determined to wreak their vengeance on the inferior grade. As for us, we had enjoyed the satisfaction of visiting the island undisturbed, and of seeing the Chinese character in its true light, that of friendliness and kindness towards foreigners. Our mandarin friends had thought us entirely ignorant of the existence of such an island; they were therefore highly exasperated that we had dared to discover it and note it in our charts. Judging from their efforts to keep Europeans ignorant of their country, they can scarcely believe that we have any knowledge of them, or are even acquainted with their most celebrated cities. How astonished were they, therefore, when we mentioned the principal districts composing the Keang-soon province, and the canals leading to Nanking. Hence they concluded that some treacherous native had betrayed his country, and brought the barbarians to the most fertile portions of the Celestial Empire. While seeing our maps, which had been made in the reign of Kang-he, they showed very little interest to become acquainted with their construction, because the names were in foreign characters.

July 5.—We revisited Shang-hae: though the wind was unfavourable, the tide enabled us to reach the place at half-past seven o'clock. We took up our quarters at the temple of the queen of heaven, where the crowds gathered around us again. I began with distributing the Scriptures to them, as the best means to promote their eternal happiness. They seized them eagerly from my hands, and immediately retired to read them leisurely.

Confounded at our unceremonious visit, the mandarins came in great haste to the temple. They were at this time more humble and yielding than before, yet they had stuck up two outrageous proclamations, which I immediately copied. They also attempted to prevent us from going into the city, but we passed through another gate, which they were unable to shut. We now bought large quantities of silk, and some trifles, to which they at first made great objections, but very soon granted to us the liberty of buying, though they nominally prohibited the shopkeepers from selling. I distributed tracts house by house, and nobody interfered. Highly grateful for the favour of the Most High bestowed upon his most unworthy servant, of being the bearer of his precious Gospel, we returned to our old quarters, where the priests who had constantly shown us great kindness, had prepared a very substantial dinner. The mandarins afforded us every facility to do our business, and we ought to be truly thankful to them, for it was the first time that they showed good will towards strangers.

It will not be amiss to remark here that Shang-hae ranks after Canton in importance. Though this may not be the only emporium near the Yang-tsze-keang, and thus the only place for importation to Keang-nan, the junks from all the southern provinces are prohibited from proceeding to the harbours north of this great river.

There is always a brisk trade carried on, which

would be much increased, if Europeans were admitted to the port. The consumption of foreign articles, among the many millions who inhabit central Asia, is very great. Hence the imports far exceed the exports; the latter consist chiefly of raw silk, silk stuffs and teas, besides manufactures fabricated by the skilful hand of the Keang-nan people. Ships bound to this place might touch at Sha-po, in Che-keang province, Hang-chew district, and at Soo-chow, a little south of Woo-sung river. This latter place is one of the most populous and delightful districts of the whole Chinese empire, and might fully claim the poetical name of Arcadia. That so large a field for mercantile enterprise has been hitherto overlooked, is really surprising. The fear of infringing Chinese laws has deterred ships from even attempting to open commercial intercourse. It is true there are obstacles, but not insurmountable; they are surely less than at New Zealand and Madagascar. If we consider the lukewarmness with which these regions, containing so many millions of immortal souls, are viewed by most of the Christian world, we are constrained to weep bitterly. Whilst blind fanaticism, nourished by attachment to popery, has found ways and means to penetrate into

these regions, we are satisfied with the bare
excuse of alleged impossibilities. If mere fanaticism can conquer the obstacles, ought we not
to expect that true Christian enthusiasm will
prevail? Can we not fully believe that the
constant prayer of the church, with a firm reliance on the divine promises, will gradually
open the way? If the heralds of Christianity
might not at first be permitted to stay, nobody
will prevent them from passing along the coast,
and the numbers to which they may thus have
access are very great, and well repay the trouble.
Let us not object that the Chinese laws of exclusion are very severe; they are nominally so,
but lose that severity in the same degree with
which they are resisted with firmness and reason.
Let it rather be remembered that these millions
of inhabitants are anxious to cultivate friendship
with Europeans, and never object to receiving
our Christian books. I speak from *facts* against
inveterate opinions; and though I am conscious
of having done but very little for the advancement of the kingdom of God in Keang-nan, yet
I am fully persuaded that my successor will
succeed better.

July 6.—Two messengers were sent from Soo-
chow in order to settle our affairs; one of them a

Foo-tseang, military mandarin with a red button, and the other a civilian, with a crystal button. We were formally invited to this audience, to bring matters to a conclusion. They were seated in the hall of the temple, opposite to our anchorage, and received us with the greatest friendship. After the usual compliments, we sat down near them, and the Foo-tseang, who was the chief speaker, inquired whether we had been at Shang-hae, and had bought the necessary articles. He rejoiced very much that we were satisfied with this visit, and had no complaint against the mandarins. Mr. L. was very eloquent in showing the reasonableness of permitting us to trade. They urged the invariable laws of the Celestial Empire as their general rule. We referred to laws still more ancient, permitting a trade to all the Chinese ports. They then requested us to represent the matter to our king, that he might send a proper person, with powers to negotiate an arrangement. When our respective sovereigns had agreed on the matter, they would rejoice to give us free permission. They ended with a declaration of the friendly feelings which they cherished towards us.

Whilst they were thus confident of having convinced us that they were our warm friends, we produced those offensive edicts which I had copied, and which breathed nothing but enmity. They were ashamed of the language in which they were couched, and would have denied the existence of such proclamations, had we not copied them only one day since. The whole conversation was conducted in a spirit of amity, the best understanding reigned throughout the whole, and we began fondly to believe that these men would take the trouble to transmit our representations to the viceroy of Keang-nan. Mr. L. deserves credit for pleading so well the cause of his countrymen; and though we did not reap the advantages of such a conference, we hope that others may be benefited by it in future. The people also, who saw that we were on so good footing with the mandarins, rejoiced at such a happy change.

In the evening we went to the opposite side of the river to visit some of the hamlets, scattered every where over this alluvial soil. The cottages are generally built among a cluster of trees, and would be very pleasant, if care were taken to keep them clean. But even the smell of the exhalations from the environs, is so offensive that one scarcely dares to enter. All the fields yield very good crops, but the number of the

inhabitants is sufficient to consume their most
abundant harvests. After distributing some books
to very attentive readers, we went higher up the
field and turned towards the fort. This threw
the garrison into consternation, and some soldiers
came out to prevent our proceeding further; but
they were very unceremoniously driven back by
the second officer of the ship, who was one of
our party. We inspected the batteries, passed
several ranks of soldiers, and finally came up to
the officers near the fort, who besought us not
to enter, because their superiors had forbidden
it. There was an open stable for the horses
belonging to the imperial cavalry; but it appeared that no care was taken of the ponies,
which constitute all their horses, but that they
were left to shift for themselves. Their barracks
outside of the fort having been destroyed by
water, they readily afforded us every comfort
in their power, which amounted to permitting us
to sit down in these stables. They repeated the
gross lie, that they were collected here for a
military review, and not solely on our account;
whilst they complained most bitterly of the literary mandarins, who left them under the open
sky. Whilst the rain poured down in torrents,
they were obliged to stand up to their knees in

mud. We consoled them in the best way we could, and answered many questions which their curiosity dictated.

To extenuate his harshness, the Taou-tae had sent a more reasonable edict on board, but as the seal was wanting, we returned it, to the great consternation of the interpreter and the mandarins. The Taou-tae afterwards was prevailed upon to imprint his official seal upon the document.

July 8.—After having bought, and received as presents, a great quantity of provisions, we prepared for our departure, (our anchorage had been lat. 31° 23′, long. 121° 20′.) The two days previous they had given the people permission to come on board. Our visitors were therefore very numerous; and I enjoyed an excellent opportunity of distributing the word of eternal life: some sick persons also were benefited. Our visit here has had a most beneficial influence upon the people; and the mandarins have learned to relax their severity. They made it their principal business to-day to praise us beyond bounds, representing our character as the most amiable on earth. But they are so despicable for falsehood, that their vain talk influences us little.

After having made them a few presents, which they hid under their clothes, we bade them farewell. They were very kind to offer us their convoy, to which we could not object.

As soon as we had left the harbour, they fired most valiantly, leaving us no doubt of their heroism; the military camps were immediately withdrawn, and the mandarins no doubt began to breathe freely. Had we come hither as enemies, the whole army would not have resisted half an hour, for they were all dispirited; and the mandarins went so far as to report that one soldier had actually died at the sight of our second mate: the war-boats are unable to keep out the smallest well-armed ship; and the people highly disapprove of the restrictions upon trade. All this we have fully ascertained, and make report of it to draw the attention of missionaries, as well as merchants, to this interesting field. At the same time, we should highly disapprove of violent measures to obtain an object, which might be gained by firmness and resolution.

As the heat has been very oppressive, and the musquitoes numerous, we were happy to leave this marshy country, where all had fallen more or less sick.

The tide being in our favour, we advanced

slowly over the banks, followed by the imperial convoy, to protect us against the pirates in our way to Canton. Captain Rees, our naval commander, in this unexplored passage, and in the most critical moments, displayed the greatest skill in extricating the vessel from most dangerous situations. By his consummate skill and coolness, he rendered the greatest service to the expedition. He has also made accurate charts of the harbours which we visited.

July 14.—Without suffering in any way from our passage near the banks of the Yang-tsze-keang, we arrived at the promontory of Shang-tung, at Wei-hae-wei, where the English embassy formerly touched, lat. 37° 8′, long. 121° 20′. We immediately landed at the island Lew-kung-taou, inhabited by fishermen, who were astonished at our sudden appearance. In walking over the hills, we experienced from the natives more than one instance of reserve and unfriendliness, which seemed depicted on every countenance. Most of the people refused or returned our books, though some had the boldness to receive and read them. The houses are built of granite, and covered with sea-weed: the people seemed very poor, and indeed poverty reigns all over Shan-tung province. They are stronger, and apparently much more healthy, than the inhabitants of the southern provinces; but the females, on the contrary, look pale and languid. Nothing can exceed the clownishness of these natives, who, though born in the land of Confucius, the great author of ceremonies, are regardless even of the common rules of decorum. The odour of garlic which proceeds from them keeps every stranger at a distance, and is often quite intolerable. But they are more honest than their southern countrymen; and, if well trained, would make good soldiers; for of all the Chinese which I have seen, they are the bravest. Necessity obliges them to seek the hospitable shores of Mantchou Tartary, where they find plenty of work, and various means of subsistence. Thither they have lately flocked in great numbers, and formed very large colonies, which greatly contribute to the prosperity of both countries. All the natives speak the mandarin dialect with great fluency; and any one who would learn to speak it perfectly, would do well to stay among them some time.

As soon as the ship had anchored, a mandarin, of very large stature, came aboard, rudely entered the cabin, and made the customary inquiries. He seemed reserved, and not a little

perplexed, at our arrival: several of his fellow-
officers followed him; and among them, a literary
mandarin, from Peche-le province, of very pleasing manners.   He was particularly anxious to
know all the places where we had touched, and
the times of each.   According to orders received
from the emperor, we were not allowed to
go on shore.   But to console us, they all spoke
largely of the poverty and insignificance of
Wei-hae-wei, and strongly recommended us to
go to Leaoutung, where we might trade extensively.

After dinner, we went ashore; and, though
strongly urged by a military mandarin to proceed
no further, we did not listen to his injunctions,
but proceeded slowly along side of a wall, till
we reached the top of a hill.   Here were two
stones, with inscriptions, from which we learned
that this city had been built during the Ming
dynasty, and repaired during the reign of Yung-
la, (1423.)   The inroads of the Japanese are
mentioned, and this is considered a firm bulwark
against their invasions.

When the mandarin perceived that we persisted in our walk, he smote his breast most furi-
ously, and seemed entirely frantic.   In walking

through the fields, sowed with wheat, onions, garlic, Barbadoes millet, and culinary herbs, we saw a team, consisting of an ass, a cow, and a mule, yoked together, which presented the most ludicrous appearance yet seen among Chinese agriculturists.   On our return, we stipulated with our mandarin guide, that provisions should be sold us; and he called an old man, who now became the speaker, and explained to us every thing relating to the place.   I had the pleasure to observe, that the more civilized part paid more regard to our Christian books than the fishermen had done, and we distributed several among them.

July 16.—Fully expecting that the mandarins would keep their word, we went on shore, but found the people backward to sell provisions, and every one willing to impose on us.   Wearied with evasions, we met the mandarins, who were seated in the area of a temple devoted to the queen of heaven.   They complained that we had taken a fowling-piece on shore, and fired it several times.   We excused ourselves by saying, that it was our constant custom to go armed in an unknown country, and that fowling was our diversion.   But after all our requests, we were obliged to depart without effecting our purpose.

We now stretched over to Corea, and boarded junks, bound to Teen-tsin: one of them was from Siam, and all the crew recognized me.

CHAPTER VI.

JULY 17.—A stiff breeze brought us in sight of Corea. A merciful Providence has protected us through many dangers, along the coast of China, and O that we were truly grateful!

Before entering on any details of our transactions with this singular nation, I will give some account of the country.

Corea, called by the natives, Chaou-seen, as well as by the Chinese, who besides name it Keaou-le, is separated from Mantchou Tartary by a wooden wall. The waters on the western coast are spotted with islands, which on the charts of the Jesuits have been blended with the main land, so that the longitude of this peninsula is placed two degrees too far westward. Those parts of the country which we saw were very fertile and well watered; but thinly inhabited, and still less cultivated. Though this was, indeed, but the outskirts of the kingdom, we cannot think the interior is as thickly inhabited as the maritime provinces of China. Their state of barbarism, cherished by the odious system of exclusion, which has no where, by a maritime nation, been carried farther than at Corea, does not admit of a numerous and flourishing population; nor do we think there are any large cities to be found.

The king may well be styled " the sovereign of ten thousand isles," for the whole coast is studded with islands of every shape. Though his kingdom is powerful enough to maintain itself independent, he has long submitted to pay tribute to the Celestial Empire four times a year.

The kingdom was known to the Chinese as early as the times of Yaou. At different periods they attacked the " middle kingdom," and often proved victorious. It was natural that they should early adopt the Chinese writing character, the use of which prevails among them to this time. Several domestic broils, which seem to have been fomented by Chinese policy, together with the variety of tribes inhabiting the country, seem to have kept this kingdom in barbarism, from which it did not emerge ; while their neighbours, the Chinese as well as the Japanese, made rapid advances in civilization. As soon as the Ming dynasty ascended the Chinese throne (A. D. 1368), the Coreans sent an ambassador to Hungwoo, the emperor, desiring the inauguration of their king with the imperial seal. This was readily granted, and Corea was henceforth considered a tributary kingdom. During the reign of Tai-kosama, the warlike emperor of Japan, Corea was repeatedly invaded by the Japanese, and finally conquered. The Chinese tried in vain to expel the Japanese, for they maintained themselves with the utmost bravery; and so far from yielding up Corea, they disquieted all the Chinese coast with their fleet. It was at this time that Christianity, or rather Popery, was first promulgated in Corea; for the generals of the Japanese, and many of the soldiery, were Christians. When Tai-kosama died, the Japanese general-in-chief withdrew to his own country (1598) after the war had raged seven years. Thus were all the fruits of the repeated victories lost to the Japanese. The Chinese did not fail to establish their authority as supreme masters, to whom all the earth should bow. Since that time the country has undergone little change. The king cannot reign without the imperial sanction, nor can he himself confirm the choice of a colleague or successor; all these must be sanctioned by the court of Peking. In other respects it is an independent kingdom, and the Chinese meddle very little with their internal administration. Its subjects are not allowed to visit other countries, nor are even Chinese admitted to settle among them. They trade with the frontiers of Japan at Tuymataou, which is opposite to the Corean island of Kin-shang. Their trade with Chinese and Tartars is carried on at Fung-hwang-ching, the frontier town of Mantchou Tartary. This traffic is conducted with great secresy and circumspection, lest one nation should spoil the other, and thus tend to subvert their ancient regulations. Nothing is more ridiculous than to see the people so tenacious of ancient and useless forms, rather than desirous to keep pace with the march of improvement.

We could never discover the staple articles of export from this country. Judging from the climate and from what we have seen, we think there must be a great variety of the productions which we find in southern Europe. The natives were very desirous to persuade us that their country produced nothing for exportation; but their trade with Japan and Mantchou Tartary proves the contrary. Full allowance should, however, be made for the uncivilized state of

the country. Instead of allowing the Chinese
to come over from Shang-tung to cultivate a
large quantity of waste but arable land, they
choose to live on salt fish rather than to have
intercourse with foreigners. As long as this
system of exclusion of which they boast continues, they must always remain in the lowest
rank of nations.

We came to anchor at Chwang-shan, an island
north of Basil's Bays. The silence of the desert
seemed to reign every where. We ventured
towards the shore, and the first thing we met
was a fishing-boat, miserably constructed, with
two natives in it clothed in rags. Though we
could not communicate with them orally, yet we
could use the Chinese character in writing. We
gave the old man a few books, and lion buttons,
which highly delighted him. As soon as we
had landed on a small island several natives
came down from a hill, wearing conical caps
of horse-hair, with jackets and trowsers similar
to the Chinese, but wider and without buttons.
Nothing could exceed the gravity of their look
and demeanour. An elderly man, who held a
staff, bade us sit down by repeating several
times " tshoa." After complying with his request, he made a long harangue, of which we

understood not a syllable, but in which he seemed very earnest. From his unequivocal gestures, and from a young man whom we had the happiness to find, who understood a few Chinese words, we afterwards learned that he was pointing out to us the regulations of his country, and the duties of strangers on their arrival.

They thought to be able, by persuasion, to keep us on the beach; but how great was their astonishment to see us hastening up the hill! When we turned in the direction of their dwellings they made a firm stand, and would by no means permit us to proceed. What suggested this precaution of not allowing us to look at their miserable clay hovels we could not find out; however, we desisted from the attempt to intrude. On the hill we found a species of lily and rose growing wild, but no appearance of the least cultivation, though the soil was evidently fertile. When we descended they offered us pipes and tobacco, and seemed satisfied with our obedience. They inquired very minutely into our ages, our surnames, and our country. The old man was anxious to impress us with the grandeur of Keaou-le-wang (king of Corea), that every body ought to fear him, and to be inspired with awe at the mention of his name.

July 18.—We started for a village which we
saw yesterday from a hill. As soon as we stepped
ashore, some persons took the trouble to conduct
us to their village. Many of them wore large
brimmed black hats most elegantly plaited. Their
frocks, made of a sort of grass cloth, reached
down to their ankles, and had very long and
wide sleeves, which served also as pockets.
Most of them wore stockings and shoes very
neatly fitted to their small feet. They are not
tall, but of middle stature, have Tartar features,
and the most symmetrical shape. They tie their
hair on the crown of the head, and if married
put a conical cap over it; but unmarried persons
wear long queues, like the Chinese, but do not
shave the head. The females, whom we saw at
a distance, wore short jackets, and had the hair
plaited in a different way, and in appearance
they were inferior to the males. Considering
the degrading state in which they are kept by
their husbands, it is no wonder that they are
destitute of those attractions which belong to the
sex in enlightened countries.

Among the people who came to us was a man
with a matchlock of European manufacture. He
had also a powder-horn, and seemed well acquainted with the use of fire-arms. We could

not make out from whence he had gotten this piece; it seemed very old, and of a superior quality. If we might conjecture that some European ship had stranded on this coast, and the natives had thus possessed themselves of some European articles, it might account for the indifference with which they examined some of our curiosities. More than two centuries ago a Dutch ship was lost upon this coast, and the crew detained for several years, till one escaped and published at Amsterdam an account of his sufferings. A few Jesuits were also permitted to enter the kingdom during the last century, but we do not remember that any European nation has traded to this peninsula. Some priests proposed to the late queen of Portugal to send an embassy hither, with some gentlemen versed in mathematics, that they might benefit the country both in a religious and scientific way. There were at that time men of high rank at the court of Corea, who had professed Christianity, and would have used their influence to promote the objects of a foreign power in establishing commercial intercourse. This plan never succeeded. According to all accounts which we could collect, there are at present no Europeans at the capital, and Christianity is unknown even by name. We do not know how far we may credit the detailed accounts of persecutions which the Corean Christians endured, and endured with heroic firmness. If so many thousands as is said had been executed on account of their belief, Christianity would live in the recollection of the natives, at least as a proscribed creed; but we could discover no trace of it. The same misanthropic system of restriction is continued till this day, nor do we know when it will please Providence to remove these insurmountable obstacles.

We were anxious to walk up to the village, but were stopped near a miserable hovel, where several natives, in a respectable dress, met us. We were desirous to barter for some cattle, which were abundant here, and were inquisitive to know the residence of a great mandarin, to whom we might hand a petition addressed to his majesty. On the plea of bearing a letter to the monarch, we wished to be treated with civility. They wrote down, " Please to communicate to us the contents." Answer, " How dare we communicate the affairs of so great a king to his subjects?" They replied, " Report it to the mandarins, and they will report it to the king." We then desired them to call a mandarin of the first rank, to whom we should communicate our intentions. They pointed out to us the residence of such an officer, who lived only a few miles to the north, and bade us get immediately under way, to free them from such troublesome company, and to gain our object. Another told us plainly, if we did not immediately retire he would call soldiers to drive us instantly away, and our lives would be endangered. I asked him what rank he held to entitle him to use such language, and threatened to report his insolence to the mandarins. This softened him, and he asked simply, " What time do you think to depart?" Several natives made the sign of beheading when we offered some trifles for their acceptance; others secretly pocketed some buttons, and one received a book, and immediately returned it, exclaiming, " pulga," which we interpreted to mean *fire*, or *burn it!* There was very little chance of giving books in a direct way.

Their conduct formed a contrast with the behaviour of the Chinese. Had we now left the peninsula, we should have reported to the world, in addition to the accounts of other travellers, that the Coreans were the most misanthropical people in the world, with courage enough to repress every intruder, so that threatening and injury were all which could be obtained there.

From our first interview with them, I very much doubted this, but had no sufficient reasons to urge in supporting my opinion of their cowardice, and willingness to yield any thing firmly demanded. Though they very plainly showed their inhospitable feelings towards us, we could yet perceive a conflict in them while treating inoffensive strangers like enemies; for the native feelings of humanity, which are in the breast of every mortal, can never be entirely eradicated.

We got under way again and visited a large fishing-boat which was at anchor. The structure of these boats is very rude, and in a high sea they are entirely unmanageable. We could not conceive how they could hold together, as no iron, not even a nail, is used to unite the parts. There is neither order nor cleanliness aboard; they are as slovenly in their persons as in their boats. As the boatmen were under no restraint from the observation of their countrymen, they showed us a great deal of cordiality. Unable to repay a present of books which we made them, they gave us tobacco leaves, highly delighted that we condescended to accept them. At every place where we afterwards met with Coreans alone, we found them as good-humoured and obliging as these fishermen. Thus we ought to ascribe the hostile feelings shown towards strangers, to the iron rules which the government inculcates. We cannot think that those signs of decapitation, made by the people on shore, were merely for pretence, but begin to believe, from the universal adoption of this gesture, that government would punish every transgressor with death, who dared to cultivate friendship with strangers.

July 23.—After coming to anchor between rocks and numerous islands, we visited one of the peaks near us. When we had left Changshan, we examined some picturesque caves formed by the dashing of the waves. There were pillars, many of them as regular as if formed by art, which were composed of a very hard, brownish basalt. Some parts had the appearance of a regular church, built in Gothic style, but in ruins; many formed small niches, and others were like the fragments of pedestals and cornices. We amused ourselves a long time among these wonderful works of nature, till some seals, which were frisking about in the bay, caught our attention. They feared no assault from us, whom they had long eyed with a great deal of curiosity; we shot and caught one, which furnished a great quantity of oil for consumption on board.

During all this time the fogs were very dense, rendering the navigation among the numerous rocks and islands dangerous. The wind often blew very fresh, and dispersed the mists for a short time, after which we were again involved in impenetrable darkness. During the afternoon, it cleared up a little, and some fishermen came from a village to the right of our anchorage, to make us a visit. They invited us to come ashore. We accepted their invitation, and hastened towards their wretched dwellings, to partake of a collation which they offered us. When we had overcome their scruples, we ascended a hill, and seated ourselves on a sloping spot in front of their houses. But to render the visit as harmless as possible, this house had been previously evacuated, and we only caught by chance the sight of a woman, who ran up the hill at full speed. We were regaled upon dried salt fish, and a sour liquor, in common use among the Tartars. But before entertaining us, they partook of the fare themselves; they were greatly troubled, therefore, that our Lascars would not taste the things offered them. They would not believe that it was religious superstition, which caused them to refuse this present; for, possessing very few religious feelings themselves, they find it hard to believe that others are guided by them. During all the time, we made many inquiries about the country, the residence of the mandarins, &c., but had the mortification to find, that, though we amply satisfied their curiosity, they gave us no satisfactory answer to the most trivial questions. All this conversation was carried on by writing the Chinese character, which, though differently pronounced by the Coreans, conveys to them the same meaning as to the Chinese.

July 24.—A large boat came along-side, and before the people came on board, they sent up a slip of paper, expressing their sympathy with us in our hardships from the winds and weather, and assuring us that they did not come to intimidate us. Those who entered the cabin called themselves mandarins, and made very free with the rum. They inquired politely our country, and remarked that we had anchored in a very dangerous place, adding, we will bring you to a bay called Gan-keang, where you may find safe anchorage, meet the mandarins, adjust the affairs of your trade, and obtain provisions. We did not follow their advice in going to-day, because the weather was very hazy, but promised to follow their direction to-morrow.

The principal man of this company was very communicative; yet he would not tell us the name of the king, but simply said that he had reigned thirty-six years, and ruled over three hundred cities. They know the Chinese money, " cash," which they said was also current among them, but they had never seen a dollar, " In our country," said they, " there is silver as well as copper found." One of them explained to us a Chinese classic in his own native dialect, reading very fluently. We showed him a Chinese statistical work, which stated that the king of Corea sent a tribute four times a year to China, and asked him whether this was true. He answered, without hesitation, this is the fact.

July 25.—The clouds dispersed, and we enjoyed again a little sunshine; our friends also returned and brought pilots aboard. When their excessive desire for spirits was satisfied, we got under way, and, with wind and tide favouring, soon reached Gan-keang, and found very convenient anchorage, sheltered from all winds. Our pilots were numerous and clamorous, since all wished to command, but only one understood the way. As soon as we had anchored, several mandarin boats came along-side. A brisk little fellow, named Yang-chih, who styled himself a mandarin, set down all the questions and answers which Teng-no, the man who came yesterday, had already recorded. All seemed cheerful and happy that we had come, and promised that we should soon have an audience of the great mandarins, to whom we might deliver the letter. The capital was stated to be only three hundred lees distant, so that we might expect a speedy answer. They were particularly anxious to gain our friendship, and gave us great hopes that we had not come in vain.

July 26.—Fresh boats came along-side; and the same questions were repeated till the two great mandarins arrived. They were both elderly men, of venerable aspect; in their dress no way distinct from the common people, except a small piece of bamboo hanging down their side, on which their rank and station were written. Both of them wore cloaks, made of transparent skin, well adapted to protect from rain; their large hats were also covered with the same material. They inquired particularly the time we sailed, and came purposely to console us for the hardships endured in so long a voyage. We had to explain to them why England was called Great Britain, and why India was called Hindostan. Their questions were very brief, and imported little;

we were therefore glad that they left us shortly afterwards. How surprised were we, when about dinner time, small dishes were handed aboard, containing dried fish, soy and liquor, which were placed upon low tables, and we were requested to sit down and partake of a meal. This peculiar mark of hospitality we regretted that we were obliged to refuse, since it was absolutely nauseous to our taste. All the sailors were invited, but nobody dared to touch what the natives themselves must have found difficult to swallow.

As we intended, as soon as possible, to deliver the letter and presents to his majesty, we employed a great part of this day in packing them up. Mr. L. very kindly requested me to make up a set of the Bible, and of all the tracts which I had, to send them in the present to his majesty. I had hitherto enjoyed the great satisfaction of seeing the people who came aboard, receive our books gladly; and now I strongly hoped that the ruler of so secluded a country might be benefited with the perusal of the oracles of God. Could he receive a greater gift than the testimonials of God's love in Christ Jesus, offered to sinful creatures? I highly rejoiced to have an opportunity of communicating to him those doctrines, which had rendered me happy for time, and, I hope, for eternity.

Accompanied by our two negotiators, Tengno and Yang-chih, we set off with the presents, consisting of cut glass, calicoes, camblets, woollens, &c., and the letter written in Chinese character, and wrapped in red silk. Arriving in front of a paltry village, we were told that the great mandarins had gone out, and that we could not expect an audience. Then, we replied, we shall wait till their return; and proceeded towards one of the lanes which led through the village. There we were met by a soldier, wearing a large-brimmed hat, with a great quantity of red hair hanging down. He held a trumpet, and as soon as he perceived us, began to blow upon it, both to give notice of our arrival, and to frighten us away. Mr. L., who was by no means intimidated by this martial music, entered into one of the houses. Meanwhile, the two mandarins, one of the military class, whose surname was Kin, and the other of the literary class, surnamed Le, both made their appearance, sitting on an open sedan chair, carried by four men. They immediately ordered that the sentinel stationed at the lanes, who had suffered us to proceed so far, should be punished. The poor fellow threw himself down upon the ground before the chair, and awaited his punishment, which was to be inflicted by blows, with an instrument similar to an oar. At this critical moment, we interceded, and told the mandarins, that if this innocent man was punished on account of us, we should immediately withdraw. Such an interposition had the desired effect, and the soldiers desisted from inflicting the punishment. The spectators were delighted with this act of humanity, and we were now going to transact our business. But the mandarins ordered that a shed should be set up on the beach, and mats spread on the sand, for us to sit upon, whilst our hosts had seated themselves on tiger skins. We very soon explained to them that such incivility, in not permitting us to enter a house to settle public affairs, quite surprised us; and that, if our letter and presents could not be respectfully received, we were ready to withdraw. This had the desired effect. They sent one of their creatures to empty a house, and finally introduced us to the *outside* of one, where we squatted down upon the " sloping place." Before we entered, a poor fellow was seized, laid prostrate before the mandarins, and received two strokes over his thighs, under the pretence of improper behaviour in public business, but, in reality, to impress us with due awe of mandarin authority.

After our formally delivering the letter and presents, they handed us raw garlic and liquor, and promised speedily to forward the things entrusted to their charge. Meanwhile, they sent us two pigs, and a little ginger and rice, aboard; a very satisfactory proof of their good intentions. Though apparently their laws do not permit foreigners to enter their dwellings, we met every where with as much friendship as could well be expected from barbarians.

Tengno and Yang-chih came during the night, to make further inquiries. They were anxious to know how many kingdoms a ship must pass, in coming from England to Corea? Of how many cantons and districts the English dominions consist? "How far does your relation with China extend? Are you also tributary to the 'middle kingdom?'"

On inquiry, we found that their whole system of government is on the Chinese model. They have the same examinations, the same ranks and offices. Anxious to ascertain how soon an answer from the capital might arrive, we were told, there was some chance in thirty days, for it was now one thousand lees distant, (yesterday it was only three hundred.) To show them the incorrectness of this assertion, we showed them the map, and pointed out the capital. Astonished at the knowledge which foreigners possessed of their country, they confessed, after some evasions, that they had told us a falsehood. Lying seems to be as common a vice here as in China. The behaviour of their mandarins is equally inconsistent as the Chinese, if not more so. When we beg, nothing is granted; when we demand, every thing is obtained.

July 27.—The names and ages of all our ship's company were again noted down with great precision. We were informed that all these things would be properly stated to the king, though we could not find the reason that his majesty was so anxious to know the name of every Lascar. They asked most minutely what communications we had at Chang-shan, why we had not delivered our letter there, and how many people we had seen. These two chiefs dined with us: the inferior one behaved very rudely; but Kin, the military man, showed much decency. We found some difficulties in procuring their permission to go on shore. As soon as we stepped ashore we were met by a soldier, who intended to stop us;

but when he saw that we hurried on, he made the sign of beheading, and ripping open the belly, as the unavoidable punishment awaiting him if he suffered us to proceed. However, our guide Tengno upbraided him, and his sour face forced itself into a smile. We walked over the whole island, of which only the small part in the immediate vicinity of the village is cultivated. The greater part is overgrown with grass and herbs, and would furnish excellent pasturage for goats; but we saw not one. In point of vegetation, the coast of Corea is far superior to that of China, where barren rocks often preclude any attempt at cultivation; but here, where the land is fertile, the inhabitants do not plough the ground. The field for botanical researches, in this remote part of the world, is very rich. On the top of the hill, we saw a stone building, which we afterwards ascertained to be a temple.

We walked over the silent habitations of the dead, which are here merely mounds of earth, thrown up without any regularity. A very venomous serpent, which infests this place, was shot by Mr. L. The natives showed great dread of them.

About nine o'clock, our usual examiners, Yang-chih and Tengno, arrived. They desired to know of what wood the ship was made, the height of the mast, the number of cabins, &c. &c. "What do you intend to do with all your cargo?" We wish to sell the whole. "What do you wish to receive in return?" Either gold or silver, copper, drugs, or any other commodity which would suit our market. To this they replied: "Our gold comes from China, our copper from Japan: we have very little silver; but iron we have. For Chinese commodities, we give paper and straw cloth." From their statement, it appeared, that the tenets of Confucius were the popular belief. They have temples erected in honour of the founder; believe his doctrines infallible; and, though they worship idols, they detest Budhism, and are unacquainted with Taouism.

In avowing their belief of the immortality of the soul, they did not explain themselves upon this important point, but grew angry when we expressed our doubts of their entertaining any serious thoughts upon so consolatory a doctrine. We never discovered in their houses any traces of idolatry, nor did we ever witness them performing any religious rites. From all it appears that they are a very irreligious nation, and by no means anxious to become acquainted with the salutary doctrines which may afford consolation

in life and death. We had frequently opportunity of speaking to them of the Saviour of
mankind, whilst we explained to them the time
of the commencement of our Christian era. They
heard and read repeatedly, that Jesus Christ,
God over all, was also their Redeemer; but their
affections were never roused. Such callousness
of heart bespeaks great degree of mental apathy
which seems to be very characteristic of the
Coreans. Yet I provided those who were willing
to receive the gospel, with books, and they promised to bestow some attention to the subject,
and took great care to keep possession of their
books. To my great sorrow, our visiters were
afterwards prohibited by the mandarins from
receiving any more books, or any thing whatever; so that they did not dare take even a
button. Previous to the issuing of this order,
however, all the officers and clerks had received
the word of life. At the same time, I had given
them small treatises on geography and history,
and I feel confident that the prohibition will
enhance the value and increase the eagerness to
read the books. At all events, it is the work
of God, which I frequently commended in my
prayers to his gracious care. Can the divine
truth, disseminated in Corea, be wholly lost?

This I believe not: there will be some fruits in the time appointed of the Lord. It is highly interesting to know, that the people even of the lowest classes can read, and delight in reading. They seem by no means so bigoted to their own, as to be jealous of the introduction of another creed. When the people saw that their chiefs received the books, they pressed forward to obtain the same gifts. This encourages us to try again to devise ways to introduce the gospel amongst a nation apparently almost devoid of any religion. Our Almighty God will remove those political barriers, and permit us to enter this promising field.

Our friends were greatly apprehensive that we might tell the mandarins what we had learned from them of their king. They said repeatedly, " Should they hear that we told you he has one wife, and that the capital is only three hundred lees distant, we shall lose our heads." By promising the most profound silence, we induced them to ask several things about our capital; but they were highly dissatisfied that we could not give the exact number of military officers stationed there.

July 30.—Two mandarins, of whom one was a general by the name of Kim, and stationed at

the Tsee-che-to district, came to visit us in order
to console us for our hardships. Both of them
were dressed in most elegant silks. Kim wore
a string of amber beads to fasten on his hat, in
which was stuck a peacock feather. They
showed much dignity of behaviour, and never
interfered in any business which did not concern the immediate object of their missions.
Our old friend, Kin, meanwhile prepared a
dinner, consisting of cakes, vermicelli, honey,
pork, melons, salad, vinegar and rice. This
time they had taken all possible care to make
the whole palatable, and we did not fail to enjoy
their hospitality. They were greatly delighted
with our cheerfulness, and that we did not refuse
the well-meant though scanty dinner of Corea.
After dining, we requested the honour of their
company to our table to-morrow. To this invitation they gave no decided answer. These
men had quite the appearance of courtiers, and,
we did not doubt, had been sent from the capital
to examine our affairs. Though we expressed
this opinion to them, they always denied it.

This afternoon we went ashore to plant
potatoes, giving them in writing the directions
necessary to follow for insuring success. Even
this act of benevolence they at first strenuously

opposed; for it was against the laws of the country to introduce any foreign vegetable. We cared very little about their objections, but expatiated upon the benefits which might arise from such innovation, till they silently yielded.

While we were engaged in explaining our motives in walking around, one of the guard in attendance on the general, who had been negligent of his duty to drive away the surrounding populace, was about to be punished in front of the place where we were sitting; but at our request he was immediately released. It seems their maxim to impress foreigners with the rigour of their discipline, that they may know how to respect such powerful mandarins.

We visited to-day the temple on the hill. It consisted of one small apartment hung around with paper, and salt fish in the middle. There was no other idol visible but a small metal dragon which rested on the ground. From the inscription on the outside, we learned that the temple was erected in the third year of Taoukwang; the names of the contributors, with their several sums, were carefully noted down in Chinese taels.

July 31.—General Kim came to-day to prohibit us from going any more on shore, because

he had received the strictest orders from his
superiors to prevent us. "You are our guests,"
said he, " and guests ought to conform to the
rules the host prescribes."   We quoted some
passages from the book of rites, which enjoin
the host to give his guest the fullest liberty to
walk about and to be at ease.   When he read
this he exclaimed, " Hota, hota!" (good, good,)
and never touched that point again.   We began
now to grow impatient at receiving no answer
to our petition, nor the provisions which we had
been desired to write down.   The general only
told us, that we ought to wait quietly till an
answer from the capital arrived.

We took a sail to-day in order to ascertain
whether we were near the continent, or among
the islands.   The spot which we visited was
covered with wood and the most excellent timber
in every direction, but we saw scarcely a human
being in the neighbourhood.   So long as we
have been here, we have not seen an orchard or
garden.   To-day we found peach trees growing
wild in the jungle, and some days since discovered wild grapes.   It is astonishing that the
inhabitants do not plant these useful trees; yet,
in all our rambles, we never saw more than one
peach tree reared by the hand of man.   They

are ignorant of wine, though they occasionally eat the grapes, which are rather sour. I described the mode in which we cultivated this excellent plant, and the pleasant beverage made of the juice of the grape. This they could hardly believe, for the wine, they said, which they had drank on board, was sweet, and therefore could not be extracted from sour grapes. On the whole, the food of this people seems to be very scanty; they eat every thing and swallow it voraciously. It is most lamentable that so fertile a soil in so temperate a climate, which might maintain its thousands, now scarcely subsists a few hundreds.

August 1.—There is a marked change in the behaviour of mandarins and people who visit us; all of them are very reserved and cautious in answering any question. Formerly we had made them sundry presents, which they gladly and gratefully received, but now they try to force them back. We suspect that some prohibiting orders from the capital have arrived, but we cannot come at the truth. Mr. L. had been daily collecting words for his vocabulary, but now they refuse to give the shortest sentence; for they fear that by learning their language, we may converse with them and influence them to adopt sounder policy.   Now and then we grow impatient at their childish reserve, and again are reconciled, for no strangers ever enjoyed such privileges here as we do.

In our excursions we came to several houses lately deserted.   There were generally two apartments in each, shaped liked ovens.   The kitchen was a separate building adjoining the house. To heat the room in winter, they had a large hole under the floor, by burning a proper quantity of wood in which, the whole apartment was kept warm.   Every house is surrounded with a fence of dry bamboo : these cottages are generally built very compact and in squares, having small lanes between the squares.   Such are the dreary abodes where the Coreans pass their life amidst filth and poverty.

We met with many individuals whose skin was regularly incrusted with dirt; many had not washed themselves for months, and were covered with vermin, which they did not hesitate to catch and to dispatch in our presence.   They scarcely possessed any thing; their utensils were clumsy; their vessels made of earthenware, of the coarsest kind imaginable; and besides these they had nothing else.   As long as we have been here, we have never seen one copper coin.

Since their mandarins are so elegantly dressed, and possess all the conveniences which their limited world affords, the people must needs be conscious of their wretchedness. In their intercourse with us they always showed a great deal of soundness of judgment. We cannot charge them with laziness, but we fear they want the necessary stimulus to exertion. Government does not permit them to enjoy the fruits of their labours; they are therefore indifferent to the possession of any thing beyond the bare necessaries of life. Would their present state have been what it is, had they been allowed intercourse with foreigners? " Exclusion" may have kept them from the adoption of foreign customs, but has not meliorated their condition. Walking over these fertile islands, beholding the most beautiful flowers every where growing wild, and the vine creeping among weeds and bushes, we accuse " the lord of nature," man, of shameful neglect; for he could have changed this wilderness into an Eden. Let the gospel penetrate into these regions, and as far as it is accepted in truth, misery will cease.

August 2.—New boats from the capital arrived very early, and we received a hint that a great mandarin was coming to make us a visit. He proved to be a literary mandarin of the third rank, wearing under his chin a beautiful string of amber. In his haughty deportment he showed all the ignorance of the peasant, and the arrogance of the barbarian. Woo, a commissioner sent to treat with us, followed him very soon. He had a very pleasing countenance, was cleanly and elegantly dressed, but discovered very little ingenuity in his questions, and was exceedingly reserved. Our visiters to-day were more numerous than on any previous day; among them were several conceited young men, who used very impertinent language. I have hitherto had constant applications for medicine. To-day I was requested to furnish a sufficient quantity for sixty old persons, all suffering under a very severe " cold."

August 5.—Woo is so minute in his inquiries, that it is difficult to answer them all. He insisted upon examining the chests of the Lascars, and all the cargo which was aboard. We gratified him in the former demand, and would have done so in the other, if he had only brought one hundred thousand dollars aboard to purchase it. In the enumeration of kingdoms passed in coming out, he insisted on the most exact catalogue, asked the time required to return to England, and come back again, &c.

August 7.—Old Kin brought back the letter and presents in a state of the utmost agitation. He said that he had endangered himself by receiving them and promising to deliver them to the king. "In a very short-time a mandarin of high rank will arrive, who will settle the whole business." We did not receive the things returned, but sent the old man disconsolate away.

We took a cruize to ascertain how far the bay where we were at anchor extended inland; for on the Jesuits' charts it is marked as entering very far into the peninsula. After having passed our usual limits of excursion, the bay became broader and broader, the country less inhabited, and the scenery very wild. We went in a northwest direction, where the bay again opened to a great extent, but the limits of which we could not discern, though we ascended a hill whence we could survey all the country around us. The people were so exceedingly shy, that they ran off in great haste as soon as they perceived us; but from the opposite shore they came off to us, and gladly received a few books. We finally ascertained that the large projecting point was an island, and separated from the main land only by a stream which disembogues into the sea. Had we gone in a north-east direction, we should very probably have arrived at the capital, or at least have approached it so near as to reach it within a few hours; for all the boats with the great mandarins came from that direction: and when stating to some of the clerks our conjecture that we had been near the capital, they first wanted to deny it, but afterwards admitted that it was true.

August 9.—We finally had the pleasure to see the royal commissioner come on board. He stated that he was sent by the treasurer, and after some introductory remarks said: " To receive your letter and presents is illegal; we ought to ascribe the mistake to the great age of the two mandarins whom you charged with this business; but as it is illegal, we cannot represent your affairs to his majesty, and accordingly returned all to you. Our kingdom is a dependent state of China; we can do nothing without the imperial decree; this is our law. Hitherto we have had no intercourse with foreigners; how could we venture to commence it now?" In our turn we asked why they had retarded our departure so very long, always requesting us to

wait for the royal answer? It was true that
they had never had any intercourse with foreign
nations except the Mantchou Tartars, Chinese,
and Japanese; but we came hither for the purpose of bringing on such an intercourse for the
mutual benefit of both nations. Besides, Corea
is no dependent state, but only tributary to
China; it has its own laws, and is by no means
ruled by the decrees of the Celestial Empire.
It reflected very little honour on a public
functionary to degrade his own country in the
eyes of foreigners, in order to evade giving a
direct refusal to their request. This remark
touched him to the heart; he was ashamed of
himself, and would have retracted the assertion
that Corea was a dependent state, had he not
written it upon paper.

The conduct of the mandarins has been most
inconsistent. At first they were anxious that we
should enter the harbour, and deliver every thing
into their charge. And when we designed to
leave immediately, they besought us to remain
and await the royal answer. Finally, they told
us that they had not reported us to the king,
though they had repeatedly assured us that it
was done. Our principal regret was at the loss
of time incurred to no purpose.

August 10.—We obliged the principal mandarins to become sureties for the deliverance of the provisions which they had promised, but never sent. It happened that some people came along-side, whom they caught and cudgelled most cruelly.

We ascended the hills of the largest islands near our anchorage, and inspected a fort built on the peak of one of them. It consists of a stone wall, and the interval filled with earth, but without any guns or martial apparatus. This island is densely inhabited, and the best cultivated which we have seen. When the inhabitants saw us, they were much alarmed lest we should see their fortifications, and great numbers ran up the hill, and surrounded us on all sides. When they found that we would enter their villages, they escorted us strictly, and turned us several times out of the right way. It seems they have received orders to do so, for at first they were very friendly, and rendered us every little service in their power.

August 11.—We heard that the people who brought the provisions had great trouble to procure them all. However, we were well satisfied with the stock which they furnished. After a desultory conversation, we handed to some of the principal mandarins a paper, descriptive of their tergiversation, and of the English character, which did not brook any disgrace. Such plain language had the desired effect; they became humble, and began to regret their assertions of the day before. Woo, the royal commissioner, lost all courage; he had committed himself too much, and could find no excuse for his faults. We stipulated that whenever an English ship came hither in distress, they should immediately furnish her sufficient provisions. To this they readily agreed, with the single condition that they should not receive pay for it. If any ship should be wrecked on their coast, we requested them to send the unfortunate sailors back by way of Peking, to which they agreed also.

We went ashore, and stated the conditions on which we hoped to leave them; but as they seemed little disposed to hearken, we left them, and visited a Corean junk in the harbour. They do not carry above two hundred tons, and seem quite unmanageable in a tempest. Even the little skill displayed by the Chinese, in the construction of their vessels, is wanting here.

Kim made the last attempt to return the letter and presents; but when he saw that we did not receive what we had once given, and what had been accepted, he praised our rule of conduct as most consistent and commendable. He lamented the mean shift to which Woo had betaken himself, by declaring his country dependent on China. He expressed his regret at our parting, and was almost moved to tears. Again we requested that any English ship touching there might be treated with civility, and supplied with provisions, to which he agreed most fully, and solemnly took his leave. Among all the officers who came on board, none behaved with such politeness and dignity as Kim. He had something commanding in his aspect; he was always grave, and answered and asked questions generally to the point. His observations were just, and his objections usually unanswerable. He expressed his deep regret that strangers should not be permitted to have any intercourse with his country, but remarked that it was not at the option of the mandarins, but could be authorized only by the king. This was nothing new to us, who well knew that in every despotic country the will of the monarch is the law of the country.

As cattle are abundant, ships touching here can always be supplied with beef; and to this the mandarins will make no objection. It is not likely that any trade of importance could be carried on with this peninsula. Though there are spacious and secure harbours, among which, Gan-keang, the place of our anchorage, holds the first rank, there are perhaps few productions for exportation, and little money to pay the surplus of imports. One should not be too positive, however, in such assertions, for a country not sufficiently known may not be sufficiently valued. We have an instance in the Sandwich islands, where a flourishing trade is now carried on, which a few years before was considered a matter of impossibility. Those parts of Corea which we have seen, have in themselves great resources; and we think that the interior is far more cultivated than the islands of the coast. Doubtless there would be a demand for British goods; for we saw they invariably prized the calico and the woollens, cloths entirely unknown among them. Nor, as the natives would have us believe, do we think that the country is so entirely destitute of silver, as to be unable to purchase annually some cargoes of European merchandise. How could the king, otherwise, pay such large sums in silver to the court of Peking?

Never did foreigners, perhaps, possess such free access to the country as we enjoyed. We hope that the communications which we transmitted, will suggest to the rulers a different line of policy from that which they have hitherto followed.

The inhabitants seem to possess sound understanding, but with great pride and apathy of feeling. The majority indulge to excess in spirituous liquors, but they swallow great quantities without becoming intoxicated. Unnatural crimes seem to be very common among them. Our notions of decency differ very widely from theirs; however, they are not so entirely lost as not to feel that they do wrong. In the great plan of the eternal God, there will be a time of merciful visitation for them. While we look for this, we ought to be very anxious to hasten its approach, by diffusing the glorious doctrines of the cross by all means in our power. The king of Corea may be said to have a Bible, which he at first refused to receive; and whether he now reads it, I am unable to say; but all the official persons about Gan-keang, and many of the common people, accepted them. The scripture teaches us to believe that God can bless even these feeble beginnings. Let us hope that better days will soon dawn for Corea.

August 17.—We passed many islands of every imaginable shape. The most southern, Ouelpoert, (lat. 32° 51′, long. 126° 23′,) is a charming spot. It is well cultivated, and so conveniently situated, that if a factory was established there, we might trade with the greatest ease to Japan, Corea, Mantchou Tartary, and China. But if this is not done, could not such an island become a missionary station? Would it not be giving a fatal blow to those hateful systems of exclusion, by establishing a mission in so important a situation? I know not how far the Corean government exercises control over the island; but I should think, that a missionary residing here, would be less subject to dangers than those in New Zealand, and the first harbingers of the glad tidings in Labrador and Greenland. One thing is true, these islands are *not inaccessible* to Christianity.

CHAPTER VII.

AUGUST 22.—Yesterday, we passed Sulphur island, from which great quantities of smoke were rising. This island seems to be entirely volcanic, and destitute of vegetation. We wished much to go ashore; but the wind blew too hard, and the sea was too high to permit us to land. After experiencing sudden gusts of wind, we arrived, to-day, safely at Napa-keang, the principal anchorage of Great Loo-choo. This island has been repeatedly visited by Europeans, and has engaged the attention of the ablest writers.

Soon after anchoring, we set out to go ashore, at the temple of Lin-hae. We saw several Japanese vessels in the harbour, and observed the junk returned which we had seen at Fuh-chow.

Some of the mandarins immediately invited us on shore. They spoke the mandarin dialect fluently, and showed us every attention, but objected strongly to our going further than the jetty. We told them, however, that we could not converse in the midst of the water, and went up to the temple without taking notice of their objections. Surrounded by a great crowd, we squatted upon the ground, drank tea, and smoked, whilst we stated whence we came, and with what intention. They showed us a cart, left by Captain Stevens, of the *Partridge*, who had been here in February. We saw also the commencement of an English and Loo-choo dictionary, written in their own and the Chinese character. In their behaviour, they are friendly and polite, though very inquisitive about the China men whom we had on board; but when they saw our wish to walk, they were highly displeased. Those whom we saw, were small in size, pleasing but effeminate in appearance. They did not hesitate to tell us lies, whenever it suited their purpose; but they were as ready to retract what they had uttered. A faint recollection of the English visiters, who had formerly been here, was all that remained to them of those past transactions. The names of Captains Maxwell and Hall were almost forgotten, and Captain Beechey was only slightly remembered. We could perceive a certain distrust, and an extreme reserve, about them, which seemed to to us unaccountable.

August 23.—The wind blew hard, and nobody came on board. In the afternoon, we landed near the place where the observatory had been erected, during the stay of the *Alceste* and *Lyra*. We were conducted by several mandarins to the temple, which at that time had been converted into a hospital by the humane Loo-chooans. Though not so picturesque as the description would lead us to suppose, it is indeed a beautiful place. We went to visit the grave of the sailor who had been buried there; and, for the information of the natives, translated the inscription into Chinese, for which they were highly grateful.

Anjah, so often mentioned by Captain Beechy, was introduced to us to-day. He spoke some phrases in Chinese; but soon recollected a few sentences of English, which he repeated very formally. He likewise was very reserved at first; but soon forgot the restrictions laid upon him, and uttered his feelings in unrestrained, and often striking remarks. They were generally so very complimentary, and so excessive in their professions of friendship, that we were at a loss how to answer all their polite observations.

I distributed to-day some books among them,

which they received very gladly. I perceived no reluctance to receive freely what we offered freely; but could plainly see, that the principal mandarins by no means wished the people to take them.

August 24.—Anjah, with Tche, and an elderly mandarin, to-day made us a visit on board, the first which we have yet received. We took an opportunity of examining their language, which seemed greatly to resemble the Japanese, so far as we could compare it with Mr. Medhurst's Japanese vocabulary. The alphabetical writing is nearly of the same form, and the letters are pronounced in the same way, with a very few exceptions. It is, therefore, not at all improbable that the Loo-chooans were originally a colony from Japan. Their present vassalage to the Chinese empire has given to the mandarin dialect a great ascendency amongst the officers, who converse among themselves almost exclusively in this dialect. Many of them told us that they had been educated at Peking, and that the mandarin dialect was also taught in schools on the island. The majority of the people understand the Chinese characters, but do not know how to read it in the mandarin dialect. The same is the case throughout Japan.

We received the first provisions, consisting of
fruits and other vegetables. The Loo-chooans
have so graceful a manner in making their presents that the value is quite enhanced by it.

To-day we visited the Japanese junk. The
substantial canvas of the sails, the broad structure of the vessel, the immense rudder, and
main-mast, which is quite disproportionate, the
spacious accommodations, were all objects of
curiosity for strangers. Most of the sailors were
naked: they were very friendly, and received
our Christian books gratefully; and we should
have gained much information from them, but
for the interference of the Loo-choo mandarins,
who were much displeased with the visit, and
endeavoured by every means to get us away
from the junk. They pictured the treachery
of the Japanese, and the danger of our lives in
becoming too intimate with them. Yet we pro-
tracted our visit as much as possible, and viewed
every part of the junk.

We found in the Lin-hae temple a great
number of mandarins, anxiously awaiting us,
where they had prepared a very palatable collation. They showed more good sense in their
conversation to-day than ever we had observed
in China. By their questions respecting the

R

trade which several European nations carried on at Canton, they discovered much geographical knowledge. They were able to converse upon politics with great volubility, and gave us to understand that they preferred the friendship of China to that of England, because the former was nearer to them. We do not doubt that they have received strict orders from China to keep strangers aloof, and to treat them with distance and reserve, yet they were too good-natured to confess it. Though they frequently alluded to their intercourse with China, at Fuh-chow, where Anjah had seen us this year, yet they disclaimed all intercourse with Japan, and said that those three junks from Satsuma, which lay in the harbour, had been driven hither by stress of weather. Several of their own craft were in the harbour, all built in the Chinese fashion, with a green head like the Fuhkeen junks.

They entered afterwards upon religious topics. When they heard that we did not worship idols, they said, " We also abhor this worship; those which you see here are the property of the Budhists, and we do not batter our heads against them." This has been the general reply of many mandarins when I inquired upon this subject.

They disavow practical idolatry, because their reason disapproves the theory, yet they do in fact persevere in their unreasonable worship.

August 25.—I had found several patients on board the Japanese junk; and therefore we set out this morning to try whether benevolence would open a free communication with that people. The patients were wasted by disease, the consequence of vice, and were very glad to receive a little assistance, for which they expressed the warmest gratitude. The Loo-choo mandarins watched them more closely than yesterday, and did not allow them even to offer us a pipe without a special permission. We gave to all the inmates who could read the Chinese character, Christian books, though the Loo-choo mandarins strongly objected to their accepting them. It was painful to see how anxious the Japanese were to conciliate our favour, and how much mortified they were when they were prevented from showing their good intentions. Whilst giving those books I earnestly prayed that they might reach Japan, to which none of our missionaries have yet had access. It is the precious word of God, which in that country also will be known ere long. I never cherish great hopes from my individual endeavours, yet I humbly hope that God in his mercy will bless those remote nations by the gift of his holy gospel. It is chiefly the work of faith, but no less, therefore, the work of God.

Wishing to finish our business very soon, we went ashore to treat with the mandarins, and while waiting for them ascended an eminence to a temple. These temples are comparatively very small, have a broad verandah around them, and large windows. We observed scarcely any idols, these being generally shut up in a small building in the back ground. The priests were always despised, yet seemed neither to want food nor clothing. They do not appear greatly addicted to idolatry, for they are too rational for this. We could never discover the reason of their objections to our distributing books among the people; but we overcame these scruples by giving them freely to all the officers as well as to the people, and after receiving them they generally came to pay us their thanks. Whenever we gave any thing else *privately* they would gladly accept it, though they have taken the books in preference; but every thing *openly* offered them was always declined. For the least thing which we gave them they offered

something in return, but their giving and receiving was all by stealth.

We tried to-day to go into the village, and,
notwithstanding their extreme anxiety to prevent
us, succeeded. We entered a house, or rather
a temple, around which the tablets of their
ancestors were very neatly arranged. We afterwards scrambled over the splendid mausoleums,
which are built in magnificent Chinese style.
Their reverence for the dead is very great;
they decorate their silent abodes with whatever
may contribute to give them a mournful appearance. From the food which was placed near
them we concluded that they were as profuse in
their offerings to the manes of their forefathers
as the Chinese are. I am anxious to know how
they will regard the treatise on the immortality
of the soul which I gave them.

August 26.—The promise which they yesterday made of sending us the provisions to-day,
they kept punctually. They were liberal also in
their gifts. We, on our part, had sent to his
majesty the king, or rather the Che-foo of the
island, a variety of presents, and among them three
Bibles, which were very well received. O that the
glorious gospel may enter the hearts of these
amiable people, and form them for heaven!

During my stay here I had an opportunity of rendering them some medical assistance, especially in cutaneous diseases. The consequence was that a doctor was sent off to us to make inquiries respecting the drugs which had been used so effectually to cure them; and with him I had a very long conversation. He was very desirous to know every particular of our pharmacology, and his inquiries bespoke much intelligence and knowledge of the Chinese pharmacopœia. After having satisfied his curiosity, and given him the most important directions in writing, I presented him with some drugs. These he refused most pertinaciously, till I sent them into the boat, and told him that I could not receive them back.

All my patients were very grateful for the assistance bestowed upon them, and to them I distributed a great many books, which were gladly received, because it was done in my cabin, where only a few spectators witnessed it.

To-day we received an answer to our request, that the mandarins should consult whether it was advisable or not that we should petition his majesty for permission to trade. They wrote back in answer, that their country was poor, and unproductive of any thing which they could give

in exchange for our imports; that besides, they
had never traded with the English, and therefore
this would be an innovation contrary to law ;
and that from the first they had been averse from
having any commercial dealings with us.

To-day we dined in the Po-tsang temple.
The most savoury dishes were placed, with much
order and taste, upon japanned tables, and presented to us in regular succession. The liquor
with which they treated us was very clear, and
of excellent flavour. We admired the good order
and propriety exhibited in the feast, among a
great crowd of spectators. Good manners seem
to be natural to the Loo-chooans.

After dinner we took a long walk among the
hills and groves of this delightful island. We
saw several women working very hard in the
fields; and the peasantry appear to be poorly
clad and in poor condition ; yet, they were as
polite as the most accomplished mandarins.
Sweet potatoes occupied the greater part of the
ground, and seem to constitute the principal
food of the inhabitants.

While our friends were rambling, I gave
books to those people who had collected in the
yard of the temple. As they were not under
the scrutiny of a mandarin, they secured to

themselves the word of life with very great eagerness. After making an additional present of a spy-glass and watch, we departed, to their great joy; for they had been much annoyed with our walking and entering villages, though they themselves laughed at their groundless fears.

We took an affectionate leave of our kind hosts. In reviewing our intercourse with them, I think that their politeness and kindness are very praiseworthy. They are, however, by no means those simple and innocent beings which we might at first suppose them to be. Upon inquiry we found that they had among them the same severe punishments as at Corea; that they possessed arms likewise, but are averse to use them. The Chinese tael and cash is current among them, but very scarce; their manufactures are few and neat; their houses and clothes are always kept clean. They are certainly a very diminutive race; and every thing which they possess or build, seems proportionably small. While the Japanese regard them with the utmost contempt, as an effeminate race, we will freely acknowledge that they are the most friendly and hospitable people which we have met during all our voyage.

August 30.—After three days' sailing, we perceived Botel Tobago, bearing north, in lat. 21° 40'. A very heavy sea and frequent showers of rain made this day one of the most gloomy which we have experienced.

September 5.—Entered Kap-sing-moon, after groping our way in a dark and stormy night. God has always protected us amidst the greatest and most imminent dangers, and his name be praised to all eternity!

Mr. L. and myself went immediately to Macao, where Dr. Morrison received us very kindly into his house.

RELIGIONS OF CHINA.

THE tie which unites the visible with the invisible world, which reaches over the distance between man and God, is religion. It is the most precious gift of God to men: by it, a world of wickedness is preserved from that desolation, which would be the immediate consequence of the absence of all true religion from the earth. But the name of religion has been often given to systems of mere falsehood and delusion; in which the adoration of the Supreme Being has been neglected for the service of his creatures; and by which man, instead of being "brought nigh," has been more estranged from God.

In our view of the religions prevalent in China, we lament that this last remark is too applicable to them. It is important, in the first place, to ascertain how much of the patriarchal religion has been retained. Few records of the belief of the ancient Chinese remain. We can

trace, however, in them, a primeval adoration
of one Supreme Being, under the name of
Shang-te. We believe that Teën, or Hwang-
teen, was adored as the great God and benefactor
of mankind. The sacrifices made to Shang-te
seem to have been in imitation of those which
Noah and his progeny offered; yet to determine
precisely how far the true knowledge of God
influenced the Chinese to worship him, as the
only fountain of all light and grace, is at this
distance of time impossible. Though there are
some passages in the Shoo-king and She-king,
which allude to the omniscience and omnipotence
of the Supreme Being, there are others more
numerous, which induce us to believe, that idolatry gained ascendency at a very early period.
We fully believe, that the sacrifices which the
Chinese sovereigns, in ancient times, offered to
Shang-te, were in imitation of that patriarchal
institution, by which every father of a family
was its priest also; but, at the same time, we
regret that many sacrifices are mentioned, which
were by no means instituted to honour the Supreme Being. Yet we believe that the records
which have come down to us were greatly and
purposely mutilated by the transcribers, and
even modelled according to the prevailing

customs of later ages.   Even the commentators on
the "Five Classics," have often explained away
divine truths in them, and substituted their own
errors as the genuine sense of the passages.
Antiquity has always been the model to which
the Chinese classic writers refer.   We are therefore led to think, that some sufficient cause must
have induced them to retrace their steps to former ages, and to admire there those things of
which they considered their own age destitute.
The rude simplicity of their ancestors seemed
principally to attract admiration; they contrasted
it with the hypocrisy of their own times, where
they found nothing to praise; but the golden
age of ancient days was all perfection.   Though
they undoubtedly overrate antiquity, yet this is
an honourable testimony in favour of the superior morals which resulted from even the partial
maintenance of the true religion ; a religion,
founded on the revelations which God made to
the progenitors of mankind, and which was
spread as far as the migration of their posterity
extended.   We can, however, by no means plead
exemption from barbarism for Chinese antiquity.
Before the times of Yaou and Shun, (2200 years
before Christ,) they lived in holes and caves,
wore garments of skins, and devoured the raw

flesh and the blood of animals. Their social order was not yet established, their dead were left unburied, a prey to wild beasts, and no written character facilitated communication. Such is the description which the Chinese authors themselves give. We doubt not that this picture of wretchedness is too highly coloured, in order to set off the merits of the emperors Yaou and Shun.

From the time of Kang-foo-tsze, (Confucius,) a new era begins. He reduced the traditions of antiquity into a system, added his own opinions, and became the moral as well as political lawgiver of his country. His writings abound in quaint sayings, striking aphorisms, practical observations, and most useful lessons to promote order and social happiness. The theory of good government is here exhibited in all its varieties. He lays particular stress upon filial piety, as the source of all political prosperity. We admire the subordination which he every where inculcates. We praise the practical tendency of much that he recommends. A system like his could never have become the prevailing doctrine of so many ages, to so many millions of his countrymen, if there had been no excellency in its foundation, and no adaptation to usefulness. The opinions of the greatest philosophers of the western world have been forgotten, or are kept in remembrance only by a few scholars; but the Confucian system is studied to this day, by many millions of people, as the only rule of conduct, and the best theory of good government. But is this system therefore perfect?

In looking through the pages of *Lun-yu*, a work which records the principal sayings of Confucius, we observe a studied silence on the existence of God, on our duty towards him, and on the worship of this adorable Being. In vain we look for the doctrine of the immortality of the soul; in vain for a description of the future state; in vain for a system of ethics which inculcate humility as a virtue most acceptable in the sight of God. Even the Chung-yung, which hints at one great truth, man's insufficiency to become truly virtuous, blends the natural heaven with the Creator of heaven, and often applies to the former what belongs exclusively to the latter. The Confucian maxim is: revere the gods of the land; pay them your respects by offering stated sacrifices; treat them all with distant politeness; discharge your duty to mankind in general, and your relations in particular. The mind of Confucius was so much engrossed with the things of this world, and with the necessity of establishing human happiness by human laws, that he entirely lost sight of the most important duty of man—gratitude towards his Creator and Preserver. His peculiar care was bestowed upon *form*, and the *material* part of man: he never pretended to enter the spiritual world, or to speak of their future destiny—

> " Where, amid the wide ethereal,
> All the invisible world shall crowd ;
> And the naked soul surround
> With realities unknown."

As soon as he has described the ceremonials of the funeral, respecting the grave which includes those corruptible remains, and the idolatrous sacrifices at the tombs, he then ceases to speak. Beyond the threshold of mortality all is darkness : not even the idea of eternity enters his mind.* We do not call him an atheist, though many of his present followers are such ; for his allusions to a superior power are often very plain ; but his ideas are very confused,

---

* His followers, " The Confucian philosophers," according to a writer in the Chinese Repository, " anticipate no future state of existence at all."

and he constantly confounds materialism with incorporeity. The principle of the reciprocate action of Yin and Yang, light and darkness, heaven and earth, the male and female principle, occurs constantly. He thus explains the pro-creation of all things by the process of nature in its generating system, and reasons away the primary cause, by confounding it with the effect. We have a perfect pantheism in the Chinese system of constituting *heaven* (Teen,) and *earth* (Te,) the gods, by which all things are made and maintained. To account for an overruling Providence, which is visible even to a heathen mind, Confucius formed, or improved the system of the Yih-king, which represents the manifold changes in nature, as well as in the affairs of the world, as produced by the mutual action of all the elements and principles of the visible world, in strict imitation of the principles of Yin and Yang.

We do not triumph in the gross aberration of unaided human understanding, in order to enhance the value of the true religion; we wish, on the contrary, to ascribe all due honour to God for sending a man like Confucius, and his most celebrated follower, Meneius, to so large a nation as the Chinese. Whatever is praiseworthy in his system, comes from God, the source of all wisdom ; and all which is evil, is the product of man's corrupt heart.

The numerous followers of Confucius could have known God; yet " they neither glorified him as God, nor were thankful, but became vain in their imaginations, and their foolish heart was darkened : professing themselves wise, they became fools." Instead of correcting erroneous notions respecting the Deity, they have even wandered so far as to deny his existence. It is true, that Tae-keih, an existence before the creation of the universe, is loaded with creative epithets in one respect, as bringing forth, uniting, and preserving all the parts. It works in conjunction with Le, *reason*, which is deified as self-existent. But while they maintain these theories, their minds actually plunge into atheism, or gross idolatry. They are callous to all which concerns man's supreme happiness, and are real Epicureans in the world. Bent on the enjoyment of this life, their only sphere of happiness, they disregard every thing which does not immediately contribute towards their earthly welfare. But when death arrives, which cuts off their prospects, they often throw themselves into the arms of a Budha or Taou priest, whom they had heretofore treated with the utmost contempt.

There is, strictly speaking, no state religion. The Confucians are latitudinarians; yet there are certain rites prescribed which must be observed by all who are in the service of the government. The emperor himself very solemnly worships heaven and earth (Teen-te); the provincial governors, the gods of the land (Shay and Tseih), with all the spirits presiding over the elements; the queen of heaven (Teen-how), who, with Lung-wang, rules also over the sea; the god of war (Kwan-te); and, above all, Confucius, and the gods of literature. The worship of their ancestors is observed by the literati with far greater strictness than by the common people. Thus we meet atheism in league with polytheism, and both in opposition to true religion.

It would be unjust to assert that all the mandarins and Confucians are equally ignorant or depraved. There are certainly many who discern some glimmerings of light; but the major part still go on in this course of mental perversion. Their fears and hopes terminate with this life, and the spring of all their actions is self-interest.

And yet China, as a nation, claims the nearest affinity to heaven; it is heaven upon earth—"*the*

Celestial Empire." They have endeavoured to model their government after nature, and the laws of the visible heavens. Even their military standards and royal palaces are supposed to have resemblance to celestial objects. With the son and vicegerent of heaven at their head, the Chinese claimed, as a religious right, interference with the governments and states which disobeyed the decrees of heaven. They punished them, they extirpated them, as a warning against all future attempts to subvert heaven's laws. Even at the present time we have instances where they confound the laws of heaven with the sordid intrigues of their own government. It is a most extraordinary fact, that a nation " without God in the world" should claim what no other nation on earth presumes to arrogate—to stand in heaven's stead in these terrestrial regions; yet this is one article of the Chinese religious-political creed.

Laou-tsze, the founder of the Taou sect, was a contemporary of Confucius. His metaphysics are far more subtle than those of Confucius, their tendency is less practical, and hence they have fewer votaries, and are understood only by the higher order of Taou priests. Though they are much less perspicuous than the Confucians, yet they speak of a future state; they glance at the existence of a Supreme Being, and urge the human mind to the practice of virtue by notions drawn from a future state of existence. Yet they do not exclude, but inculcate idolatry. The San-shing, or *three precious ones in heaven*, has evidently reference to the mystery of the Trinity, of which tradition has found its way even to China. The Yuh-hwang, or Shang-te, the supreme emperor and most honourable in heaven; Pih-te, the northern emperor; Hwa-kwang, the god of fire, and a whole train of lares, penates, and other inferior gods, demonstrate sufficiently, that without the aid of divine revelation, we never know the only true God. Their Taou, *reason*, or the essence of all reason, and the fountain whence all reason flows, coincides in many respects with the *logos* of the Platonic school.

We do not pretend to exhibit here all the absurdities which are so amply detailed in the works of this sect. We consider the Taou sect as the mystics of the heathen world in China. The birth of their founder is related as a miraculous event. He lived a retired life, and clothed his doctrines in subtle, and often unintelligible language. We find there a system of demons and of demoniacal agency; a description, or rather some hints of the state of a human being separated from the body; control of the passions as the most worthy object of our care, and the direct way to felicity. Alchemy employs the researches of their most celebrated priests; animal magnetism, which has made so much noise in Europe, is known to those who are farthest advanced in their doctrines, and is often shamefully abused. They pretend to possess the liquid which confers immortality; they impose upon the common people, and always act with a very mysterious air. Lofty in pretensions, and nice in their speculations, they hunt after phantoms, and lose themselves in the abyss of uncertainty.

Budhism, a foreign religion introduced about seventy years after Christ, is far better adapted to the common people, and has therefore the most numerous followers. The system of idolatry which this doctrine enjoins is very gross, but the idols are not obscene. Consistent Budhists are atheists. While they tolerate idolatry in every shape, and adopt every known idol, they reduce the whole universe to a self-existent machinery, which moves without the intervention of any agent. Every particle of this great universe is an emanation from the vast vacuum, into which all visible things will gradually be absorbed. The souls of men and of beasts continually transmigrate till they arrive at the highest pitch of tranquillity, the summit of happiness—to be swallowed up in nonentity.   Budha, with his numerous disciples, have trodden this path before, and have safely reached the vacuum, and his true disciples now ought to imitate them. Their gods are as numerous as human invention can make them.   Above the thrones are the San-paou-fuh, or the three precious Budhas; the goddess Kwan-yin, who nourishes all things; the holy mother, or queen of heaven; and nameless other deities, which deform the monstrous system.   The moral precepts of their religion are very minute, and some of them are excellent. To subject passion to reason, and to curb the lusts, appear to be the object at which they aim. Their forbearance to take life in any case is carried to extremes.   The way which they mark as the shortest that leads to happiness is, perfect silence, utter apathy of feeling, and entire cessation from thought and action.   As soon as a man ceases to be man by becoming as unfeeling as a stone, he enters the portals of happiness.   Their paradise in a future world is a splendid garden, with trees of gold, and birds of the same among the branches, singing in perpetual melodious strains. Sweet odours impregnate the air of this celestial region; nectar flows in the rivers; and eternal day excludes the night. But their Tartarus (hell) is the haunt of unspeakable misery. The condemned are strangled, sawn asunder, boiled in caldrons, frozen, and in other ways tormented, till they arrive at a new metempsychosis. Their monasteries, nuns, and friars, are very numerous; their priests generally very ignorant; their system despised by every one, but maintained for want of a better. Budhism is the refuge of all when this world is receding, and the horrors of death oppress the guilty soul. Its literature is in verse.

The present dynasty seems to have supported the authority of the Lamas. As the Monguls are much attached to this creed, which is either Budhism, or varies very slightly from it, it forms a part of the Chinese policy to support the influence of the Thibetian Grand Lama, whose authority may prove a check to the wild inhabitants of the steppes (plains) of Central Asia.

The Chinese national festivals are numerous, and nothing can exceed the splendour and clamour with which they are celebrated. Their gods are then visited, their temples decorated, their future destiny consulted. The feast of the tombs, and the birth-days of gods and heroes, constitute numerous occasions of mirth and festivity, which a nation so sensual as the Chinese demand for the gratification of their appetites. These pastimes begin with offerings of burning incense, and prostrations to the gods, and end in revelry, drunkenness, and gambling. Their gods are treated with the odour of the viands placed before them, while they themselves consume the more substantial part.

To venerate the dead, and to keep up an affectionate remembrance of the worthy who have gone before us, is the duty of every mortal; but to offer sacrifices to the manes of their ancestors, and to prostrate before the tablets created to their memory, is a gross idolatry. This is the universal practice in China; the law enjoins such idolatry; Confucius taught his disciples to serve the dead as they would serve the living; and he who omits this sacred duty, is stigmatized as the veriest wretch in existence.

So general degradation in religion, makes it almost impossible that females should have their proper rank in society. They are the slaves and concubines of their masters—live and die in ignorance—and every effort to raise themselves above the rank assigned them, is regarded as impious arrogance. We should not mention this under the head of religion, did not Confucius designate to females an inferior station, and use every argument to render them mere cyphers in society. Taouism and Budhism join in this endeavour, so destructive to social and human happiness. As long as the mothers are not the· instructors of their children, and wives are not the companions of their husbands, the regeneration of this great empire will proceed very slowly.

Astrology, divination, geomancy, and necromancy, prevail every where in China. Though some of these practices are forbidden by the government, yet the prohibitions are never carried into effect. The Chinese wear amulets, have tutelar deities, enchanted grounds, &c. all the offspring of blind superstition. We lament the deep degradation of human nature in a nation endowed with sound understanding, and no wise destitute of reflecting minds. We, at the same time, cannot avoid noticing their general apathy towards all religious subjects. They are religious, because custom bids them be so. Forms and ceremonies are the whole which occupy

s

their minds, their hearts scarcely ever participate in any religious worship. That the doctrines of Confucius have greatly contributed to form the national character in this respect, is doubtless the fact. With him every thing is form, and the outward ceremony is worship. Earthly pursuits fill the whole mind of a Chinese; to gain money, to obtain honour, to see his name propagated in his offspring, are the objects for which he constantly strives. When he has gained his end, he relaxes in energy, and calmly enjoys his felicity. He dreads death as the destroyer of all bliss, and frequently builds splendid temples to avert the indignation of the gods on account of his ill-gotten gain. There are few exceptions to this general assertion, that, in religious matters, the Chinese are among the most indifferent people on the earth.

In the writings of the Chinese sages, we may see a fair specimen of the degree of knowledge in natural religion, to which the human mind may arrive without the aid of revelation. Philosophers in Europe, and even missionaries in China, have endeavoured to make them speak the language of a heathen acquainted with Christianity. The ancient writers, their commentators, and the literati of the present day, would not

even *understand* the sentiments which are ascribed to them. The most simple truth of
Christianity, which even a deist acknowledges,
is unintelligible to a Chinese mind, void of any
other ideas except those drawn from their own
classics. We may here exclaim with St. Paul,
" Where is the wise ? where is the scribe ? where
is the disputer of this world? hath not God made
foolish the wisdom of this world? For after
that in the wisdom of God the world by wisdom
knew not God, it pleased God by the foolishness
of preaching to save them that believe."

In the enumeration of the different religions
which are known in China, we ought to mention
the Jews and Mohammedans. The former are
said to have entered China under the dynasty of
Han, two hundred years before Christ. They
have diminished in number, and at present possess only one synagogue, at Kae-fang-foo, the
capital of the province Honan. The little which
we know of them, rests upon the authority of
Gozani, a missionary; we have never met with
any, nor with any allusions to them in the
Chinese books, from which we might infer their
existence.

The Mohammedans are more numerous; in the
western provinces bordering on Mohammedan

countries, there are great numbers. They are distinguished from the Chinese heathen only by their abstinence from certain meats, and by disclaiming idolatry. In this latter article, however, they are not so rigid but that they conform occasionally to the common ceremonies of their countrymen.

CHRISTIANITY IN CHINA.

CHRISTIANITY, that heavenly gift, has been graciously bestowed on many nations. The first disciples were deeply imbued with zeal for the conversion of the world; and so long as the Holy Spirit actuated them, Christianity was extended. Congregations sprung up among most of the nations known at that time to the civilized world; but we have no account that the truth of the gospel penetrated as far as China. Afterwards, when the church was rent by the disputes of cold-hearted orthodoxy, and the Nestorians were persecuted by the other parties, many subjects of the Roman empire, who confessed this creed, fled to Persia, or went from Armenia to the regions of the " inaccessible Caucacus." From hence they promulgated their faith among the Tartars of those extensive steppes, which form a barrier to the Chinese empire. That Christianity should thus have found its way to China is by no means incredible; and seems to be probable from some remarks of the early traveller, Marco Polo, who frequently mentions the Nestorian heretics, whom he met as well in Tartary, as in other parts of Asia which he visited. Some missionaries from the Syrian churches of Hindostan or India might also have entered China. This the Jesuits strive to prove from a Syriac inscription, found at Se-gnan-foo, in Shense province. Though we rather doubt the authenticity of much of this inscription, we do not consider it improbable that some Christian missionaries entered a country, to which teachers of heathenism were invited from Hindostan. The silence of the Chinese historians on so important an event, tends not at all to discredit the supposition; for on that ground, we might as well deny, that popery ever entered China, during a later period, because their annals scarcely mentioned the fact. The coincidence of many pagan rites with the ceremonies of a corrupted Christian church, makes us firmly believe, that Christianity in a most corrupt form, was once known to a few individuals. It was afterwards blended with Budhism and Taouism, tincturing some of the tenets of those systems. That most lamentable state, into which many inhabitants of the Caucacus have fallen, who were formerly Christians, is an example corroborative of the truth of our conjectures. But the efforts of the Nestorians to extend Christianity could be but feeble; their ignorance prevented them from proclaiming the whole gospel; they mistook a mere acceptance of their creed for living faith; they taught ceremonies instead of pure and undefiled religion, and the traces of such missionary efforts must necessarily have been soon effaced. When the Christian world had to contend with the almost irresistible torrent of Mohammedanism, nothing could be done for China, except by the isolated efforts of Nestorians. The empire of the Monguls was afterwards extended over a great part of Asia, under the banner of the celebrated Gen-ghis-khan. China was subjected to the sway of the grandson of this great warrior, Cublai, or, as the Chinese call him, Hurih-peih-lee, (1296.) The Monguls in the west soon came into contact with the Europeans, who were threatened with invasion. Pope Inno cent IV. therefore sent them an embassy (1246) to persuade the Mongul emperor, Kayer-khan, to become a convert. Visionary as such a scheme might appear, it was worth the trouble to try to accomplish by persuasion what arms could not effect. Though the message was then rejected with disdain, yet the western Mongul rulers of their unwieldy empire soon were forced to request the aid of the crusaders to repel the impetuous assaults of the Mohammedans, the enemies both of heathens and Christians. Several ambassadors passed between the grand Khan and Saint Louis, then on a crusade. This mutual friendly understanding emboldened Louis to send Rubruquis, a Capuchin friar, to the grand Khan to attempt his conversion. Though all these efforts proved abortive, the attention of Europe towards this distant land, which now began to bear the name of the empire of Katay, was constantly kept alive. The authentic, though marvellous accounts published by Marco Polo, of his travels in this empire, which were afterwards confirmed by the reports of the royal Armenian traveller, Hayton, greatly roused the spirit of discovery to explore this wonderful country.

From the moment when the Portuguese found the way to India, a new era begins. They had scarcely taken Malacca when they sent several ships to China (1517), to form a treaty of commerce. After many reverses they established themselves at Macao (1537).

We see now issuing forth from all the Roman Catholic countries of Europe, a host of missionaries to convert China. Amidst so great a variety of character were men of great talents, fervent zeal, and exemplary patience, together with many stupid, bigoted, and worldly-minded labourers. Though all the orders vied with each other in taking a large share in missionary labours, none could send so able agents as that of the Jesuits; for they had the superintendence of schools in Europe, they possessed a deep knowledge of human nature, and always selected proper agents for the work or trust to which they were deputed. It would be very uncharitable to condemn them all; the grace of God must have been stronger in the hearts of some than Jesuitism. Should we not believe that their cheerful endurance of sufferings, yea, of death, was founded on better principles than blind and headstrong adherence to superstitious tenets? We leave this to the Judge of the world to decide, whilst we humbly hope that their unwearied zeal will find many imitators among Protestant missionaries, who, with simplicity and truth in their hearts and lips, will show greater

s 3

fervour and wisdom in proclaiming the glorious gospel, than their predecessors did in
propagating the legends of saints, and establishing the ceremonies of the Romish church.

Francis Xavier, the man who first attempted
to enter China, surely possessed a warm heart,
and a mind patient to endure all sufferings for
the cause which he had espoused.   When dying
in the sight of that land for which he had prayed
so earnestly, he left to his followers his zeal and
perseverance for imitation.   That he has been
canonized and deified was no fault of his ; he
was a most extraordinary man, but only an
instrument of the Lord; and his name had
been better buried in oblivion on earth, while
written with glowing letters on the book of life
in heaven.

The Portuguese, always anxious to promote
the tenets of their religion, had established
several ecclesiastical dignitaries in India, as well
as at their new-founded city, Macao.   Alexander
Valignan, Superior-general of the missions of
India, who resided at Macao, expressed his deep
regret that so large a country as China should
not be enlightened by Christianity.   Subsequent
events show that his zeal, though misguided,
was sincere.   The success of his efforts to sur-

mount forbidding obstacles proves that ardent zeal, coupled with perseverance, may effect the most difficult enterprises. What would have been the glorious result if these men had promoted the kingdom of Christ, instead of extending the dominion of the pope; if they had taught the word of God, rather than the commandments of men!

Alexander Valignan chose the most able men for the establishment of the mission in China. M. Ruggiero and M. Ricci, by stratagem and by the greatest sacrifices, gained a footing in China, and the latter persevered to the last. To zeal and prudence well balanced, he joined a thorough knowledge of the religion which he promulgated, and acquaintance with mankind. He was well versed in the mathematical sciences, and knew how to insinuate himself into favour. His acquisitions in the Chinese tongue are truly astonishing, for he wrote with classical elegance on several subjects, and discussed philosophy and religion. He was abundant in resources, and seemed at no loss how to put down his inveterate enemies, who appear to have been numerous. Canton province was the first scene of his labours; thence he removed to Keang-se, and afterwards settled at Nanking, whither multitudes of people came to hear him, and to admire his talents. Presents to a large amount opened the way for him to Peking. He had every where made converts, but he laboured no where with so great success as at the capital. Even several mandarins believed his doctrines, and the number of converts increased daily. There is still extant a confession made by candidates for baptism, before they received the ordinance. It is very probable that Ricci drew it up. We cannot perceive that lively faith in the Saviour constitutes the marrow of these confessions. It is a renunciation of idolatry, without a reception of the " faith of the Son of God" as the only preservative against it.

Among his most illustrious converts was Paul Syu, a minister of the cabinet. This man was constant in his profession, and became an able defender and supporter of the Roman Catholic creed. Having received this religion from conviction, he maintained it against all the assaults of its enemies; while he valued its doctrines, he showed a superstitious regard for its ministers. His youngest daughter, Candida, improved upon the zeal of her father. During these abundant labours of Ricci, others of his fellow-labourers had entered into the harvest. For these she obtained permission to stay; she protected them against the extortions of the mandarins; she herself founded thirty handsome churches in different parts of the province. The province of Keang-nan alone contained ninety churches, forty-five oratories, and three kinds of congregations. The missionaries translated into Chinese, " Reflections upon the Evangelists;" " Scholastic Summary of St. Thomas;" " The Commentaries of Borodius;" with sundry lives of saints; all together, one hundred and thirty volumes. These she printed at her expense. Alas! the pure gospel, without comment, was never published. The lives of saints were distributed to the people, but not the life of the adorable Saviour of mankind. Not satisfied with common means to propagate the doctrines of the church, she persuaded some blind persons, who stood at the public places, and told fortunes, to preach the tenets of popery, instead of continuing to impose upon the credulity of the people. She ordered them to be properly instructed for this purpose. When they had sufficiently exhorted their auditors, they bade them repair to the missionaries. After having received the most distinguished marks of imperial favour, and bestowed upon the embellishment of altars, and for the relief of the poor, the ornaments presented her from the emperor, she died, the most celebrated patroness which Romanism ever numbered in China.

Agatha, a female of equal rank, and wife of a mandarin who had been viceroy of four different provinces, imitated her zeal, and frequently protected the teachers against the attacks of fanatic heathen.

The missionaries were desirous to introduce all the superstitions, as well as the excellent institutions of their church. While they held assemblies, and instituted congregations, in honour of the holy Virgin, they had also assemblies where the most fervent Christians meditated upon the sufferings and death of our Saviour; a meditation worthy of all Christians.

The unconquered zeal, which prompted them to hazard life in order to promote religion, cannot be entirely ascribed to bigotry. Some heavenly flame must have burned in the hearts of some individuals, else the fire would soon have become extinct. Though there is an immense rubbish of " wood, hay, and stubble," there will surely be found, also, some " gold, silver, and precious stones."

The rapid progress of the missionaries drew

forth a persecution against them from the priests of Budha and Taou. Yet, as these have never much influenced government, it had scarcely any serious consequences. Their most dangerous enemies were the priests of their own religion, of the other different orders, all hostile to the Jesuits, the only order which at the commencement had any missions in China. Their arrogance, cunning, and contempt of all the other orders, who were indeed very far inferior to them, procured them many most inveterate enemies. Even during the life-time of Ricci, their animosities broke out at Macao; and a friar was mean enough to accuse them to the government, of a conspiracy to subvert the Chinese empire. A heavy tempest now clouded their prospects; but it was averted by a mandarin, who arrived at Canton, and successfully refuted this calumny; but not till Martinez, a very worthy man, had been beaten to death as a traitor. Shortly after, Ricci died, (1610) lamented both by Christians and heathen. He had introduced the lax rule, of permitting Chinese converts to retain some superstitious rites in honour of Confucius, and of their ancestors, that they might the more easily be gained over: for a true Chinese will hardly part with the worship of his fathers.

This indulgence became subsequently the source of innumerable evils, and ended in the annihilation of very many missions.

The approaching armies of the Tartars, which threatened utter subversion of the empire, caused the emperor, Wan-leih, to recall the missionaries, whom he had expelled, at the instigation of a mandarin at Nanking, who had very cruelly persecuted them. Shortly afterwards the great Father Schaal was called to Peking, in the reign of Tsung-ching, (1628.) He was a man equal in perseverance and zeal to Ricci, and superior in scientific acquirements. Towards the close of the Ming dynasty, robbers laid the country waste, and the Tartars were invited to assist the Chinese in expelling them. They readily agreed to free the Chinese from these lawless bands, but at the same time they conquered those to whose aid they had come. The adherents of the Ming dynasty established themselves in the southern provinces, and chose an emperor from the imperial family. The mother, son, and wife of this emperor, Yung-leih, were Christians, and many ladies of the court followed this religion. They even wrote a letter to Pope Alexander VII., in which they showed their submission to the church, and their gratitude for being numbered with the holy flock. Though their influence very soon ceased—for their state was conquered by the Tartars—yet the reigning Tartar emperor, Shun-che, showed great respect towards Adam Schaal, who rendered himself highly useful as a mathematician.

To him it was owing that a numerous host of missionaries were invited, who spread themselves into all the provinces. Among them, was Father Verbiest, a man who subsequently gained so great renown. At the death of Shun-che, a persecution shook the Christian churches in all the provinces: even Schaal was imprisoned, and sentenced to death. However, he triumphed over his enemies, gained the favour of the new emperor, Kang-he, to whom he had been appointed instructor, and died esteemed by all parties. Verbiest trod in his steps, ingratiated himself at court, and accommodated himself still more to the usages of the Chinese. The persecutions had ceased, and a number of French Jesuits entered China, among whom were Gerbillon, Tachard, Bouvet, and Le Compte. When the emperor heard of their landing at Ning-po, he sent for them, and made several of them the constant companions of his joys and his troubles. These men filled up the place vacated by the death of Verbiest, (1688,) on whom hereditary nobility had been conferred, for his services rendered the emperor. But their enemies also never slept. Scarcely had the conflict ceased between the Pope and the king of Portugal, respecting the investiture of bishops, when the viceroy of Chi-keang province raised against them a fiercer persecution than any which they had previously suffered. He insisted upon enforcing all the old edicts against Christianity. So-san, a powerful minister of state, vigorously expostulated against it. At first, he received no answer; and the viceroy grew more furious in his persecutions; pulled down the churches, imprisoned the members, and seized on the preachers. After long petitioning, the missionaries succeeded in obtaining a favourable edict from the emperor, who, notwithstanding the murmurs of the tribunal of rites, showed himself their protector and friend. From this moment, Roman Catholicism began to triumph. The Jesuits built a splendid church within the palace, which drew upon them the denunciation of the imperial censors; but they were not dismayed, so long as they possessed the imperial patronage. Unhappily for the progress of their doctrines, another dispute broke out, between the Jesuits and Dominicans, which threatened the entire extirpation of Christianity. The old questions were revived, whether the worship at the tombs, and the honours bestowed on Confucius, and the adoration of Teen, were not real idolatry? An unbiassed mind would have answered, Yes; and would have added, that the denomination Teen, *heaven*, was understood as the material heaven; for most of the Chinese have no idea of an invisible world. Yet the Jesuits found, that if they acted on these rigorous rules, they would lose all which they had gained with so immense trouble, and therefore connived at these superstitious rites in their converts. Even the holy father, and his legate Tournon, who had come to China expressly to settle these disputes, could not succeed. The Jesuits maintained their ground, while their opponents contested every inch with them. Finally, Mezzabarba arrived in China, (1720,) and issued the strictest orders to discontinue all superstitious worship and rites; but as no one wished to yield, the matter was never adjusted. The death of Kang-he put a stop to all these contentions: the most flourishing congregations were very soon scattered; for Yung-ching, who succeeded to the throne in 1722, was the declared enemy of Christianity, and persecuted it systematically. Upon an accusation brought before the viceroy of Fuhkeen province, the missionaries were banished from the country, and their churches were condemned to be demolished. In vain they struggled to protect their numerous congregations, which had spread through all the provinces: their intrigues, their prayers, and all their endeavours proved ineffectual. From other persecutions the churches had recovered; but this was a death-blow. The missionaries continued to enter the country secretly, and to promote their religion by means of native teachers. Yet the congregations were always decreasing; and when the order of the Jesuits was abolished, there were no men of great talent, who could maintain the respectability of a teacher at court. Though some missionaries always resided at court, as mathematicians and artisans, yet they were too closely watched, to make any progress in the work of teaching religion.

Keen-lung, who ascended the throne in 1736, was far better inclined towards Europeans; yet reiterated persecutions disturbed the peace of the Christians, and rendered the most ardent endeavours of the missionaries abortive.

Notwithstanding the many marks of private regard which Keen-lung showed them, they remained, as a sect, exposed to the caprice of the local mandarins, who often persecuted them with great fury. After the coronation of Kea-king, (1795,) the successor of Keen-lung, the missionaries had far more to suffer; for he hated Christianity more bitterly than any of his predecessors had done. The sufferings of many were most intolerable. Many congregations were again paganized for want of teachers; others were dispersed, and only a few could maintain themselves. An imprudent act of making maps of the empire, from which to decide their contentions respecting the sphere of their operations, roused the cruel monarch to the highest pitch of jealousy. He punished the author, and endeavoured by every means to repress the efforts of the missionaries. Since the accession of the present emperor, Taou-kwang, (1821,) nothing serious has befallen the Christians. They have been tolerated, but not encouraged. The number of missionaries now sent from Europe, is comparatively small. The French send the largest number; the Roman " Propaganda" next; the Spanish recruit their missions in Fuhkeen province from Manilla. The Portuguese were permitted to maintain a mission at Peking, while the French claim Se-chuen as their sphere. Till this day, the Italians, Spanish, Portuguese, and French, keep up expensive establishments at Macao, in order to maintain their missions in the interior. Taou-kwang has never denounced Christianity; he has rather connived at it silently; but has never showed any predilection for it, or wish to know its doctrines.

Protestant nations for more than a century had reaped the benefits of trade with China, before attempting to bless her in return by introducing the gospel. This heavy debt which pressed upon them, was either unthought of, or they imagined it useless to attempt any thing while the country was shut against foreigners. The example of the Catholic missionaries showed facts in opposition to such opinions. If they could penetrate China, if by perseverance they had gained access to all the provinces, why should Protestants despair, without one trial, of an enterprise like this?

As soon as the God of all grace had moved the minds of his people, in Great Britain, to send abroad the heralds of salvation, China was also remembered. But it was so late as 1807, when the London Missionary Society sent the first messenger of peace to this benighted country. They found in Dr. Morrison, a man eminently fitted for the great work. He had an ardent desire to serve his Saviour, and perseverance to continue the labours which his zeal for the salvation of souls had projected. Under the guidance and help of his Lord, who graciously protected him from numerous enemies, he studied, without being discouraged, the Chinese language, which offers great difficulties to the student; and has translated the Holy Scriptures, a work which the Roman Catholic missionaries, during their labours for more than two hundred years in China, had never executed. His appointment of translator to the British factory in China, secured to him a place not so much exposed to the malice of his enemies. He completed also a dictionary under the patronage of the East India Company, the directors of which defrayed the expenses of publication. This will always remain a standard work, and has already been one of the most effectual means of paving the way for others to acquire the language.

In the year 1813, a second labourer arrived. Dr. Milne, a man of great piety and talent, reached Macao, from which he was driven away

by order of the Portuguese government. He
subsequently visited Java and Malacca, at which
latter place it was finally resolved to fix a station.
This has been eminently blessed by becoming
the depository of numerous tracts and Bibles,
which have been distributed all over the Indian
Archipelago, and in some parts of China. A
college has also been established here, by the
munificence of Dr. Morrison and other persons
who took an interest in the welfare of China.
The object of this institution was to teach the
English language to Chinese, and the Chinese to
European and other students, and that both may
be benefited by religious and scientific knowledge.
It has greatly aided the cause of Christianity,
and has assisted many Europeans to acquire the
Chinese language, while it has also constantly instructed some Chinese lads both in their own and
the English language. Numerous schools were
established; new labourers arrived; and though
Dr. Milne sunk into the grave, after the most
judicious and persevering exertions for the diffusion of Christianity, others carried on the work
undismayed. Collie, at Malacca, as a scholar,
and Medhurst at Java, as a scholar and labourer,
will always rank high as Christian missionaries.
Other stations were established at Rhio, Batavia,

Singapore and Penang; finally, a mission to Siam was undertaken and will be maintained.*

At the present time it appears probable that our great Lord and King will shortly open the door to China. Though many true Christians may consider that this is not soon to be expected, we are of a different opinion; although conversant with the almost insurmountable obstacles which oppose, we humbly trust that an Almighty hand will remove them.

The authority of our Saviour, who is exalted above all principalities and powers, and has received all power in heaven and earth, whilst

* The American churches have also taken up the cause of China. Messrs. Bridgman and Abeel were their first missionaries. Mr. Stevens has also arrived at Canton, intending to preach to the European and American seamen at that port, and also to prepare himself for missionary labour among the Chinese. Messrs. Tracy and Williams have just sailed from America on the same benevolent enterprise. Mr. Bridgman has a lithographic press, which he is using in printing scripture-sheet, and other tracts. He has also contemplated publishing an edition of the Chinese Bible, at the expense of American Christians. The labours of these zealous missionaries have been recently encouraged by a grant of three thousand dollars from the American Bible Society, and of two thousand dollars from the American Tract Society. And several private individuals, in America, have cheerfully pledge themselves to Mr. Gutzlaff, to supply his whole demands of medicines and books, to be distributed by himself for thed temporal and spiritual welfare of the Chinese.

T

he has given his promise that the earth shall be filled with his knowledge, warrants to us the happy issue of every endeavour made in his name to promote his eternal glory. We would earnestly beseech Christians at home, to send out new labourers, filled with the Holy Spirit, imbued with humility, willing to suffer and to die for the great cause. There is nothing impossible with God. A soul fully penetrated with his eternal love, and living in constant communion with Him, knows the extent of the divine promises, which never mention impossibilities. O, we wish to see such labourers in the vineyard! If the Romish missionaries could brave the dangers of penetrating into the heart of China, under the auspices of some tutelar saint, how much more may we, by trusting the living God, who created heaven and earth and all the powers therein! It is our earnest wish, our constant prayer, our feeble endeavour, to convince our fellow Christians, that China is not inaccessible to the operations of missionaries.

JOURNAL

OF A

𝕍𝕠𝕪𝕒𝕘𝕖 𝕒𝕝𝕠𝕟𝕘 𝕥𝕙𝕖 ℂ𝕠𝕒𝕤𝕥 𝕠𝕗 ℂ𝕙𝕚𝕟𝕒,

FROM THE PROVINCE OF CANTON TO LEAOU-TUNG IN
MANTCHOU-TARTARY;

1832-33.

JOURNAL

THIRD VOYAGE ALONG THE COAST OF CHINA, &c.

_____

AFTER much consultation with others, and a conflict in my own mind, I embarked in the *Sylph*, Capt. W. commander, and A. R., Esq. supercargo, Oct. 20th, 1832. The *Sylph* was a fast sailing vessel, well manned and armed. She had to beat up against a strong north-east monsoon, and to encounter very boisterous weather before reaching her destination, Teentsin and Mantchou Tartary. From the moment we left Macao roads, we had to contest our whole course against wind and current. Furious gales, accompanied with rain and a tremendous sea, drove us several days along the coast, threatening destruction to our barque. But God who dwelleth on high did not forsake us; and though often engulphed in the deep, his almighty hand upheld our sinking vessel. Only one Lascar was swept away; we heard his dying groan, but could lend no assistance. It was a dark, dismal night; we were thoroughly drenched with water; horror hovered around us. Many a wave swept over our deck, but those which dashed against our poop were really terrible; three of them might have sunk us.

October 26th, we lay to under a double reefed sail, and then ran into Ke-seak (Ke-shih) bay, on the east coast of Canton province. The harbour is lined with rocks. The coast is bleak and studded with granite; the interior is very fertile. Many villages and cities are visible from this place. We were soon visited by the fishermen, a boisterous and rough sort of people. In exchange for their fish, we gave them rice, but they were never satisfied with the quantity. Perceiving, however, that the barter yielded them a great profit, they brought vegetables, and offered themselves as brokers. Although this was an imperial naval station, they were by no means frightened by the presence of his Majesty's officers. They received my books gladly, frequently repeating their thanks, and promising to circulate them far and wide amongst their friends. In this voyage I was provided with a choice stock of books, three times the number which I had in the preceding voyages.

During the night the wind subsided, and for the first time we enjoyed repose. The next evening we visited Kap-che (Ka-tsze), a little to the east of Ke-seak. Here I was hailed by my friends, who called me their townsman, and expressed their delight in seeing me come back again. Books were in great demand, and the genuine joy in receiving them was visible in every countenance. I had been here a few months before, and travelled through many a village with the word of God in my hand. It had drawn the attention of many, and the interest now manifested was truly encouraging.

The weather becoming gradually fair, though the wind was contrary, we were able, by tacking, to advance slowly. When we passed Namao (Nanaou) in Fuhkeen, we saw occasionally large villages and cities along the coast, at which we could only gaze, and were obliged to put into Lae-ao (Nae-aou) bay. This is in the northern part of Fuhkeen, lat. 26° N.; and long. 120° E.; a very excellent harbour, and almost land-locked. Anxious to proceed on our voyage we weighed anchor early next morning. The inhabitants in the neighbourhood who had never seen a ship, came off in boats, but being rather distrustful they kept aloof. When I hailed them they approached nearer and nearer, but by the time they came along-side, we had already got under way. Tendering a book to an intelligent looking man, he was at first surprised at the strange gift, but then turning to his countrymen he read it aloud. Their attention was instantly drawn towards him : other requests were made, and within a few minutes the ship was surrounded by clamorous applicants. The Captain was beckoning them away and loosened the painters, but they clung to our tackle and declared, " We must have these good books, and will not move without them." Such determination had the desired effect; I gave them freely what they so earnestly craved, and they went away exulting.

November 8th, we put into Pih-kwan, on the frontiers of Chekeang, in lat. 27° 11'; long. 120° 22' E. This harbour is spacious, and by changing the berth, affords shelter against all winds. Here we visited several junks which were on their way to Shang-hae. When books were offered to the crews, they refused to accept them, upon the plea of having nothing to give us as an equivalent; and upon hearing that they might receive them as a present, they made many bows, and said that they took them upon credit.

Innumerable native craft are always seen plying about, as we approach the emporiums of Keangnan and Chekeang. These coasters seem to be an aquatic race, preferring the briny element to the comforts of the shore. Of all the Chinese fishermen, which is a very numerous class of people, the natives of Fuhkeen are the most enterprising and daring. The greater part of the Chinese coast is visited by them; they brave all dangers for a scanty livelihood, and suffer the severest hardships to return to their families with five dollars after the toils of a whole year. Want and their lawless inclinations have frequently converted them into pirates; even at this moment they are the terror of the whole Chekeang coast.

We had now (Nov. 15th) reached Keang-nan; the winds were variable, and a month after our departure we saw the promontory of Shantung, and were beating towards Mantchou Tartary. It was now a year since I had been there; we landed at Fung-ming, a place to the south of Kae-chow. Some Shantung emigrants, which here constitute the most numerous part of the population, were quietly walking along the shore, when they saw "these strangers" start up to view. Instead of being startled they looked very gravely at us, and after having satisfied their curiosity in regard to our origin, they went on with their work. We had had a long conversation with the owner of a house, who had posted himself right in the way to prevent our entering his dwelling. I now thought it high time to make them a present of some books. When they found that I really intended to *give* these to them, they changed their tone, became friendly and hospitable. We entered their hovels, of which the oven constituted the principal part, and, in fact, seems to be the drawing-room, bed, and kitchen. Pigs, asses, and goats lodged in an adjoining room very comfortably. Our host had provided a quantity of fuel from the stalks of the cotton plant, which grows here very abundantly. He had a very numerous and healthly family of children dancing with delight about the strangers. Every body was well dressed in seven-fold jackets and skins, and seemed also to be well fed; for the country abounds in all the necessaries of life, and has abundance of produce for exportation. When we left the people, now grown more familiar with us, they pressed forward to receive the word of eternal life, and were by no means deficient in compliments and thanks for the precious gift.

A few hours afterwards we arrived in the bay of Tung-tsze-kow, in lat. 39⁰ 23′ N., long. 121⁰ 7′ E., where we found a large fleet of junks, bound to the southern provinces, but now lying at anchor. They were all loaded with Mantchou produce. The people on board seemed open-hearted, and answered our questions with great frankness. Their unanimous advice was, not to proceed farther to the north, because we should there meet with ice.—I can bear witness to their readiness to receive the tidings of salvation. Though their utter ignorance of Christianity opposed a strong barrier to their understanding our brief conversations, yet the books will speak to them at leisure. They may be only partly perused, or even some of them may be thrown away; yet many a tract and Bible will find readers, and impart knowledge necessary to the salvation of the soul. Filled with these thoughts we visited the valleys and hills around the bay. Very few traces of idolatry were visible in their houses; we saw only one temple dedicated to the queen of heaven, with the trophies of her saving power hung up—some junks in miniature. A few blind men were the overseers. We found here a very intelligent people, who made rational inquiries of us, and who also read our books.—Nothing struck them so much as the construction of a watch. The fine calico of our shirts, and the broad cloth of our coats, also struck their fancy very much; but for their want of money they would have bought these at a high price.

The valleys along this coast present an alluvial soil. In no part of the world perhaps does the sea recede so rapidly and constantly as in Leaoutung and Pih-chih-le. Every year adds to the land some fertile acres, and makes the navigation more dangerous. We walked along an estuary which runs a considerable distance into the country. Large flocks of goats were browsing upon the remnants of grass which the retiring autumn had left. The people were much frightened when they saw us entering the villages; many of their houses were very bare and comfortless. I here learned, to my great surprise, that the people had become apprehensive that we were about introducing Roman Catholicism. Though I explained to them the wide difference between our respective tenets, they shook their heads and began to disbelieve my statement. The people in the junks, however, were all attention, and gladly received the gospel. We had, from an eminence, a full view of the adjacent country. None of the existing charts gives a correct outline of the coast; the south-western extremity does not run out into a promontory, but ends in a bluff headland, about a degree in breadth. Many islands are scattered along the coast, but the water is shallow, seldom exceeding ten fathoms.

On the 28th of Nov., we arrived in the roads of Kae-chow. Upon examination, we found it impracticable to anchor so close in shore as to protect us from the strong northerly gales; we therefore bore away for Kin-chow and the Great Wall. Whilst we were anticipating the pleasure we should experience in beholding this ancient structure, we ran upon a sand-bank, which was entirely unknown to all of us. The ship knocked very heavily upon a hard sand bottom, and our apprehension both of losing keel and rudder, and of springing a leak, were by no means groundless. Backing the sails and throwing part of the cargo overboard, proved ineffectual to set us off; the vessel settled in

the sand, and remained immovable. The next
morning a fierce north wind blew from the ice-
fields of Kamtchatka down the bay; the water
decreased, the ship fell over on her beam-ends,
and all our Lascars were disabled by cold from
doing any work. During these hours of peril,
our almighty God consoled our hearts so that
we were enabled to remain cheerful, and to hope
and pray for the best.

After having failed in all our efforts to get her
off, a party of volunteers was made up, and
departed for Kae-chow to procure assistance
from the mandarins. The land was more than
twenty-five miles distant, the cold most intense,
and we had thirteen helpless Lascars in the boat.
Entirely covered with ice, we arrived at a head-
land and were received most humanely by some
fishermen and a priest, but found no mercy before
the mandarins. One of the Lascars was frozen
to death, the others were on the verge of eternity. Never did I so well understand the 28th
chapter of Acts; *we* also were received into
cottages, and a fire was kindled to thaw our
clothes.

Whilst we were on shore endeavouring to
hire some lighters, the ship got off by the interposition of God, who had ordered the south

wind to blow, thus driving up more water upon the bank. His name be praised to all eternity —for we were very near utter destruction. I had afterwards an interview with a Mantchou officer of high rank; even he, though a heathen, ascribed our escape to " supreme heaven." When we returned to the ship, we again ran the risk of perishing with cold; for the north wind rose on a sudden, and the cold became so intense that every thing congealed.

Dec. 3d, our ship was coated inside as well as outside with solid ice. After several hours of labour we succeeded in getting up the anchor, and took a speedy farewell of these dismal regions. At our re-entering Tung-tsze-kow bay, we saw a great number of junks at anchor. We were hailed by the kind natives, who procured for us provisions and fuel, which the mandarins had *promised*, but had never furnished. The absence of their rulers rendered them more friendly; they did every thing in their power to oblige, and showed themselves worthy of our trust. There is here a great field for christian enterprise. The inhabitants show much sound understanding, and are free from that degrading superstition which reigns in southern Asia. Though every grove and high place was full

of idols and images, and every eminence adorned
with a temple, the people were not utterly enslaved by superstitions.   In their habits and
behaviour, they appeared very much like our
peasantry : some of their farms were in excellent
order, and plenty reigns everywhere.—Kae-chow
city, which we visited, is situated about ten miles
in the interior, surrounded by a high wall, and
thickly inhabited; it is a place of extensive
trade, but the houses are low and ill-built.   The
Chinese colonists, which are by far the most
numerous part of the population, are very industrious ; whilst the Tartars live at their ease,
and enjoy the emoluments of government.   I
consider Mantchou Tartary as a very hopeful
field for missionary enterprise, and humbly hope
that it will soon attract the notice of some Society.

Unable to remain any longer in these northern
latitudes, we bore away for Shantung.   However, as we there found the cold rigorous, we
steered for Shang-hae, in the southern part of
Keangsoo province.   Though keeping about
eighty miles distant from the shore of Keangnan,
we nearly ran upon a bank of the Yellow River.
It is very apparent, that the immense sand-flats
of Keangnan extend a great distance from the
low coast; but this coast, as well as the greater

part of Shantung and Pih-chih-le, is entirely unknown to any European navigator. We arrived (December 11th) near the entrance of the channel, which leads between shoals and sand-flats to the Woo-sung river, on which Shang-hae is situated; here we were detained for three days by contrary winds. The air was darkened, and the storm raged throughout the dismal days and nights. The motion of the ship was very great, the sea dashing violently against her weather-side.

When at last the thick clouds cleared away, and the sun shone out in his lustre, the sea still running very high, we perceived a junk in distress. She had lost both her masts and anchors, and was drifting like a log upon the wide ocean. Several Chinese vessels were in our neighbourhood, but only one approached her, and after perceiving her helpless state, bore away with one of her crew. It was time now for us to retaliate in the christian way; for when we were in distress, nobody came to save us, and we had now an excellent opportunity of executing Christ's commands in Matt. v. 44. We manned a boat and ran along-side, but were nearly swamped by the huge waves. The crew, twelve in number, stretched out their hands for assistance, and with piteous cries intimated their dangerous situation. The first thing which they handed to us, was an image of the queen of heaven, the patroness of Chinese navigators. At this extraordinary instance of heathenish delusion, I grew impatient, as we had not a moment to lose; I called to them, " Let the idol perish, which can neither save itself nor you." We snatched up four men into the boat and returned towards the ship. The idol was drowned, but all the men were saved. As soon as they reached our ship, the captain of the junk fell on his knees before Mr. R. the supercargo. We directed him to adore the true God, and render him thanks for deliverance. When we had saved their clothing, and a small part of their cargo, the water had almost risen between decks, and we set fire to the vessel.

After many reverses, having entered the Woosung river, we drew up a memorial addressed to the principal magistrate of Shang-hae district, and delivered the Chinese, who were natives of Tsung-ming island, to his care. We had immediately an interview with admiral Kwang, the naval commander of this station; he was very friendly, made numerous inquiries respecting Mr. L. the supercargo of the *Amherst*, and offered his services for our accommodation. During the time which we staid in the river, or lived at Shang-hae, I had frequent opportunities of visiting those places where I had been six months ago. The people appeared even more friendly than before. In the villages, they inquired whether I had brought new books with me, and were eager to obtain them. After distributing a few, the demand grew more urgent, so that I could scarcely show my face in any of the villages without being importuned by numerous crowds. Most joyfully did they receive the tidings of salvation, though still ignorant of the glad message, " To you is born a Saviour."— As it is a custom with them to expose their dead near their houses, they are constantly reminded of their mortality.

The mandarins never directly interfered with my distributing books or conversing with the people. After having issued the severest edicts against having any commercial dealings, they gave us *full permission to do what we liked*. When they saw that their inflammatory placards had not the desired effect, they changed their tone, praised our conduct in rescuing twelve Chinese, but gave also their paternal advice to the people, to have nothing to do with the

barbarians. Meanwhile an imperial edict had
arrived, enjoining the officers to treat us with
compassion, but not to supply us with *rice or
water*. They acted up to the letter of these
peremptory injunctions, but sent great quantities
of live-stock, flour, &c., aboard, with the sole
condition of not paying for them. As we were
rather short of provisions, we accepted their
stores.

This central part of China is very fertile,
being a continuous plain of a black, loamy soil,
well irrigated by numerous ditches and canals.
The population is immense, and if we ought to
judge from the numerous children which we saw,
it is on the increase. Shang-hae appears to be
the greatest emporium of the empire. We
found there more than a thousand junks moored
opposite the city, and others were arriving whenever the weather permitted. We may call it the
gate of central Asia, and especially of the central
provinces of China. During the time we remained in the port, (from Dec. 25th, 1832, till
Jan. 5th, 1833,) though it is situated in latitude
31° north, the weather was rather severe, the
thermometer seldom rising above 33.

Jan. 5th we sailed from this port, shaping our
course for Cha-poo, a harbour on the north

coast of Chekeang, in lat. 30⁹ 37'. Until you come to the high lands which form the harbour of this city, the whole coast from the Yellow River is very flat, and scarcely visible even with the ship close in to the land. The sea is everywhere receding from the land, so that the flats formed along the shore, which are dry at low water, constitute a barrier to the whole coast, and are gradually becoming arable soil. We tried to reach the shore a few miles north of Cha-poo, but even our jolly-boat got aground, and we must have waded more than a mile through the mud, before we could reach the shore. But from Cha-poo the country becomes hilly, with undulating ridges, and continues so for a long distance, with little variation.

Cha-poo is the only place from whence the imperial monopoly with Japan is carried on. It has a tolerable harbour, with considerable overfalls. The rise and fall of the tide is very great, so much so that the smaller junks are left high and dry at low water. Together with its suburbs, the town is perhaps five miles in circuit, built in a square, and intersected by numerous canals, which are connected with the Hang-chow river. Nothing can exceed the beautiful and picturesque appearance of the surrounding region.

We may say, that as far as the eye can range, all is one village interspersed with towering pagodas, romantic mausoleums, and numerous temples. The adjacent country is called the Chinese Arcadia; and surely if any territory in China is entitled to this name, it is the tract around Hang-chow and Cha-poo. It seems that the natives also are sensible of their prerogative in inhabiting this romantic spot. They have tried to improve upon nature, and have embellished the scenery with canals, neat roads, plantations, and conspicuous buildings. We found nowhere so much openness and kindness as among them. Their intelligent inquiries respecting our country were endless, and they seemed never satiated with our company.

When we first landed, an armed force was drawn up along the shore. The soldiers had match-locks and burning matches ready for a charge. A Tartar general had placed himself in a temple to superintend the operations. Being accustomed to the fire of Chinese batteries, which seldom do hurt, and knowing that their match-locks cannot hit, we passed the line of their defence in peace. The soldiers retreated, and the crowds of people in the rear being very dense, a great part of the camp was overrun and pressed down by the people, so that the tents fell to the ground. After this outset, nothing disagreeable occurred; we were at full liberty to walk abroad and converse with the people, and were only occasionally troubled with the clamorous entreaties of some officers. But after an interview with a messenger from the Lieutenant Governor at Hang-chow, (a very sensible, courteous officer,) and several other mandarins, we came to an understanding.

In one of our excursions I took a box of books with me. We had visited a temple upon a high hill which overlooks all this populous region. The temples might be called *elegant* by the Chinese, if the abominations of idolatry did not render such an epithet inapplicable. When I took the books out of the boat, and handed a copy to a man of respectable appearance, he read aloud the title, and all at once the crowd rushed upon me, hundreds stretching out their hands to receive the same gift. Within a few minutes the store was exhausted, but the news spread with great rapidity. We saw the people sitting for six hours together on the brow of a hill opposite to which our vessel was lying at anchor. As soon as they saw us approaching near to the shore, they ran down the hill with great velocity, grasped the books from my hands, and sped towards their friends in the surrounding villages. If ever our christian books have been read with attention, it was here at this time. We took a wide range in the adjacent country, and were really astonished at the general knowledge which these silent preachers had spread. —Let us not boast of such an extraordinary instance of the diffusion of knowledge, nor deny to curiosity her full share in this stir; yet after all this, the gospel must be said to have flown here on eagles' wings. We leave the result to God, and wish to revisit those places, not to exult selfishly in the great changes which may have taken place, but to praise our Redeemer, that he has given to these millions the means of knowing the way of eternal life.

January 14, we changed our station and came to anchor under an island. The curiosity to see the ship was greater here than at our former place, and being less embarrassed by the presence of the mandarins, we were able to live more quietly and to extend our intercourse with the people. A temple built on the island under which we lay, is very spacious, and presents a real labyrinth. The whole island is picturesque, and appears to have been designedly chosen on this account. We saw here an edict posted up, forbidding the possession of arms on any account, and threatening decapitation to all who dared to disobey this regulation. The priests had for a long time been desirous to get hold of a few christian books, but when they could not obtain them, they almost wept for disappointment; I had previously landed on the opposite shore, where I was surrounded by multitudes, who did not cease importuning me till they had gotten every book out of my hands. There were very few individuals who could not read, so that we may entertain the well-founded hope, that even the smallest tracts will be perused to advantage. We enjoyed the society of the natives very much. Combining intelligence and cordiality, they lost no opportunity of showing their friendship, or of making pointed inquiries. What a field for missionary exertion do they present! Their hearts are open to the impression of truth, and their doors for the reception of its messengers. We humbly trust in the wise government of God, (which can defeat all the restrictive laws of the most crooked policy,) that the doors to these parts will be soon thrown open.

Though it was now winter, and often severe weather, the country to the south-west presented the most attractive views. From a temple, which being imperial had a gilded spire, we used to look down upon the surrounding valleys. With the priest, a very cunning man and a fine pattern of Chinese politeness, I had a very long conversation upon religion. As soon as I touched upon some points which concerned a higher world, he was dumb. As to the religious creed of other nations, he appeared to be a perfect latitudinarian.

On the 17th of January, we got under way for Kin-tang, an island which we had visited in the *Lord Amherst*. The cold being very piercing, some of our crew died. As the mandarins had previously taken possession of the anchorage in the inner harbour, we took care not to have any thing to do with them. The natives being under the immediate control of their rulers, were rather distrustful; however they recognized me, and had great numbers of diseased people, of whom they requested me to take charge. The state of the poor, and in general of all the common people, is very wretched during the winter. In Europe we have firesides and comfortable rooms; but these miserable beings can neither afford nor procure fuel. Every shrub is cut up; every root is dug out; and the hills, which in other countries are generally covered with wood, are bare or only planted with a few fir-trees. To supply the want of fire, they carry fire-pots in their hands with a few coals in them. They dress in five or six thick jackets, which are stuffed with cotton, and thickened with numerous patches put upon them; indeed, many are only patchwork, but they keep the body warm, and this is all that is required. The Chinese are generally dirty in their habits; and the consequences both of warm clothing and uncleanliness are a great many cutaneous diseases — often very serious when they have become inveterate. It ought to be an object with a missionary who enters this field, to provide himself with large quantities of sulphur and mercurial ointment, and he may be sure to benefit many.

It has always been my anxious desire to give medical help whenever it was practicable. However, the sufferers are so numerous that we are able to assist only a very small portion of the number. I should recommend it to a missionary about to enter China, to make himself perfectly acquainted with the diseases of the eye. He cannot be too learned in the ophthalmic science, for ophthalmia is more frequent here than in any other part of the world. This arises from a peculiar, curved structure of the eye, which is generally very small, and often inflamed by inverted eye-lids. Often while dealing out eye-water to a great extent, and successively examining the eye, I have wished to establish a hospital in the centre of the empire, in some place easy of access by sea and by land. I know scarcely one instance of a clever medical man having given himself up to the service of this distant nation, with the view of promoting the glorious gospel and the happiness of his fellow-men. There have been several gentlemen, both at Macao and Canton, whose praiseworthy endeavours to alleviate suffering have been crowned with much success. Yet we want a hospital in the heart of China itself, and we want men who wish to live solely for the cause.

We went farther towards the southern parts of this island, where I began my christian operations, which were attended with ample success. We have walked over many hills, and gone through numerous valleys, carrying in our hands the sacred Scriptures, which found ready readers. Surely we could not complain of their want of politeness, for all doors were open for us, and when the people reluctantly saw that we would not enter their hovels, they brought tea out to us, forcing us to take some of this beverage.

From this island we shifted our anchorage to Ke-tow point, a head-land on the main. A great many tea plantations are found here, and for the first time we have seen the plant growing wild. This district is cultivated only in the valleys; the mountains furnish a good deal of pasture, but the Chinese keep only as many cattle as are indispensably necessary for the cultivation of the fields.

When I first went on shore, the people seemed distrustful of receiving the word of salvation; some of them hinted that our books merely contained the doctrines of western barbarians, which were quite at variance with the tenets of the Chinese sages. I did not undertake to contest this point with them, but proceeded to administer relief to a poor man who was almost blind. He was affected with this unexpected kindness, and, turning towards me, said, "Judging from your actions your doctrines must be excellent, therefore, I beseech you, give me some of your books; though I myself cannot read, I have children who can." From this moment the demand for the word of God increased, so that I could never pass a hamlet without being importuned by the people to impart to them the knowledge of divine things. In the wide excursions which I took, I daily witnessed the demand for the word of God. The greatest favour we could bestow upon the natives, was to give them a book, which as a precious relic was treasured up and kept for the perusal of all their acquaintance and friends.

Having remained here seven days, we then departed for other parts of the Chusan group. The weather during this time was generally dark and stormy. February 4th, we arrived at the island Poo-to, lat. 30° 3′, long. 121°.

At a distance, the island appeared barren and scarcely habitable, but as we approached it, we observed very prominent buildings, and large glittering domes. A temple built on a projecting rock, beneath which the foaming sea dashed, gave us some idea of the genius of its inhabitants, in thus selecting the most attractive spot to celebrate the orgies of idolatry. We were quite engaged in viewing a large building situated in a grove, when we observed some priests of Budha walking along the shore, attracted by the novel sight of a ship. Scarcely had we landed when another party of priests, in common garbs and very filthy, hastened down to us, chanting hymns. When some books were offered them, they exclaimed, " Praise be to Budha," and eagerly took every volume which I had. We then ascended to a large temple surrounded by trees and bamboo. An elegant portal and magnificent gate brought us into a large court, which was surrounded with a long row of buildings—not unlike barracks,—but the dwellings of the priests. On entering it, the huge images of Budha and his disciples, the representations of Kwan-yin, the goddess of mercy, and other deformed idols, with the spacious and well adorned halls, exhibit an imposing sight to the foreign spectator. With what feelings ought a missionary to be impressed when he sees so great a nation under the abject control of disgusting idolatry? Whilst walking here, I was strongly reminded of Paul in Athens, when he was passing among their temples, and saw an altar dedicated " To the unknown God." For here we also found both a small hall and an altar covered with white cloth, allotted to the same purpose. I addressed the priests, who followed us in crowds, for several hundreds belong to this temple; they gave the assent of indifference to my sayings, and fixed their whole attention upon the examination of our clothes. It was satisfactory, however, to see that the major and intelligent, part of them were so eagerly reading our books, that they could not find a few moments even to look at us. The treatise which pleased them most, was a dialogue between *Chang* and *Yuen*, the one a Christian and the other an ignorant heathen. This work of the late much-lamented Dr. Milne, contains very pointed and just remarks, and has always been a favourite book among the Chinese readers.

The high priest requested an interview. He was an old deaf man, who seemed to have very little authority, and his remarks were common-place enough. Though the people seemed to be greatly embarrassed at our unexpected appearance, their apprehensions gradually subsided; meanwhile we had the pleasure of seeing our ship coming to anchor in the roads. Having therefore renewed my stock of books with a larger store, I went again on shore. At this time the demand was much greater, and I was almost overwhelmed by the numbers of priests who ran down upon us, earnestly begging at least a short tract, of which I had taken great quantities with me; I was very soon stripped of all, and had to refuse numerous applications.

We afterwards followed a paved road, discovering several other small temples, till we came to some large rocks, on which we found several inscriptions hewn in very large letters. One of them stated that China has sages! The excavations were filled with small gilt idols and superscriptions. On a sudden we came in sight of a still larger temple, with yellow tiles, by which we immediately recognized it as imperial. A bridge, very tastefully built over an artificial tank, led to an extensive area paved with quarried stones. Though the same architecture reigned in the structure of this larger building as in the others, we could distinguish a superior taste and a higher finish. The idols were the same, but their votaries were far more numerous; indeed this is the largest temple I have ever seen. The halls being arranged with all the tinsel of idolatry, presented numerous specimens of Chinese art.

These colossal images were made of clay, and tolerably well gilt. There were great drums and large bells in the temple. We were present at the vespers of the priests, which they chanted in the Pali language, not unlike the Latin service of the Romish church. They held their rosaries in their hands, which rested folded upon their breasts; one of them had a small bell, by the tinkling of which their service was regulated; and they occasionally beat the drum and large bell to rouse Budha to attend to their prayers. The same words were a hundred times repeated. None of the officiating personages showed any interest in the ceremonies, for some were looking around, laughing and joking, whilst others muttered their prayers. The few people who were present, not to attend the worship but merely to gaze at us, did not seem in the least degree to feel the solemnity of the service. Though we were in a dark hall, standing before the largest image of Budha, there was nothing impressive; even our English sailors were disgusted with the scene. Several times I raised my voice to invite all to adore God in spirit and in truth, but the minds of the priests seemed callous, and a mere assent was all which this exhortation produced. Though the government sometimes decries Budhism as a dangerous doctrine, we saw papers stuck up, wherein the people were exhorted to repair to these temples in order to propitiate heaven to grant a fertile spring; and these exhortations were issued by the emperor himself. What inconsistency!

This temple was built during the time of the *Leang* dynasty, several centuries ago, (about A. D. 550,) but it has undergone great repairs; and both under the last and present dynasties has enjoyed the imperial patronage. It was erected to emblazon the glorious deeds of the goddess of mercy, who is said to have honoured this spot with her presence. On the island are two large, and sixty small temples, which are all built in the same style, and the idol of Kwan-yin holds a prominent station among her competitors. We were told, that upon a spot not exceeding twelve square miles, (for this appears to be the extent of the island,) 2000 priests were living. No females are allowed to live on the island, nor are any laymen suffered to reside here, unless they be in the service of the priests. To maintain this numerous train of idlers, lands on the opposite island have been allotted for their use, which they farm out; but as this is still inadequate, they go upon begging expeditions not only into the surrounding provinces, but even as far as Siam. From its being a place of pilgrimage also the priests derive great profits. Many rich persons, and especially successful captains, repair thither to express their gratitude and spend their money in this delightful spot. For this reason the priests have large halls and keep a regular establishment, though they themselves live on a very sparing diet. We never saw them use any meat; few are decently dressed;

and the greater part are very ignorant, even respecting their own tenets. We saw many young fine-looking children, whom they had bought to initiate them early into the mysteries of Budhism. They complained bitterly of the utter decay of their establishment, and were anxious to obtain from us some gift. To every person who visits this island, it appears at first like a fairy land, so romantic is every thing which meets the eye. Those large inscriptions hewn in solid granite, the many temples which appear in every direction, the highly picturesque scenery itself, with its many-peaked, riven, and detached rocks, and above all a stately mausoleum, the largest which I have ever seen, containing the bones and ashes of thousands of priests, quite bewilder the imagination.

After having examined all the localities, we endeavoured to promulgate the doctrines of the gospel. Poo-to, being a rendezvous for a numerous fleet of boats, gave us great facility in sending books to all the adjacent places. Nor were the people very slow in examining us and our books. When their minds were satisfied upon the subject, they became excessively clamorous for christian books. At first I had brought my stores on shore, but finding that the great crowds bore me down and robbed me of every leaf, I entered into a boat and sat down, while multitudes of boisterous applicants were on the shore.   They now waded and even swam in order to get near me, and carried off in triumph the precious gift.   Thousands and thousands of books have thus been scattered, not in this place only, but they have found their way into the provinces, for some persons took them purposely for importation.   He who oversees and directs all, will send these harbingers of salvation with eagle-swiftness to all parts.

In order to satisfy my mind respecting founding a depository for Scriptures and tracts in one of the temples, I took my station in the great hall which leads into the large temple.   At this time I had taken the precaution of guarding my back by the wall, that I might not be thrown down by the crowd.   Within a few minutes the priests thronged around me.   Though they were urgent, they behaved politely, and begged, almost with tears, that I would give them a few tracts.   How joyfully did they retire with the books under their arms!

Thus we passed many days here, and the demand for the word of God, not indeed *as such*, but as being a new doctrine, increased daily more

and more.   We afterwards visited several other
islands belonging to the Chusan group, which
teemed with inhabitants.   There are less obstacles here to the promotion of the gospel than
in many islands in the Pacific.   They are far
more populous, and their inhabitants are very
thriving people, noways deficient in natural
understanding.   English vessels visited them
occasionally, during the last century, but they
have never been accurately known by any European navigator; therefore we took the trouble
to explore them as far as circumstances would
permit.   The great Chusan has high towering
hills, and splendid fertile valleys, some of which
are alluvial ground.   There are perhaps one
million of inhabitants.   Besides other places on
its coast, we visited Sin-kea-mun, a fishing village, with a harbour sheltered from all winds,
but the very seat of iniquity.   The natives here
crowded on board; they wanted books, and insisted upon having them; my great stock being
almost exhausted, they offered money and besought me not to send them empty handed away.
On one occasion I had taken some on shore;
several sailors acted as my safe-guard, to prevent
my being overpowered by the crowd.   We ran
for a long distance to escape their importunity,

but finally they overtook us, and I was literally plundered. Those who gained their point, returned shouting, whilst the others left me with a saddened heart, and uttering reproaches that I had not duly provided for their wants. For days I have been solicited, but I could not satisfy the craving desire. I promised to return with a larger supply, and hope that God will permit me to re-enter this sphere.

After staying a considerable time on the coast of Seang-shan, on the main, we reached Shih-poo, in latitude 29° 2', on the 1st of April. I can scarcely do justice to this place, delightfully situated as it is at the bottom of a bason, having one of the best harbours in the world, entirely formed by the hand of God. Hitherto the weather had been very boisterous and cold, a thick mist filling the air. We had been weeks without seeing the sun; even in March, and in this latitude, we had storms. But now the spring was approaching, the wheat fields stood in the blade, and the blossoms of the peach-trees perfumed the air. To ramble at such a season surrounded by such scenery is true enjoyment, and draws the heart powerfully towards the Almighty God. The mandarins had now given up the principle of disturbing us from mere jealousy, and they will perhaps never try to interfere with us any more. So fruitless have been all their attempts to deter us from any intercourse with the natives, that the more they strove to effect their purpose, the more we gained our point, and the readier we were received by the natives.

We delayed some time on the coast of Fuhkeen. We arrived at a time of general scarcity; the greater part of the people were living upon sweet potatoes, dried and ground; for the revolution, or rather rebellion, in Formosa, had prevented the grain-junks from bringing them the customary supplies from that island. Some of the poor peasants lived upon the ears of the green wheat, roasted and boiled like rice. This scarcity had given rise to piracy and highway robbery. We spent some time in a village inhabited by pirates, but received no injury. Notwithstanding all these disasters, the Fuhkeen men are the same enterprising class which they have been for centuries, engrossing all the trade of the coast. We look for the time when they will be brought to the obedience of the gospel, and become the medium of communication with all parts of China. I had here also an opportunity of scattering the light of divine truth, though on a smaller scale, for we staid only a short time.

In our excursions we examined Kin-mun, a large island to the north of Amoy harbour. Here were immense rocks piled upon each other, just as though done by human hands. Though very sterile, it has at least 50,000 inhabitants, who are enterprising merchants or sailors. Several places of considerable importance we may be said to have discovered, for they are not known to any European else, nor were they ever visited by Europeans, if we except Jesuits. As it is not my intention to give any geographical sketches, I refrain from enumerating them. However, as our commercial relations are at the present moment on such a basis as to warrant a continuation of the trade all along the coast, we hope that this may tend ultimately to the introduction of the gospel, for which many doors are opened. Millions of Bibles and tracts will be needed to supply the wants of this people. God, who in his mercy has thrown down the wall of national separation, will carry on the work. We look up to the ever blessed Redeemer, to whom China with all its millions is given; in the faithfulness of his promises, we anticipate the glorious day of a general conversion, and are willing to do our utmost in order to promote the great work.

After a voyage of six months and nine days, we reached Lintin, near Macao, on the 29th of April. Praised be God for all his mercies and deliverances during such a perilous voyage!

THE END.

R. CLAY, PRINTER, BREAD-STREET-HILL.

771868

Printed in Great Britain by
Amazon.co.uk, Ltd.,
Marston Gate.